C0-AUK-720

The Early Modern Englishwoman:
A Facsimile Library of Essential Works

Series II

Printed Writings, 1641–1700: Part 1

Volume 2

Life Writings, II

The Early Modern Englishwoman: A Facsimile Library of Essential Works

Series II

Printed Writings, 1641–1700: Part 1

Volume 2

Life Writings, II

Selected and Introduced by
Elizabeth Skerpan-Wheeler

General Editors
Betty S. Travitsky and Patrick Cullen

Ashgate

Aldershot • Burlington USA • Singapore • Sydney

Published by
Ashgate Publishing Ltd
Gower House
Croft Road
Aldershot
Hants GU11 3HR
England

Ashgate Publishing Company
131 Main Street
Burlington, VT 05401–5600 USA

Ashgate website: http://www.ashgate.com

British Library Cataloguing-in-Publication Data
The early modern Englishwoman : a facsimile library of
essential works
Series 2: Printed writings, 1641–1700, part 1: Vol. 2: Life
writings, II
1. English literature – Early modern, 1500–1700 2. English
literature – Woman authors 3. Women – Biography – Early
works to 1800 4. Women – England – History – 17th century –
Sources
I. Skerpan-Wheeler, Elizabeth II. Travitsky, Betty
III. Cullen, Patrick
820.8'09287

Library of Congress Cataloging-in-Publication Data
The early modern Englishwoman: a facsimile library of essential works. Part 1. Printed writings, 1641–1700/general editors, Betty S. Travitsky and Patrick Cullen.

See page vi for complete CIP Block 00–64295

The image reproduced on the title page and on the case is from the frontispiece portrait in *Poems. By the Most Deservedly Admired Mrs. Katherine Philips* (1667). Reproduced by permission of the Folger Shakespeare Library, Washington, DC.

ISBN 0 7546 0209 5

Printed in Great Britain by Antony Rowe Ltd, Chippenham, Wiltshire.

CONTENTS

Life Writings I:

Preface by the General Editors
Introductory Note
Frances Cook(e), *M[ris] Cookes Meditations*
Susanna Parr, *Svsanna's Apologie against the Elders*
Katherine Evans and Sarah Cheevers, *This is a Short Relation*
Katherine Sutton, *A Christian Womans Experiences*
Anne Gerard Wyndham, *Clavstrvm Regale Reseratvm*
Sarah Davy, *Heav'n Realiz'd*

Life Writings II:

Preface by the General Editors
Introductory Note
Theodosia Alleine, 'A Full Narrative' (in *The Life and Death of Mr. Joseph Alleine [1671]*)
Anne Wentworth
A True Account
A Vindication
Mary Penington, 'Mary Penington her Testimony' (in *Works of the Long-Mournful and Sorely Distressed Isaac Penington*)
Mary Rowlandson, *A True History* (London, 1682)
Hannah Allen, *A Narrative of God's Gracious Dealings*
Barbara Blaugdone, *An Account of the Travels*
Susannah Blandford, *A Small Account*

Library of Congress Cataloging-in-Publication Data
Life writings. Volume 2 / selected and introduced by Elizabeth Skerpan-Wheeler.
p. cm. -- (The early modern Englishwoman. Printed writings, 1641-1700, Part 1 ; v. 2)
Includes bibliographical references.
Contents: A Full Narrative [Theodosia Alleine] from The life and death of that excellent minister of Christ Mr. Joseph Alleine / [Theodosia Alleine] -- A true account of Anne Wentworths being cruelly, unjustly, and unchristianly dealt with by some of those people called Anabaptists / [Anne Wentworth] -- A vindication of Anne Wentworth / by Anne Wentworth -- Mary Penington, her testimony concerning her dear husband / [Mary Penington] from The works of the long-mournful and sorely-distressed Isaac Pennington -- A true history of the captivity & restoration of Mrs. Mary Rowlandson, a minister's wife in New-England / [Mary Rowlandson] -- A narrative of God's gracious dealings with that choice Christian Mrs. Hannah Allen / [Hannah Allen] -- An account of the travels, sufferings & persecutions of Barbara Blaugdone / [Barbara Blaugdone] -- A small account given forth by one that hath been a traveller for these 40 years in the good old way / Susannah Blandford.
ISBN 0-7546-0209-5
1. Christian women--Religious life--England. 2. Autobiography--Women authors. 3. Women--England--History--17th century--Sources. I. Alleine, Theodosia. A Full Narrative from Life and death of that excellent minister of Christ Mr. Joseph Alleine. II. Wentworth, Anne. True account of Anne Wentworths being cruelly, unjustly, and unchristianly dealt with by some of those people called Anabaptists. III. Wentworth, Anne. Vindication of Anne Wentworth. IV. Penington, Isaac, 1616-1679. Works of the long-mournful and sorely-distressed Isaac Penington. Selections. V. Penington, Mary, 1625-1682. Mary Penington, her testimony concerning her dear husband. VI. Rowlandson, Mary White, ca. 1635-ca. 1711. True history of the captivity & restoration of Mrs. Mary Rowlandson, a minister's wife in New-England. VII. Allen, Hannah, fl. 1683. Narrative of God's gracious dealings with that choice Christian Mrs. Hannah Allen. VIII. Blaugdone, Barbara, 1608 or 9-1704. Account of the travels, sufferings & persecutions of Barbara Blaugdone. IX. Blandford, Susannah. Small account given forth by one that hath been a traveller for these 40 years in the good old way. X. Skerpan-Wheeler, Elizabeth, 1955- XI. Title: Life and death of that excellent minister of Christ Mr. Joseph Alleine. XII. Title: True account of Anne Wentworths being cruelly, unjustly, and unchristianly dealt with by some of those people called Anabaptists. XIII. Title: Vindication of Anne Wentworth. XIV. Title: Mary Penington, her testimony concerning her dear husband. XV. Title: True history of the captivity & restoration of Mrs. Mary Rowlandson, a minister's wife in New-England.. Title: Narrative of God's gracious dealings with that choice Christian Mrs. Hannah Allen.. Title: Account of the travels, sufferings & persecutions of Barbara Blaugdone.. Title: Small account given forth by one that hath been a traveller for these 40 years in the good old way.. Series.

BV4527 .L54 2000 vol. 2
274.2'07'0922--dc21

00-64295

PREFACE
BY THE GENERAL EDITORS

Until very recently, scholars of the early modern period have assumed that there were no Judith Shakespeares in early modern England. Much of the energy of the current generation of scholars has been devoted to constructing a history of early modern England that takes into account what women actually wrote, what women actually read, and what women actually did. In so doing the masculinist representation of early modern women, both in their own time and ours, has been deconstructed. The study of early modern women has thus become one of the most important—indeed perhaps the most important—means for the rewriting of early modern history.

The Early Modern Englishwoman: A Facsimile Library of Essential Works is one of the developments of this energetic reappraisal of the period. As the names on our advisory board and our list of editors testify, it has been the beneficiary of scholarship in the field, and we hope it will also be an essential part of that scholarship's continuing momentum.

The Early Modern Englishwoman is designed to make available a comprehensive and focused collection of writings in English from 1500 to 1750, both by women and for and about them. The three series of *Printed Writings* (1500–1640, 1641–1700, and 1701–1750), provide a comprehensive if not entirely complete collection of the separately published writings by women. In reprinting these writings we intend to remedy one of the major obstacles to the advancement of feminist criticism of the early modern period, namely the limited availability of the very texts upon which the field is based. The volumes in the facsimile library reproduce carefully chosen copies of these texts, incorporating significant variants (usually in appendices). Each text is preceded by a short introduction providing an overview of the life and work of a writer along with a survey of important scholarship. These works, we strongly believe, deserve a large readership—of historians, literary critics, feminist critics, and non-specialist readers.

The Early Modern Englishwoman also includes separate facsimile series of *Essential Works for the Study of Early Modern Women* and of *Manuscript Writings*. These facsimile series are complemented by *The Early Modern Englishwoman 1500–1750: Contemporary Editions*. Also under our general editorship, this series will include both old-spelling and modernized editions of works by and about women and gender in early modern England.

New York City
2001

INTRODUCTORY NOTE

Readers coming to the volumes of *Life Writings* looking for intimate details or stories tracing their subjects from birth to adulthood will be disappointed. Early modern women and men represented their lives very differently from twentieth-century autobiographers. Writers today describe the process by which they have come to be what they believe they are: distinctive, unique individuals. In contrast, early modern writers sought connections between particular events in their lives and the larger pattern of Christian salvation. These writers frequently omit the names of their husbands and children, mentioning them in passing as they focus on the most important part of their lives–their quest for salvation. Their narratives interconnect their experiences and feelings with scriptural passages as they attempt to understand daily life in spiritual terms. The persons most frequently described are those who make the greatest impact on the writers' spiritual development. While modern writers strive to emerge from their context, these early modern writers attempt to justify and then subsume themselves in divine history.

With one exception, all the women represented in *Life Writings* would have been considered by their contemporaries religious radicals–Independents, Baptists and Quakers. All lived through an extremely turbulent time in English history. The English Revolution (1642–1660) saw the temporary disestablishment of the Church of England, the rise of open religious experimentation and regular interpretation of political events in religious terms. Restoration of the Stuart monarch in 1660 brought harsh laws against Protestant Dissenters from the reestablished Church, forbidding unlicensed preaching and worshipping, and requiring prison terms for religious lawbreakers. A few of the writers collected here spent time in prison, and the works are marked by a sense of persecution, interpreted as spiritual challenge. Response to a palpable threat is a common theme. Mary Rowlandson, the best known of these writers, describes the months she spent as a captive of North American Indians, while Katherine Evans, Sarah Cheevers and Barbara Blaugdone endure prison as a result of preaching the faith of the Society of Friends. Hannah Allen faces a different kind of captivity in a prolonged fight with depression. Anne Wentworth encounters the hostility of an entire congregation when she decides to leave a bad marriage; Susanna Parr is excommunicated for disagreeing with her pastor. Frances Cook has her faith severely tested by a terrible storm at sea. Katherine Sutton, Sarah Davy and Susannah Blandford recount their battles with doubt and their coming to refreshed understanding of their faith. Elizabeth White (d. 1669) recounts her crises of faith, her spiritual growth, and the challenges it entailed. However, *The Experiences of Gods Gracious Dealing with Mrs. Elizabeth White* (Wing W 1762), published in Glasgow by Robert Saunders in 1696, could not be included here because the condition of the two extant copies precludes reproduction. Theodosia Alleine and Mary Penington offer testimony to the hardships their clergyman husbands endured as a result of defying the Stuart government's religious laws. The lone exception, Anne Gerard Wyndham, tells a pure adventure story of the wartime rescue of Prince Charles from the hands of the parliamentary army by herself, her husband, and several other royalist men and women. While she seeks no religious explanation for events, Wyndham follows the pattern of the other writers in subordinating details about herself to the particulars of her narrative.

The works have been arranged in chronological order so that readers may get a sense of the progression of the historical events surrounding the writers as well as the gradual emergence of the Quakers as the newest of the Independent sects and the continuity over time and place of particular themes and methods of exposition. With the exception of Rowlandson's captivity narrative, these works are making their first complete, unexcerpted modern appearance.

Frances Cook(e) (fl. ?1646–60)

Little is known of the life of Frances Cook, other than that she was the wife of John Cook, barrister and chief prosecutor in the trial of Charles 1, executed in 1660 for his role in the regicide. Frances visited John in the Tower of London before his execution; his letter to her is printed in *A Complete Collection of the Lives, Speeches, Private Passages, Letters and Prayers of those Persons Lately Executed* (1661), edited by S.W. Possibly the Frances Cutler John Cook married in 1646, Frances was the mother of a daughter, Freelove. In January 1650, while John and Frances Cook were traveling to Ireland so that he could assume his newly appointed position as Chief Justice to the Court of Munster (which he held until 1654), they encountered the terrible storm that is the subject of Frances's book, and of one by John, also.

Mris. Cookes Meditations

Mris. Cookes Meditations is printed in 4°, with a title page of ornamented printer's rules and central ornament. Frances's book was published together with her husband's, *A True Relation of Mr Iohn Cook's Passage by Sea from Wexford to Kinsale and of the Great Storm and Eminent Danger*, in 1650 at Corke and reprinted in London by Thomas Brewster and Gregory Moule. John's book went through a second edition in 1652, but Frances's exists only in the first printing. While both editions of John's book exist in numerous exemplars, probably because of the fame or notoriety of its author, only four exemplars of Frances's book survive. There are no modern editions. Her efforts at understanding the experience through her reading of scripture and her concluding psalm, modeled on the psalms of David, place her firmly in the Protestant tradition of spiritual autobiography. Students of literature and gender may wish to read Frances's narrative together with John's: the existence of both narratives provides a rare opportunity to compare the responses of a woman and man with similar sympathies to the same event.

The base copy reproduced in Volume 1 is the exemplar owned by The British Library. It was selected for both its clarity and its inclusion in the famous collection of bookseller George Thomason, universally recognized by seventeenth-century scholars as the most inclusive collection of books and pamphlets from the revolutionary period.

Susanna Parr (fl. 1635–69)

Married and the mother of seven children, Susanna Parr was living in Exeter when in 1657 she and another woman, Mary Alleine, were–for asserting themselves, speaking in church, and hearing the minister of another congregation–excommunicated from the Baptist fellowship headed by Lewis Stucley (or Stycley) of which Parr herself had been a founder. Her actions apparently precipitated by the death of one of her children around 1654, Parr, together with Mary Alleine and Alleine's husband Toby, a prominent serge-maker, criticized Stucley's increasingly radical, separatist ministry. The incident prompted six pamphlets, including Parr's work and a tract by Toby Alleine. A full account of the episode appears in Patricia Crawford, *Women and Religion in England 1500–1720.*

Svsanna's Apologie against the Elders

Svsanna's Apologie Against the Elders was published in Oxford by Henry Hall for T. Robinson, on 12 May 1659, according to the bookseller George Thomason, who made the note on his own copy of the book. An 8° edition, without distinguishing ornaments, the book went through one printing and exists in only four exemplars. Written in response to verbal and published accusations, Parr's book coherently argues her case, dividing the text into a Narrative, which lays out the circumstances surrounding her excommunication, and a Vindication, which provides a meticulous refutation of all the charges published against her. The book opens with Parr's own preface 'To the Impartiall Reader'. While pleading the infirmity of her sex, Parr insists on speaking for herself, providing the voice missing from the pamphlets written about the case by the male participants. In presentation and argumentation, Parr's work compares favorably with those of other political and religious controversialists. An excerpt appears in Graham *et al.*, *Her Own Life: Autobiographical Writings by Seventeenth-Century English Women.*

The base copy reproduced in Volume 1 was chosen for its availability, clarity, and inclusion in the noted Thomason Collection, owned by The British Library.

Katherine Evans (d. 1692) and Sarah Cheevers (d. 1664)

Both members of the Society of Friends, Katherine Evans and Sarah Cheevers were married and the mothers of several children when in 1658, while traveling to Alexandria to preach, they were detained in Malta, where they subsequently spent three years in the captivity of the Inquisition. Redeemed after three years through the actions of Daniel Baker and other Friends, they returned to England by 1663 and continued to publish accounts of their experiences. A determined spiritual seeker from a well-to-do family, Evans had by her own account been a Lutheran, Baptist, Independent and Puritan before joining the Friends. Evans's husband, John, died in prison in 1664; she herself lived until 1692. About Cheevers, whose family home was in Slattenford, or Slaughterford, Wiltshire, and whose husband's name was Henry, little else is known. Several letters by both Evans and Cheevers appear in Besse.

This is a Short Relation

This is a Short Relation of Some of the Cruel Sufferings (For the Truths Sake) of Katharine Evans & Sarah Chevers is a cheaply printed 4° with a densely printed, descriptive title page ornamented by printer's rules, printed in London for Robert Wilson in 1662, while the women were still in prison. The title page and Daniel Baker's introductory 'Epistle to the Readers' clearly indicate that the publication is both an attempt to enlist support in the campaign to free Evans and Cheevers and an argument against the charge that Friends were Roman Catholics and agents of the Pope. As the title suggests, it is not a single account; rather, it is a complex and dazzling intermingling–in changing voices–of personal narratives, copies of letters by Evans and Cheevers and others, hymns, and connecting commentary by Baker. After their return to England in 1663, Wilson published a revised and expanded edition under the title of *A True Account of the Great Tryals and Cruel Sufferings* (8°), which included a description of the process by which the women regained their freedom and appended a narrative of the experiences of fellow Friend George Robinson, captured while traveling to Jerusalem. In the same year, Wilson also published Evans's revised version of her experiences, titled *A Briefe Discovery of God's Eternal Truth and a Way Opened to the Simple Hearted Whereby They May Come to Know Christ and His Ministers, from Antichrist and His Ministers* (4°). Five exemplars exist of *Short Relation*, two of *A True Account* and four of *A Briefe Discovery*. Versions of the narratives were reprinted twice in the eighteenth century, but there are no modern editions. The writings of Evans and Cheevers illustrate the spiritual gender equality within the Society of Friends, as readers may see by comparing the women's accounts of captivity to those of Barbara Blaugdone, in Volume 2, and of George Robinson, as well as to numerous letters to Friends collected by the Society and preserved at the Friends House Library in London and in the libraries of Swarthmore and Haverford Colleges in the United States. An excerpt from *A True Account* appears in Graham *et al.*, *Her Own Life: Autobiographical Writings by Seventeenth-Century English Women*.

The base copy reproduced in Volume 1 is the Huntington Library copy of *This is a Short Relation*, the earliest version of the narrative, and the clearest copy available.

Katherine Sutton (fl. 1630–63)

Katherine Sutton, a married woman and the mother of several children, was praised by the Baptist minister Hanserd Knollys for the depth and sincerity of her faith. Her experiences with family life, including the death of one child and disagreements with her husband, contributed to the intensity of her spiritual quest. Inspired by dreams and visions and blessed most especially, she felt, by her 'gift of singing', which she dated to February 1655, she composed both narratives and hymns. The manuscripts of some of these were lost in a shipwreck in a crossing to Holland around 1662 and rewritten for *A Christian Womans Experiences*.

The text, a 4° edition, was printed by Henry Goddæus in Rotterdam. The title page bears a beautifully detailed printer's ornament. The book opens with a preface by Knollys, who was passing through Rotterdam around 1663, continues with the narrative proper, and concludes with Sutton's address to the 'Courteous Reader' and several of her hymns which, Sutton asserts, were composed spontaneously and presented without revision. This text went through one edition; three exemplars exist. There are no modern editions, although there is some discussion of the hymns in Ian M. Mallard (1963), 'Hymns of Katherine Sutton', *Baptist Journal*, January (pp. 23–33). Sutton's text is a spiritual autobiography comparable to John Bunyan's *Grace Abounding to the Chief of Sinners*, stressing the author's conviction of sin and her quest for grace, punctuated by a series of hardships. Knollys, who may have been impressed by Sutton because of her gift of singing (his last published work defends the right of women to sing in church) and who would prove to be the nemesis of Anne Wentworth (see Volume 2), cautions readers about 'some suddain and unexpected Transition' in Sutton's writing, but offers its lack of polish as evidence of 'Heavenly communications'. Sutton echoes Knollys's concern about style in her concluding address to the readers, but urges them to judge the quality of her work for themselves, guided by the spirit.

Owned by Cambridge University Library, the base copy of this very rare book, reproduced in Volume 1, is distinguished for its clear, legible printing.

Anne Gerard Wyndham (1632–98)

Alone of all the women in these two volumes, Anne Gerard Wyndham was a committed royalist. The daughter of Thomas Gerard of Trent, Somersetshire, she married Col Francis Wyndham, also of Trent, whose mother had cared for the young Prince of Wales before the civil wars. Both Anne and her husband actively participated in hiding the future Charles II after the royalist defeat at the Battle of Worcester (1650). In May 1667 Anne petitioned the king for a pension in recognition of the help she and her husband gave him. The book may have been an attempt to support the petition. Wyndham counted several aristocrats among her friends and acquaintances, including Lord Henry Wilmot, later Earl of Rochester.

Clavstrvm Regale Reseratvm

Wyndham's narrative, *Clavstrvm Regale Reseratvm*, or *The Kinges Concealment at Trent* is a brief, 4° volume, with a title page in script and without other ornament, published in London for William Nott in 1667. It opens with a dedicatory epistle to the Queen, Catherine of Braganza, and explains why the book is appearing in 1667, rather than at a date closer to the actual events. The remainder of the text is a third-person narrative describing how Wyndham, her husband and others designed and carried out their plot to rescue Prince Charles. Wyndham explains that her story provides the missing piece of a larger narrative of Charles's escape, already published, and that this narrative, originally written by her husband, remained in the king's custody until he himself gave permission to publish it. While the book went through only one printing, it survives in eleven known exemplars. It was also reprinted in its entirety in the third edition of Thomas Blount's *Boscobel* (1681). There is no modern edition. Her dedication to the queen places Wyndham among a significant group of royalists who, although not part of the court, played a crucial role in sustaining and unifying opposition to the governments of the 1650s. Her book appeared at the time of the Second Dutch War (1666–67), when supporters of the king, who at no time in the 1660s trusted in a universal royalism, were publishing works designed to make the king the center of popular patriotism. Wyndham's narrative–depicting a young and vulnerable prince dependent upon the goodwill of his people, and subjects willing to undergo risk and hardship for their prince–thus indirectly serves the interests of contemporary politics.

Of the surviving eleven exemplars, the copy owned by The Huntington Library was chosen for reproduction in Volume 1 because of its legibility and availability.

Sarah Davy (?1635–67)

Characterized as a young gentlewoman by her publisher, Sarah Davy was born Sarah Roane around 1635. When she was eleven years old, her mother died, precipitating the spiritual journey that is the subject of Davy's book. She married around December 1660 and died after a long illness in 1667. Her book was published posthumously.

Heaven Realiz'd

The text, printed in 8°, with a simple, unadorned title page, was published in 1670, probably in London, by A.P., who also contributed an extensive introduction. The text includes personal narratives, reflections on Davy's experiences and meditations on religious subjects; it concludes with several hymns and a table of contents. Printed only once, the text exists in five exemplars. As presented by A.P. (tentatively identified by Elaine Hobby as Baptist clergyman Anthony Palmer), the book is at once a book of devotions, a memorial and a didactic example for other young persons, who are living 'in an Age of the *great corruption of youth*, when Religion is made a by-word and a scorn'. While the text of Davy's book is highly personal, carefully describing the stages in the author's spiritual growth, A.P. emphasizes the exemplary nature of the writing of 'a blessed Soul (now in Heaven)' and addresses 'all sort of Readers' in the preface, decrying the morals of the age. For A.P., the value of Davy's writings is their testimony that her spiritual life gave her the rewards otherwise denied her in her short life. A.P.'s framing of Davy's text may be contrasted to Daniel Baker's handling of the letters and narratives of Katherine Evans and Sarah Cheevers. Evans and Cheevers clearly shared the same goals as Baker. While Davy intends to serve as an example, it is A.P. who gives her life and text their polemical cast. Excerpts from *Heaven Realiz'd* appear in Graham *et al.*, *Her Own Life: Autobiographical Writings by Seventeenth-Century English Women*.

Although the British Library copy reproduced in Volume 1 has been cropped too closely and is bound too tightly for perfect reproduction, the other exemplars are too fragile to reproduce.

Theodosia Alleine (fl. 1653–77)

Her birth and her marriage placed Theodosia Alleine at the center of the Dissenting community in mid-seventeenth-century England. Born at Ditcheat, Somerset, the daughter of clergyman Richard Alleine (1611–1681), Theodosia married relative and clergyman Joseph Alleine (1634–1668) in 1659. Educated at Oxford, Joseph began his ministry in 1654 as assistant to the Reverend George Newton at Taunton. Theodosia ran a school for local children while her husband conducted church activities. Ejected from his position in 1662, Joseph began evangelizing and in the next several years was repeatedly jailed. His health failed and, after repeated illnesses during which he was nursed by Theodosia, Joseph died in 1668 at the age of 34. Theodosia survived him by at least sixteen years, during which she remarried. She died before 1685.

'A Full Narrative of His Life'

The book *The Life and Death of Mr Joseph Alleine* was first published in London in 1671 in 8°. Although many bibliographics list Theodosia as the author, the text is in fact a series of testimonials to Joseph written by many prominent puritan clergymen, including Richard Baxter, father-in-law Richard Alleine, George Newton, and Richard Fairclough. It concludes with several of Joseph's letters and his funeral sermon. Theodosia contributed the sixth chapter: 'A full Narrative of his Life from his silencing to his Death; by his Widow Mrs. Theodosia Alleine, in her own words; wherein is notably set forth with what patience he ran the race that was set before him, and fulfilled the Ministry that he had received in the Lord'. Theodosia's chapter, included in this volume, incorporates one of her husband's speeches, an 'Exhortation to his Fellow Sufferers', delivered in prison before they, but not he, were released.

The book proved to be extremely popular. It was reprinted once in 1671 (five exemplars surviving from the two printings), three times in 1672 (a total of twenty-four exemplars), once in 1673 (seven exemplars), once in 1677 (nine exemplars) and once in 1693 (two exemplars). The 1672 printings corresponded to the publication of Joseph's book *An Alarum to the Unconverted* which, according to the *Dictionary of National Biography*, sold 20,000 copies in its first edition, and another 50,000 in 1675 when it was reprinted as *Sure Guide to Heaven*. *The Life and Death of Mr. Joseph Alleine* thus presented an exemplary life of a puritan clergyman at a time when Dissenters were subject to harsh laws and governmental repression.

In contrast to the works of many of the other writers in these volumes, Theodosia's account reached an exceptionally wide audience. Her narrative is the sixth of nine chapters, all testifying to the high moral character of Joseph. The unidentified editor stresses the difficult circumstances of all the writers, commenting that two anonymous chapters were 'written by two Conformable Ministers' who clearly ran a risk of losing their livings if their friendship with Joseph were known. The same editor advises readers that Theodosia had prepared her contribution as notes to be used by 'a worthy Divine' in his own work, but he and others 'upon perusal, saw no reason to alter it, but caused it to be printed as it is'. Theodosia's chapter is noteworthy for the honesty with which she describes the hardships of life married to a man who appeared at times to be more devoted to the church than to his family. Moreover, it presents a rare example of a woman writer 'framing' the words of a man, as Theodosia inserts Joseph's 'Exhortation' in the middle of her chapter. The inclusion of her chapter in the commemorative volume dignifies both the private life of a public figure and the insights of an articulate woman.

'A full Narrative of his Life', excerpted from *The Life and Death of Mr Joseph Alleine*, and reproduced in Volume 2, is taken from the fine copy owned by Cambridge University Library, one of the few surviving exemplars of the first printing of 1671.

Anne Wentworth (fl. 1650s–77)

Married around 1653 and often in failing health, Anne Wentworth led a difficult life with her husband until her healing and conversion in 1671 (Old Style 1670). From that time onwards, her marriage worsened until, after considerable provocation, she left it in 1674 (Old Style 1673). Her actions precipitated great public arguments with her Baptist church in London, headed by Hanserd Knollys. These experiences prompted her to write the two works discussed here as well as *England's Spiritual Pill* (?1678) and *The Revelation of Jesus Christ* (1679). Several of her letters appear in *CSPD* 1677.

True Account

Wentworth's first publication was *A True Account of Anne Wentworths Being Cruelly, Unjustly, and Unchristianly Dealt with by Some of those People Called Anabaptists*, a 4° edition, printed in 1676, probably in London, with a simply-designed title page. It bears the author's name not only on the title page but at the end of the narrative. Only two exemplars exist, and the work went through only one printing. The text itself is a narrative describing Wentworth's view of her miserable marriage and the harsh judgment she received from members of her church. It also is noteworthy for its insistence that God's word was never meant to justify the mistreatment of a wife and that she had a right to redress of grievances.

The base copy of this extremely rare book reproduced in Volume 2 is owned by the Folger Shakespeare Library.

A Vindication

The following year saw the publication of *A Vindication of Anne Wentworth, Tending to the Better Preparing of All People for Her Larger Testimony, which is Making Ready for Publick View*. This text, a 4° edition, includes a supporting but unsigned letter 'by an eminent Christian' and a hymn by Wentworth, called by her a 'Song of Tryumph'. Like her previous work, this text was printed once. Two exemplars survive. In this work, Wentworth elaborates on her previous narrative, this time presenting more scriptural references to underscore the rightness of her leaving her husband. The supporting letter calls attention to *A True Account*, asking Baptist preachers 'Can you prove that God hath not spoken to her and by her? No, you dare not produce that Book of hers ... you too well know it would demonstrate her to be in the Truth, and your selves shameless Lyars'. Readers may compare Wentworth's two books to Susanna Parr's *Svsanna's Apologie Against the Elders* (in Volume 1). Both assert their right to independent action and challenge criticism of them based on gender, but for Wentworth gender is at the heart of her dispute with her church as she makes the case for her right to leave her marriage. Excerpts appear in Graham *et al.*, *Her Own Life: Autobiographical Writings by Seventeenth- Century English Women*.

The base copy of this very rare book reproduced in Volume 2 is the exemplar owned by The British Library. The sole other existing copy, owned by the William Andrews Clark Memorial Library, is cropped at the top, affecting page numbers.

Mary Penington (c. 1625–82)

The daughter of Anne (Fagge) and Sir John Proude, Mary Penington was born around 1625 in Kent and was orphaned by 1628. The heiress of both her parents, trained as an oculist and druggist, she married Sir William Springett in 1642. He became a colonel in the parliamentary army, dying in 1644. Mary and William had two children, including daughter Gulielma Maria, who later became the wife of prominent Quaker William Penn. In 1654 Mary married the clergyman Isaac Penington, son of Isaac Penington, Alderman and Lord Mayor of London in 1642, who was subsequently imprisoned for his antiroyalist activity and died in the Tower of London in 1661. At some time subsequent to their marriage, Mary and Isaac joined the Society of Friends. By 1656 her house at Chalfont St Peter (Buckinghamshire) had become a meeting house. Isaac wrote extensively for the Society, and, after he died in 1679, his works were collected and published. After his death Mary wrote several manuscript accounts of her life which she prepared for her family and which were published by Quaker printers in the late eighteenth and early nineteenth centuries: *A Brief Account of My Exercises from Childhood* (1668–80), published in a work by Christopher Taylor (1797); and *Some Account of the Circumstances in the Life of Mary Penington, from Her Manuscript, Left for Her Family* (1821, 1848). Mary died in 1682 and was buried next to her husband at Jordans, Buckinghamshire. The Chalfont Meeting was established with assistance from Mary's estate.

'Mary Penington her Testimony'

'Mary Penington her Testimony concerning her Dear Husband' was her only work published in her lifetime. It is a two-page account that forms part of the preface to *The Works of the Long-Mournful and Sorely-Distressed Isaac Penington, Whom the Lord in his Tender Mercy, at length Visited and Relieved by the Ministry of that Despised People, called Quakers*, a handsomely-produced folio volume published in London by Benjamin Clark in 1681. Mary's text accompanies the testimonies of many prominent Quakers, including George Fox and the Peningtons' son-in-law William Penn. Mary is the only woman represented. *The Works* was frequently reprinted throughout the eighteenth and nineteenth centuries. Sixteen exemplars of the first edition survive. In a concluding note, Mary comments that she wrote her account 'between 12 and 1 at night, while I was watching with my sick child'. Her text focuses on Isaac's character, especially his '*hidden life*', known only to herself and God. Like Theodosia Alleine, Mary Penington offers her unique perspective as a further way of understanding and appreciating her husband. Unlike Alleine, Mary describes her great sense of loss and the companionate nature of her marriage.

Because of its high degree of legibility, the exemplar owned by The Huntington Library was chosen as base copy for Volume 2.

Mary Rowlandson (?1635–1711)

Although she was probably born in England, Mary Rowlandson is best known as one of the earliest American writers. Born around 1635, she was the daughter of John White, one of the founders of Lancaster, Massachusetts, where her family moved in 1653. Around 1656 she married Joseph Rowlandson, minister of Lancaster, with whom she had four children. Little is known of their lives until 10 February 1676 (Old Style 1675) when Mary and her children were captured by Indians in an attack on Lancaster that was part of King Philip's War. Mary was moved several times by her captors, living with them until she was ransomed in May. Her three surviving children were released shortly thereafter. In the following year she and her husband moved to Wethersfield, Connecticut, where he was called to the ministry. According to the *Dictionary of American Biography*, Wethersfield voted Mary an allowance when her husband died in 1678. Remarried in 1679 to Captain Samuel Talcott, she died in 1711.

A True History of the Captivity & Restoration

The first edition of Rowlandson's narrative was published in Boston in 1682, under the title *The Soveraignty & Goodness of God ... Being a Narrative of the Captivity and Restauration of Mrs. Mary Rowlandson*. Only fragments survive. A second edition, 'Corrected', was printed in Cambridge, Massachusetts by Samuel Green in 1682 and reprinted in London in the same year under the title *A True History of the Captivity & Restoration of Mrs. Mary Rowlandson, A Minister's Wife in New-England*. In the English version, but not the American, Mary's narrative is framed by an opening preface, signed "Per Amicum", and concludes with what is identified as Joseph Rowlandson's last sermon. Six exemplars survive of the American edition, twelve of the English. The existing copies of the American edition, an 8º, are in poor condition: the type is still clearly legible, but many pages are torn or have portions missing. The extant copies of the English edition, a 4º, are in much better condition, although the typeface is smaller and more difficult to read than in the American edition. One of the earliest books by an American woman, Rowlandson's work is also one of the first examples of the New World captivity narrative. Its form and sensibility established many of the features repeated in subsequent narratives through the nineteenth century. The book went through some thirty printings before the advent of modern editions, and remains one of the most frequently anthologized works of early American literature. The American edition most recently has been edited by Neal Salisbury for the Bedford Series in History and Culture (Boston: Bedford, 1997). Because of its pivotal position in both American and European history, the book continues to attract extensive critical attention. Of all the works in these two volumes, Rowlandson's is the only one with a substantial secondary bibliography. Earlier twentieth-century scholars studied the text as a step in the formation of a national identity. Recent studies have considered Rowlandson's narrative as a microcosm of colonialism, seeing in her text the psychological damage feared by Europeans in their encounters with alien 'others'; and as a vehicle for self-assertion amid conflicts of gender roles and expectations. Both feminist and historical scholars have incontrovertibly established Rowlandson's work as a key text in the development of modern identity.

Because of the poor condition of existing American editions and many of the London editions, the London edition owned by The Huntington Library has been chosen as base copy for Volume 2.

Hannah Allen (fl. before 1670–83)

Born around 1638, Hannah Allen was the daughter of John Archer of Snelton, Derbyshire, and his wife, the daughter of William Hart of Uttoexeter Woodland, Staffordshire. Her father died when she was a child, and she was raised partly by her mother in Snelton and partly by her paternal aunt in London. Around 1654 she married the merchant Hannibal Allen, who died at sea around 1662. This event precipitated a serious depression, from which Allen suffered for several years, aided by her relatives, several members of the clergy and her Baptist faith. Some time after 1667 she married Charles Hatt of Warwickshire; she died before 1683.

A Narrative of God's Gracious Dealings

The account of Allen's depression, *A Narrative of God's Gracious Dealings with that Choice Christian Mrs. Hannah Allen*, published with the running title *Satan's Methods and Malice Baffled*, was printed in 8° in London by John Wallis in 1683. The text begins with an extensive, anonymous preface describing the exemplary nature of the mental struggles of this 'Now-glorified Soul' who presumably died before publication. The narrative follows, giving a detailed description of the onset and progress of Allen's depression and its treatment, and concludes with several scriptural passages that Allen found especially comforting. Seven exemplars exist of this work, and apparently all are missing pages 75 through 78. There are no modern editions. The preface to the work explicitly urges the reader to regard this narrative as an aid in combatting what the writer perceives to be a common problem confronting the faithful: the depression that sometimes arises from an overwhelming conviction of one's own sinfulness. The writer compares Allen's experiences to those of '*an eminent and holy Minister of Christ, that once counted himself a Reprobate*' and finds in their experiences strong reasons to avoid sin and assert one's commitment to one's faith in light of the irreligion of the times. Like the work of her sister Baptist Katherine Sutton, Allen's text may be compared to Bunyan's *Grace Abounding to the Chief of Sinners* and other Baptist spiritual autobiographies, many of which describe encounters with despair. Allen's experiences are noteworthy because they form the principal subject of her book and because she describes at length the efforts of others to respond to her with compassion. As presented, her depression was the central, formative experience in her religious life, challenging her as others were challenged by prison and government persecution. Excerpts appear in Graham *et al.*, *Her Own Life: Autobiographical Writings by Seventeenth-Century English Women*.

Although it is severely cropped, we have chosen as base copy for Volume 2 the exemplar owned by The British Library because of its superior legibility. Unfortunately it, like all other known exemplars, is missing pages 75–78.

Barbara Blaugdone (1609–1704)

A determined Quaker traveler and preacher, Barbara Blaugdone was probably born in Bristol around 1609. She died in London in 1704 at the age of 95. Introduced in 1654 to the Society of Friends by John Audland, husband of Anne Audland, who herself was a distinguished pamphleteer for the Friends, Blaugdone journeyed throughout England and Ireland 'on my own Purse', facing such hardships as robbery, whipping, death threats and an accusation of witchcraft. Imprisoned for her religious activities in 1655, 1664, 1681 and 1683, Blaugdone occasionally supported herself as a schoolmistress.

An Account of the Travels

Blaugdone's sole publication, *An Account of the Travels, Sufferings & Persecutions of Barbara Blaugdone*, was published in small 8° by Quaker printer Tace Sowle in London in 1691. The book has a plain, unadorned title page and begins with Blaugdone's narrative, with no intervening prefatory matter. Four exemplars survive. There are no modern editions. Blaugdone gives very few details of her own life before her conversion. In effect, her life begins at that point, and her narrative is filled with specific references to people and places, and to the events that frequently sent her to prison. The text is a chronicle of the author's determination to preach in the face of opposition and hardship, once even being accused of witchcraft. Her method of presenting her experiences compares to Katherine Evans and Sarah Cheevers's narrative of their own experiences in captivity. All confront others who do not share their religious convictions but, in contrast to Rowlandson's account of her captivity, reproduced in Volume 2, all three Quaker women emphasize not their loss of freedom but their efforts to assert and witness publicly for their faith.

The base copy reproduced in Volume 2, chosen for its legibility, availability, and association with the Society of Friends, is owned by the Friends House Library.

Susannah Blandford (fl. 1658–1700)

The S.B. of the title page of *A Small Account* is believed to be Susanna Blandford, a follower of the Quaker preacher William Rogers from Northamptonshire. S.B. was born around 1658, brought up in the Church of England, began to suffer from spiritual troubles in her teens and experienced conversion at the age of 24. She was married, had several children and also wrote *A Small Treatise Writ by One of the True Christian Faith; who Believes in God and in his Son Jesus Christ*, published in London in 1700.

A Small Account

Blandford's personal narrative, *A Small Account Given Forth*, was printed in 8°, in 1698, probably in London. The book opens with a brief preface by Blandford declaring her desire to share her experiences with others. The narrative follows, and the text concludes with a poem and several postscripts defending the beliefs and actions of the Quakers. The book was published once; three exemplars survive. There are no modern editions. In contrast to the works of other Quaker women included in these volumes, Blandford includes no account of prison or physical hardship. She emphasizes instead her spiritual journey, the teachings that most influenced her and her opposition to extensive preaching, especially by women. The concluding postscripts exemplify her confidence in discussing the politics of religion in a climate unfavorable to Dissenters.

Chosen for its availability and legibility, the exemplar owned by Cambridge University Library is reproduced in Volume 2.

References

Wing C 6008 [Cook(e)], Wing P 551 [Parr], Wing T 935 [Evans and Cheevers], Wing S 6212 [Sutton], Wing W 3772 [Wyndham], Wing D 444 [Davy], Wing A 1011B [Alleine], Wing W 1355A [Wentworth, *True Account*], Wing W 1356 [Wentworth, *Vindication*], Wing P 1149 [Penington], Wing R 2094 [Rowlandson], Wing A 1025 [Allen], Wing A 410 [Blaugdone], Wing B 3163A [Blandford]

Bell, Maureen, George Parfitt, and Simon Shepherd (eds) (1990), *A Biographical Dictionary of English Women Writers 1580–1720*, Boston: GK Hall

Besse, Joseph (1753), *A Collection of the Sufferings of the People Called Quakers, for the Testimony of a Good Conscience*, 2 vols, London

Bevan, Joseph Gurney (1831), *Memoirs of the Life of Isaac Penington; to which is Added A Review of His Writings*, Philadelphia: Thomas Kite

Blain, Virginia, Patricia Clements, and Isobel Grundy (eds) (1990) *The Feminist Companion to Literature in English: Women Writers from the Middle Ages to the Present*, New Haven and London: Yale University Press

Blount, Thomas (1681), *Boscobel, or, The Compleat History of His Sacred Majesties Most Miraculous Preservation after the Battle of Worcester, 3 Sept. 1651*, 3rd ed., 2 vols, London

Crawford, Patricia (1993), *Women and Religion in England 1500–1720*, London: Routledge

Derounian-Stodola, Kathryn Zabelle and James Arthur Levernier (1993), *The Indian Captivity Narrative, 1550–1900*, Twayne's United States Authors Series, 622, New York: Twayne Publishers; Toronto: Maxwell Macmillan Canada

Ebersole, Gary L. (1995), *Captured by Texts: Puritan to Postmodern Images of Indian Captivity*, Charlottesville and London: University Press of Virginia

Edwards, Karen (1997), '*Susanna's Apologie* and the Politics of Privity', *Literature and History*, 6

Graham, Elspeth (1990), 'Authority, Resistance and Loss: Gendered Difference in the Writings of John Bunyan and Hannah Allen' in Anne Laurence, W. R. Owens and Stuart Sim (eds), *John Bunyan and his England, 1628–88*, London and Ronceverte: Hambledon Press

Graham, Elspeth (1996), 'Women's Writing and the Self' in Helen Wilcox (ed.), *Women and Literature in Britain, 1500–1700*, Cambridge and New York: Cambridge University Press

Graham, Elspeth, Hilary Hinds, Elaine Hobby, and Helen Wilcox (eds) (1989), *Her Own Life: Autobiographical Writings by Seventeenth-Century English Women*, London: Routledge

Greene, David L. (1985), 'New Light on Mary Rowlandson', *American Literature*, 20

Hobby, Elaine (1992), '"Discourse So Unsavory": Women's Published Writings of the 1650s' in Isobel Grundy and Susan Wiseman (eds), *Women, Writing, History 1640–1740*, Athens: University of Georgia Press

Hobby, Elaine (1988), *Virtue of Necessity: English Women's Writing 1646–1688*, London: Virago

Jansen, Sharon (1996), *Dangerous Talk and Strange Behavior: Women and Popular Resistance to the Reforms of Henry VIII*, New York: St. Martin's

Knollys, Hanserd (1691), *An Answer to a Brief Discourse Concerning Singing in the Publick Worship of God in the Gospel-Church* [London]

Mack, Phyllis (1992), *Visionary Women: Ecstatic Prophecy in Seventeenth-Century England*, Berkeley: University of California Press

Mallard, Ian M. (1963), 'Hymns of Katherine Sutton', *Baptist Journal*, January

Mendelson, Sara Heller (1985), 'Stuart Women's Diaries and Occasional Memoirs' in Prior, Mary (ed.), *Women in English Society 1500–1800*, London and New York: Methuen

Pratt, Mary Louise (1992), *Imperial Eyes: Travel Writing and Transculturation*, London and New York: Routledge

S., W. (1661), *A Complete Collection of the Lives, Speeches, Private Passages, Letters and Prayers of those Persons Lately Executed*, London

Smith, Joseph (1867), *A Descriptive Catalogue of Friends' Books, Or Books Written by Members of the Society of Friends, Commonly Called Quakers, From their First Rise to the Present Time*, 2 vols, London: Joseph Smith, rpt (1970) New York: Kraus Reprint Co.

Warburton, Rachel M. (1999), 'Not a Description of Sodom's Glory: Quaker Women Travelers and Biblical Geography', Women and Knowledge in the Seventeenth Century, Renaissance Society of America Annual Meeting, The J. Paul Getty Museum and Research Institute, 27 March

ELIZABETH SKERPAN-WHEELER

'A full Narrative', excerpted from *The Life and Death of Mr. Joseph Alleine* (Wing A 1011B), classmark U*.7.178[1], is reproduced by permission of the Syndics of Cambridge University Library. The text block of the original measures 131 × 79 mm.

Readings where the Cambridge University Library copy is obscure:

63.17 his
63.18 sent
63.19 so
63.22 lost
63.23 not
63.30 ceeding
63.33 mer
63.34 the
63.35 creased
63.39 But
63.40 ten
65.28 day
65.30 Bed
65.31 and
65.32 to
65.33 ters
65.24 to
65.35 his
65.38 met
65.39 at
67.1 respect
67.2 ferers
67.16 thing
67.22 time
67.27 ving
81.11 me
81.12 your
81.27 visit
81.28 them
81.33 fearing
81.34 hoping
93.1 me
93.3 long
93.7 Husbands
97.3 and
97.4 panted
97.5 to
97.6 in

Mr Bates

THE Life and Death Of that Excellent MINISTER OF CHRIST

Mr JOSEPH ALLEINE,

Late Teacher of the CHURCH of *Taunton* in *Somerset-shire*, Assistant to Mr. NEWTON.

PROV. 10. 7.

The memory of the just is blessed: but the name of the wicked shall rot.

Printed *Anno Domini* 1671.

CHAP. VI.

A full Narrative of his Life, (from his Silencing till his Death) by his Widdow Mrs. Theodosia Allein, *in her own words, wherein is notably set forth, with what patience he ran the Race that was set before him, and fullfilled the Ministery that he had received of the Lord.*

BEfore the *Act for Uniformity* came forth, my Husband was *very earnest day and night with God*, that his way might be *made plain* to him, that he might not desist from such Advantages of saving Souls, with any scruple upon his Spirit; In which when he saw those *Clauses* of *Assent*, and *Consent*, and *Renouncing the Covenant*, he was *fully satisfied*: But he seemed so *moderate before*, that both my self and others, *thought* he *would have Conformed*: He often saying, *he would not leave his work for small or dubious Matters*: But seeing his way *so plain* for quitting the publeck *Station that he held*, and being throughly perswaded of this, that the Ejection of the Ministers out of their Places, did not disobleige them from Preachieg the Gospel, nor the People from attending upon their Ministery, as his Book Intituled, *A Call to* Archippus, sheweth, after that Black and Mournful Sabbath, in which he took his Farewell (with much affection) of his beloved People. He presently took up a firm Resolution to go on with his Work in *private*, both of *Preaching*, and *Visiting* from House to House, till he should be carried to Prison, or Banishment, which he counted upon, the Lord assisting him: And this Resolution without delay he prosecuted; for the *Thursday* after he appointed a *Solomne Day* of *Humiliation*, when he Preached to as many as would adventure themselves with him at our own house: But it being then a strange thing to the most Professors to Suffer, they seemed much affrighted at the threatenings of Adversaries; so that there was not such an appearance at such opportunities as my Husband expected: whereupon he made it his work to converse much with those he perceived to be most

timmertimerous, and to satisfie the scruples that were on many amongst us; so that the Lord was pleased in a short time to give him such success that his own People waxed bold for the Lord, and his Gospel: and multinudes flocked into the Meetings at whatsoever season they were, either by day or night; which was a great incouragement to my Husband, that he went on with much vigour and affection in his Work, both of *Preaching*, and *Visitting*, and *Catechising* from house to house.

He went also frequently into the Villages and Places about the Townes where their Ministers were gone, as most of them did flye, or at the least desist for a considerable time after *Bartholomew* day: Whereever he went the Lord was pleased to give him great success; many Converted, and the generallity of these annimated to cleave to the Lord and his ways.

But by this the Justices rage was much heigtehned against him; and he was often threatened, and sought for; But by the power of God, whose work he was delighted in, was preserved much longer out of their hands then he expected: For he would often say, If it pleased the Lord to grant him three Mon: his Liberty before he went to Prison he should account himself favoured by him, aud should with more chearfulness go, when he had done some work. At which time we sold off all our Goods, prepareing for a Goal, or Banishment, where he was desirous I should attend him, as I was willing to do, It alwaies having bin more greivous to me to think of being absent from him, then to suffer with him.

He also resolved when they would suffer him no longer to stay in *England*, he would go to *China*, or some remote Part of the World and publish the Gospel there.

It pleased the Lord to indulge him, that he went on in his work from *Bartholomew* day till *May* the 26*th* after: Though often threatened, yet he was never interrupted, though the People both of the Town and Country were grown so resolute that they came in great multitudes, at whatever season the *Meeting* was appointed; very seldom missing twice a Sabbath, and often in the week: I know that he hath *Preached* fourteen times in eight dayes, and ten often, and six or seven ordinarily in these Months, at home and abroad, besides his frequent converse with Souls. He then laying aside all other

Studyes which he formerly so much delighted in, because he accounted his time would be but short. And the Lord (as he often told me) made his work in his Ministry far more easie to him, by the supplyes of his Spirit both in Gifts and Grace, as did evidently appear both in his *Doctrine* and *Life*; he appearing to be more Spiritual, and Heavenly, and affectionate then before, to all that heard him, or conversed with him.

When he was taken up for Prison, he was not only contented, but joyful to suffer for the Name of Jesus and his Gospel, which was so dear to him; Intimating that God had given him much more time then he expected, or askt of him, and that he accounted it cause of rejoycing, and his honour, that he was one of the first called forth to suffer for his name.

Although he was very suddenly Surprised, yet none could discern him to be in the least moved.

He was upou a *Saterday* in the Evening about six a clock seazed on by an *Officer* of our Town, who had rather have been otherwise Imployed, as he hath often said; but that he was forced to a speedy Execution of the Warrant, by a Justice's Clerk, who was sent on purpose with it to see it Executed, because he feared that none of the Town would have done it.

The Warrant was in the Name of three Justices, to Summon him to Appear forthwith at one of their Houses, which was about two Mile from the Town, but he desired liberty to stay and Sup with his Family first, supposing his Entertainment there would be such as would repuire some Refreshment: This would not be granted, till one of the Chief of the Town was bound for his speedy Appearance: His Supper being prepared, he sat down eating very heartily, and was very chearful, but full of holy and gracious Expressions, sutable to his and our present state, After Supper, having Prayed with us, he with the Officer, and two or three Friends accompanying him, repaired to the Justice's House, where they lay to his Charge, that he had broken the Act of Uniformity by his Preaching; which he denied, saying: That he had Preached neither in any Church, nor Chappel, nor place of publick Worship, since the 24*th.* of *August*, and what he did was in his own Family, with those others that came there to hear him. When that would not do, they Accused him for being at a Riotous tons Assembly; though there were no Threats, nor dangerous Words, no Staves, nor Weapons, no Fear so much as pretended to be struck into any man, nor any other Business met about, then Preaching and Prayer. Here he was much Abused, receiving many Scorns, and Scoffs from the Justices, and their Associates, who were met to hear his Examination, also from the Ladys and other Gentlemen, who called him often Rogue, and told him he deserved to be Hanged, and if he were not, he should be Hanged for him: With many such like Scurrilous passages, which my Husband received with much Patience, and seeming, as they apprehended by his Countenance, to slight their Threatnings; they were more Inraged at him, they urged him much to Accuse himself, which they seeing they could not bring him to; and having no Evidence as appeared after: Yet did make his Mittimus for to go to the Geal on *Monday* Morning, after they had detained him till Twelve at Night, abusing him beyond what I do now distinctly remember, or were fit to Express.

Assoon as he returned, it being so late about two a Clock, he lay down on the Bed in his Clothes' where he had not slept above two or three Hours at the most, but he was up, spending his time in Converse with God, till about Eight a Clock; by which Hour, several of his Friends were come to Visit him: But he was so watched, and the Officer had such a charge, that he was not suffered to Preach all that Sabbath, but spent the day in discoursing with the various Companys, that came flocking in from the Town, and Villages, to Visit him; Praying often with them, as he could be permitted. He was exceeding chearful in his Spirit, full of Admirations of the Mercys of God, and incouraging all that came to be bold, and venture for the Gospel, and their Souls; notwithstanding what was come upon him for their sakes: For as he told them, he was not at all moved at it, nor did not in the least repent of any thing he had done, but accounted himself happy, and under that Promise *Christ* makes to his, in the 5th. of *Matthew*, that he should be doubly and trebly blessed now he was to suffer for his sake: And was very earnest with his Brethren in the Ministry, that came to see him, that they would not in the least desist when he was gone, that there might not be one Sermon the less in *Taunton*; and with the People to attend the Ministry with greater Ardency, Diligency, and Courage, than before; assuring them how sweet and comfortable it was to him, to consider what he had done for God, in the Months past: And that he was going to Prison full of Joy, being confident that all these things would turn to the furtherance of the Gospel, and the Glory of God.

But he not being satisfied to go away and not leave some Exhortations with his People, he appointed them to meet him abone One or Two a Clock in the Night, to which they shewed their readiness, though at so unseasonable a time: There was of Young and Old, many Hundreds, he Preached and Prayed with them about three Hours.

And so with many yernings of his Bowels towards them, and theirs toward him, they took their farewel of each other; a more affectionate Parting could not well be.

About Nine a Clock, he with two or three Friends that were willing to accompany him, set out for *Illchester*: The Streets mere Lined on both sides with People, and many followed him a foot some Miles out of the Town, with such Lamentations (that he told me after) did so affect him, that he could scarce bear them; but the Lord so strengthened him, that he passed through them all with great Courage, and Joy, labouring both by his chearful Countenance and Expressions, to encourage them.

He carried his Mittimus himself, and had no Officer with him; but when he came there, he found the Goaler absent, and took that oportunity to Preach before he went into the Prison; which was accounted by his Adversaries, a great addition to his former Crime. Assoon as the Goaler came, he delivered his Mittimus, and was clapped up in the *Bridewel* Chamber, which was over the common Goal. When he came to the Prison, he found there Mr. *John Norman*, late Minister of *Bridgwater*, who for the like cause, was Apprehended and Committed a few days before him (a Man who for his singular Abilities in Preaching, his fervent Zeal and holy boldness in the Cause of Christ, his Constancy to his Principles in the most Wavering and Shaking times, joyned with an exemplary Carriage and Conversation, was deservedly had in great Repute among the People of God in these *western*

parts;

parts; and indeed there were very few that knew him, either among the sober Gentry, or Commonalty, but for his eminent Parts, and spotless Life, had great respects for him.) There were also Five more Ministers, with Fifty *Quakers*, which had all their Lodgings in the same Room, only parted with a Mat, which they had done for a little more Retirement. It was not long after before Mr. *Coven*, and Mr. *Powel*, with Eight more, were brought into the same place, being taken at Meetings; which made their Rooms very straight, and it was so nigh to the upper part of the Prison, that they could touch the Tiles as they lay in their Beds; which made it very irksome, the Sun lying so hot on it all the day, and there being *so many* of them, and so much Resort continually of Friends, they had very little Air, till they were forced to take down the Glass, and some of the Tiles, to let in some Refreshment. But here they were confined to Lie and eat their Meals, and had no place but a small Garden, joyned to the place where all the common Prisoners were, which was no Retirement for them, they having there and in their Chamber, the constant noise of those Wretches, except when they slept; who lay just under them, their Chains ratling, their Tongues often blaspheming, or else Roaring and Singing by Night, as well as in the day: And if they went into the Courts of the Prison, there was the sight of their Clothes hanging full of Vermin, and themselves in their Rags and Chains: Bnt that which was most grievous to them, they had no place to Retire to God in, neither alone, nor together. They were also much mollested by the *Quakers*, who would frequently disturb them by their Cavils, in the times of their Preaching, Praying, and Singing. and would come and work in their Callings just by them, while they were in Dutys, which was no small disturbance to them: And the want of the Air was more to my Husband, than to most of them, because he always Accustomed himself both in *Oxford*, and after, to spend his most secret Hours abroad in by Places, in the Fields, or Woods.

Assoon as he came into the Prison, he Preached and Prayed, that he called the *Consecration* of it. After he had spent a day or two in the Prison, being willing to have me either in the Town, or there, to attend him, and to keep company ny with his Friends, who came frequently to Visit him, he then began to fit up his Lodging; having prevailed with the Keeper for one Corner which was more private than the rest, to set his Bed in, about which he made a little Partition by some Curtains, that so he might have some Conveniency for Retirement. This was much comfort to him, and after a few Weeks, he got leave of the Keeper to go out a Mornings and Evenings a Mile or more, which he did constantly, unless the Weather or his Keepers fury did hinder him.

Their Diet was very good and sufficient, and sometimes abundant, by their Friends kindness. Here they Preacht once a day constantly, sometimes twice, and many came dayly to hear them Eight or Ten Miles round about the Country, and Multitudes came to Visit them; it being a strange sight to see Ministers laid in such a place. Their Friends were exceeding kind to them, endeavouring by their frequent Visits, and provisions for Diet, and supplys of Money, to make their Prison sweet to them.

But my Husband's Labours were much increased by this, spending all the day in Converse, he was forced to take much of the Night for his Studies, and secret Converse with God.

Thus he with my Brother *Norman*, and his Company, with their fellow Prisoners, continued in that place for four Months, being tossed from Sessions to Assizes. On the 14*th*. of *July* following, he was brought to the Sessions held at *Taunton*, and was there Indited for Preaching on *May*, the 17*th*. but the Evidence against him was so slender, that the Grand Jury could not find the Bill, so that he was not brought to his Answer there at all: And his Friends hoped he should have been Dismissed, it being the constant practice of the Court, that if a Prisoner be Indited, and no bill found, he is Freed by Proclamation. But however, my Husband was sent to Prison again until the Assizes, and to his Friends that earnestly expected his Inlargement, he said, *Let us bless God that his Will is done, and not the will of such Worms as we.*

August, 24*th*. He was again Indited at the Assizes, and though the Evidence was the very same, that at the Sessions was by the Grand Jury, judged Insufficient, yet now at the Assizes, the Bill was by them found against him. So was he had to the Bar, and his Inditement read, which was to this

purpose:

purpose: That he upon the 17th. day of *May*, 1663. with Twenty others to the Jurors unknown, did Riotously, Routously, and Seditiously, Assemble themselves together, contrary to the Peace of our Soveraign Lord the King, and to the great Terrour of his Subjects, and to the evil Example of others. Unto which, his Answer was, That as to Preaching, and Praying, which was the truth of the Case, of these things he was Guilty, and did own them as his Duty; but as for Riotous, Routous, and Seditious Assemblies, he did abhor them with his Heart, and of these he was not Guilty. At last he was found Guilty by the Petty Jury, and was Sentenced by the Judge, to pay an Hundred Marks, and to Lie in Prison till Payment should be made. Sentence being pronounced against him, he only made this brief Reply: *That he was glad that it had appeared before his Country, that whatsoever he was Charged with, he was Guilty of nothing but doing his Duty, and that all did appear by the Evidence, was only that he had Sung a Psalm, and Instructed his Family, others being there, and both in his own House: And that if nothing that had been urged would satisfie, he should with all Cheerfulness, and Thankfulness, accept whatsoever Sentence his Lordship should pronounce upon him, for so Good and Righteous a Cause.* Thus from the Assizes he was sent to Prison again, where he continued a whole Year wanting but Three days.

But the *Winter* coming on, they were willing to try if they could have the favour to be removed to the *Ward*, this place being like to be as *Cold* in the *Winter*, as it had been *Hot* in the *Summer* (there being no Chimney in the whole Chamber) which with some difficulty they obtained; and then had more comfortable Accommodations in all respects.

Here they had very great Meetings, Week-days, and Sabbath-days, and many days of Humiliation, and Thanksgiving. The Lords-days many Hundreds came. And though my Husband, and Brother *Norman*, had many Threats from the Justices, and Judges, that they should be sent beyond Sea, or carried to some Island, where they should be kept close Prisoners; yet the Lord preserved them by his Power, and thus ordered it, that their Imprisonment was a great furtherance to the Gospel, and brought much Glory to him, both by their Preaching, and Conversing with Souls: In which they

they had great Success through his Blessing on their Labours. My Husband having here more Freedom, made a little Book, Entitled *A call to Archippus*, to stir up his Non-conforming Brethren, to be diligent at their Work, whatsoever Dangers and Sufferings, they might meet withal: And because he could not go to his Flock, he had prepared for them, *The Synopsis of the Covenant*, which was after placed into one of my Fathers Books.

And for the help of the Governours of Families, in their Weekly Catechising those under their charge, he *Explained all the Assemblies shorter Catechism*, to which he *Annexed* an affectionate Letter, with Rules for their daily Examination; which were Printed and Dispersed into all their Houses by his Order, while he was a Prisoner. He also Writ many Holy, and Gracious, and Affectionate Letters to all his Relations, and many other Friends, to many Churches of Christ in other parts and places, both far and near.

His Sufferings that he underwent for the sake of the Gospel, could neither remit his Zeal, nor abate his Activity for God, but he would gladly imbrace all Opportunities of doing him Service. The Minister who was appointed to Preach at certain times to the Felons in the Prison: being by Sickness disabled for that Work, he freely performed that Office among them, as long as he was permitted; earnestly Exhorting them by Repentance towards God, and Faith toward our Lord Jesus Christ, to secure the Eternal welfare of their Souls; freely bestowing upon them according to his Ability for their Relief, that by doing good to their Bodys, he might win upon them to receive good for their Souls. He was very forward to promote the Education of Youth, in the Town of *Juelchester*, and Country adjacent, freely bestowing Catechisms on those that were of poor Families, to Instruct them in the Principles of Religion; stirring up the Elder to Teach, and incouraging the Younger to Learn. He was a serious and faithful Monitor to his fellow Sufferers, if he espied any thing in any of them that did not become the Gospel for which they Suffered.

Here, as elsewhere, he was a careful redeemer of his time, his constant practice was early to begin the day with God; rising about Four of the Clock, and spending a considerable

part

part of the Morning in Meditation and Prayer, and then falling close to his Study in some Corner or other of the Prison, where he could be private. At times, he would spend near the whole Night in these Exercises, not putting off his Clothes at all, only taking the Repose of an Hour or two in his night Gown upon the Bed, and so up again. When any came to Visit him, he did not entertain them with needless Impertinent discourse, but that which was Serious, Profitable, and Edifying, in which he was careful to apply himself to them, according to their several Capacities, whether Elder, or Younger; Exhorting them to those gracious Practises which by reason of their Age, or Temper, Calling, or Codition, he apprehended they might be most defective in, and dehorting them from those Evils they might be most prone, and liable unto. He rejoyced that he was accounted worthy to Suffer for the Work of Christ, and he would Labour to Incourage the Timerous and Faint-hearted, by his own and others Experience, of the Mercy and Goodness of God in Prison, which was far beyond what they could have thought, or expected. He was a careful observer of that Rule of the Lord Jesus, *Mat.* 5. 44. *Love your enemies, bless them that curse you, do good to them that hate you, and pray for them that despitefully use you, and persecute you.* It was none of his practice to Exclaim against those that were the greatest Instruments of his Sufferings, but to pity their condition, requesting for them, as the Martyr *Stephen* did for those that stoned him, *That God would not lay this sin of theirs to their charge.* The greatest harm that he did wish to any of them, was, *That they might throughly be Converted and Sanctified, and that their Souls might be saved in the day of the Lord Jesus.*

In all his Imprisonment, at present I could not descern his Health to be the least Impaired, notwithstanding his abundant Labours; but cannot but suspect, as the Phisitians judged, that he had laid the foundation for that Weakness, which *suddenly after surprised him, and was his death.*

At his returnfrom the Prison, he was far more *earnest in his work than before*; yet willing to preserve his Liberty among his people, who had no Minister that had the Oversight of them, though some came and Preacht while he was absent; And the people flocked so greatly after him, that he judged

it

it best to divide the Company into Four, and resolved to Preach Four times each Sabbath to them: But finding sensibly that would be too hard for him, his Strength much decaying, he did forbear that Course, and Preacht only twice a Sabbath as formerly, and often on Week-days at Home and in the Country; and spent what time he had else from his Studying, in private Converse with God, as formerly he had done: Pressing all that feared the Lord, especielly those that were of a more weak and timerous Spirit, to a life of Courage and Activity for God, and to be much in helping one another, by their Converses, now Ministers were withdrawn; and to be much in the work of Praises and Thanksgiving to God, rejoycing and delighting themselves in him; and with chearfulness and readiness, denying themselves for him, and resigning themselves and all they did injoy, to him: Letting the World know, they could Live comfortably on a God alone, on his Attributes, and Promises, though they should have nothing else left.

He was very urgent with those that were Unconverted, to look with more care after their Salvation, now they were removed from them that longed for it, and had watched for their Souls; using this as an Argument often, that now they were fallen into the hands of such, *many* of which, if not *most* of them, had neither *Skill* nor *will* to save Souls: And setting home upon them with most tender Affections, what miserable Creatures they were while Unregenerate, telling them how his Heart did yearn for them, and his Bowels turned within him for them; how he did pray and weep for them, when they were asleep, and how willingly he had suffered a years Imprisonment: Nay, how readily he could shed his Blood to procure their Salvation. His Councels and Directions were many, and suted to the several states of those he thus Conversed with, both as to their degree and place, and their sins and wants, and would be too long to Recite, though I can remember many of them.

But it pleased the All-wise God, to take him off from the eager persuit of his Work, and designs for him, by visiting him in the later end of *August*, with much Weakness; so that he had not above three Months time after he came out of Prison: For he going about Sixteen Miles, at the Request of a Society

Society, whose Pastour was not able to come among them to Preach, and to Administer a more solemn Ordinance; he was so disabled, that he was not able to perform the great and chief Work, though he did adventure to Preach, but with much Injury to himself, because he would not wholly disappoint the people, who came so far as many of them did: With much difficulty after three or four days, I made way to get him home to *Taunton*, where we then Sojourned, and presently had the best Advice the most able Phisitians, both in, and round the Town, could give, who Advised together, and all Judged it to be from his abundant Labours, and the Preaching too soon after his Meals; as he did, when he Preacht four times a Sabbath, whereby he had so abated the Natural heat of his Stomach, that no Food would digest, nor oftentimes keep within him: He would assure us, he was in no pain, but a constant Discompsure in his Stomach, and a failing of his Appetite, that he could not for many Weeks, bear the sent of any Flesh-meat, nor retain any Liquours, or Broths, so that he Consumed so fast, that his Life seemed to draw to an end: But the Lord did so bless the means, that he Recovered out of this Distemper, after two Months time, but so lost the Use of his Arms from *October*, till *April*, that he could not put off, nor on his Clothes, nor often Write either his Notes, or any Letters, but as I wrote for him, as he dictated to me: He was by all Phisitians, and by my earnest beseechings, often diswaded from Preaching, but would not be prevailed with, but did go on once, and sometime twice a Sabbath, and in his private Visiting all that *Winter*; in the *Spring*, the use of his Arms returned, for which he was exceeding thankful to the Lord; and we had great hopes of his Recovering, and making use of further Remedies, he was able to go on with more freedom in his Work: And the *Summer* following by the use of Mineral Waters in *Wiltshire*, near the *Devises*, where he was born, his Strength was much Increased, he finding great and sensible good by them.

But he adventuring too much on what he had obtained, his Weakness returned frequently upon him the next *Winter*, and more in the *Spring* following, be seised as he was at the first: But it continued not long at a time, so that he did Preach often to his utmost strength (nay, I may say, much beyond the

stre-

strength) he had, both at Home and Abroad; going into some remote parts of the Country, where had been no Meetings kept all that time the Ministers had been out, which was two Years: And there he ingaged several of his Brethren, to go and take their Turns, which they did with great Success.

He had also agreed with two of his Brethren to go into *Wales* with them, to spread the Gospel there; but was prevented in that, by his Weakness increasing upon him: It was much that he did, but much more that he desired to do.

He was in this time much Threatned, and Warrants often out for him, and he was so far from being disturbed at it, that he rejoyced; that when he could do but little for God, because of his Distempers, God would so far honour him, that he should go and suffer for him in a Prison. He would often with chearfulness say, They could not do him a greater kindness: But the Lord was yet pleased to preserve him from their Rage, seeing him not then fit for the inconveniences of a Prison.

The Five Mile Act coming in Force, he removed to a place called *Wellington*, which is reckoned five Miles from *Taunton*, to a *Dyer's* House, in a very obscure place, where he Preacht on the Lords Days, as he was able: But the vigilant Eyes of his old Adversarys were so watchful over him, that they soon found him out, and resolved to take him thence, and had put a Warrant into the Constables hand to Apprehend him, and sent for our Friend, and threatned to send him to Goal for Entertaining such persons in his House: So my Husband returned to the House of Mr. *John Mallack*, a Merchant, who Lived about a Mile from *Taunton*, who had long solicited him to take his House for his Home: we being in such an unsetled state, my Husband thought it best to accept of his courteous Offer: But many of his Friends were willing to injoy him in the Town, and so earnest, that he did to satisfie them, go from one to another, staying a Fortnight, or three Weeks, or a Month at each House; but still took Mr. *Mallacks* for his Home: This Motion of his Friends he told me (though it was troublesome for us to be so unsettled) he was willing to embrace, because he knew not how soon he might be carried again from them to Prison, and he should have oppertunity to be more

more intimately Acquainted with them, and the state of their Souls, and of their Children, and Servants, and how they perform their Duties each to other in their Families.

He went from no House without serious Counsels, Comforts, or Reproofs, as their Conditions called for; dealing with all that were Capable, both Governours, and others particularly, acquainting them faithfully, and most affectionately, what he had seen amiss in any of them.

He went from no House that was willing to part with him; nor had he opportunity to answer the Requests of half that Invited us to their Houses: So that he would often bless God, and say with holy Mr. *Dod*, *That he had a hundred Houses for one, that he had parted with*; And though he had no Goods, he wanted nothing, his Father cared for him in every thing, that he Lived a far more pleasant Life, than his Enemies, who had turned him out of all: He was exceedingly taken with Gods Mercy to him, in Mr. *Mallack's* entertaining him and me so Bountifully, the House, and Gardens, and Walks, being a very great delight to him, being so Pleasant and Curious, and all Accommodations within sutable, so that he would often say, That he did as *Dives*, fare deliciously every day: But he hoped he should Improve it better than he did; and that God had inclined him to take care for many Poor, and for several of his Brethren in the Ministry; and now God did Reward him, by not suffering him to be at the least Expence for himself, or me.

He was a very strict observer of all Providences of every day, and did usually reckon them up to me before we went to Sleep, each Night, after he came into his Chamber and Bed, to raise his own Heart and Mind, to praise the Lord, and to trust Him, whom we had such experience of, from time to time.

The time of the Year being come for his going to the Waters, he was desirous to set one day apart for Thanksgiving to God, for all his Mercies to him and them, and so to take his leave of them.

Accordingly on the 10th. of *July*, 1665. divers of his Brethren in the Ministry, and many of his Friends of *Taunton*, met together to take their leave of him before his departure, at the House of Mr. *Mallack*, then Living about a Mile out of

F the

the Town. Where after they had been a while together, came two Justices, and several other persons attending them; Brake open the Doors by force (though they might have Unlatched them if they had pleased) and with Swords came in among them. After much deriding and menacing Language, which I shall not here Relate, having taken their Names, Committed them to the Custody of some Constables, whom they charged to bring them forth the next day at the *Castle Tavern*, in *Taunton*, before the Justices of the Peace there. The next day the Prisoners appeared, and answered to their Names; and after two days tedious Attendance, were all Convicted of a Conventicle, and Sentenced to pay three Pounds a piece, or to be committed to Prison threescore days. Of the Persons thus Convicted, but few either paid their Fines, or suffered their Friends to do it for them. My Husband, with Seven Ministers more, and Forty private Persons, were Committed to the Prison of *Ivelchester*: When he together with the rest of his Brethren, and Christian Friends, came to the Prison, his Carriage and Conversation there was every way as Exemplary, as in his former Confinement. Notwithstanding his Weakness of Body, yet he would constantly take his turn with the rest of the Ministers, in Preaching the Gospel in the Prison; which Turns came about the oftener, though there were Eight of them there together, because they had Preaching and Praying twice a day, almost every day they were in Prison, besides other Exercises of Religion, in which he would take his part.

And although he had many of his Flock confined to the Prison with him, by which means he had the fairer Opportunity of Instructing, and Watching over them, for their Spiritual good; yet he was not forgetful of the rest that were left behind, but would frequently visit them also, by his Letters, full of serious profitable Matter, from which they might Reap no small benefit, while they were debarred of his Bodily presence. And how greatly Solicitous he was for those that were with him (that they might be the better for their Bonds, walking worthy of the many and great Mercies they had enjoyed during their Imprisonment; that when they came home to their Houses, they might speak forth, and live forth the Praises of GOD, carrying themselves in every

respect

respect as becomes the Gospel, for which they had been Sufferers) you may clearly see by those parting Counsels that he gave them that Morning that they were Delivered, which I shall Recite in his own Words, as they were taken from his Mouth in Short-hand, by an intimate Friend, and fellow Prisoner; which you may take as followeth, *&c.*

Mr. Joseph Allein, *his Exhortation to his Fellow Sufferers, when they were to be Discharged from their Imprisonment.*

DEarly beloved Brethren, my Time is little, and my Strength but small, yet I could not consent that you should pass without receiving some parting Counsel, and what I have to say at Parting, shall be chiefly to you that are Prisoners, and partly also to you our Friends, that are here Met together. To you that are Prisoners, I shall speak something by way of Exhortation, and something by way of Dehortation.

By way of Exhortation.

First, Rejoyce with Trembling in your Prison Comforts, and see that you keep them in a Thankful Remembrance. Who can tell the Mercies that you have received here? My time, nor strength, will not suffice me to Recapitulate them. See that you rejoyce in GOD, but rejoyce with trembling. Do not think the Account will be little for Mercies, so many and so great. Receive these choice Mercies with a trembling hand, for fear least you should be found guilty of misimproving such precious Benefits, and so should Wrath be upon you from the Lord. Remember *Hezekiah*'s case, great Mercies did he receive, some Praises he did return, but not according to the Benefit done unto him; therefore was wrath upon him from

 the

the Lord, and upon all *Judah* for his sake, 2 *Chron.* 32. 24. Therefore go away with a holy Fear upon your hearts, least you should forget the loving Kindness of the Lord, and should not render to him according to what you have received.

Oh my Brethren, stir up your selves to render Praises to the Lord: You are the people that GOD hath formed for his Praise, and sent hither for his Praise; and you should now go Home as so many Trumpets to sound forth the Praises of GOD, when you come among your Friends. There is an Expression, *Psal.* 68. 11. *The Lord gave the Word, great was the company of them that published it.* So let it be said of the Praises of GOD now, great was the company of them that published them. GOD hath sent a whole Troop of you here together, let all these go home and sound the praises of *GOD* where ever you come; and this is the way to make his Praise glorious indeed. Shall I tell you a Story that I have read: There was a certain King that had a pleasant Grove, and that he might make it every way delightful to him, he caused some Birds to be Caught, and to be kept up in Cages, till they had Learned sundry sweet and Artificial Tunes; and when they were perfect in their Lessons, he let them Abroad out of their Cages into his Grove, that while he was walking in this Grove, he might hear them singing those pleasant Tunes, and teaching them to other Birds that were of a wilder Note. Brethren, this King is *GOD*, this Grove is his Church, these Birds are your selves, this Cage is the Prison; *GOD* hath sent you hither that you should Learn the sweet and pleasant Notes of his Praise: And I trust that you have Learned something all this while, *GOD* forbid else. Now *GOD* opens the Cage, and lets you forth into the Grove of his Church, that you may Sing forth his Praises, and that others may Learn of you too. Forget not therefore the Songs of the House of your Pilgrimage, do not return to your wild Notes again; keep the Mercy of *GOD* for ever in a thankful Remembrance, and make mention of them humbly as long as you live; then shall you answer the end for which he sent you hither: I trust you will not forget this place. When Queen *Mary* died, she said, *That if they did Rip her up, they should find* Callis *on her heart.* I hope that men shall find by you hereafter, that the Prison is upon your heart, *Illchester's* upon your heart.

Secondly

Secondly, Feed and Feast your Faith upon Prison Experiences. Do not think that GOD hath done this only for your present supply. Brethren, GOD hath provided for you, not only for your present supply in Prison, but to lay up for all your Lives, that experience that your Faith must live upon, till Faith be turned into Vision. Learn dependance upon GOD, and confidence in GOD, by all the Experiences that you have had here, *because thou hast been my help* (saith the Psalmist) *therefore under the shadow of thy wing will I rejoyce.* Are you at a loss at any time, then remember your Bonds. We read in Scripture of a time when there was no *Smith* in all *Israel*, and the *Israelites* were fain to carry their Goads, and other Instruments, to be sharpened down to the *Philistines*: So when your Spirits are low, and when your Faith is dull, carry them to the Prison to be sharpened, and quickned. Oh how hath the Lord confuted all our fears! Cared for all our necessitys! The Faith of some of you was sorely put to it for Corporal necessitys: You came hither not having any thing considerable to pay for your Charges here, but GOD took care for that: And you left poor miserable Families at Home, and no doubt but many troublesome thoughts were in your minds, what your Families should do for Bread, but GOD hath provided for them.

We that are Ministers left poor starvling Flocks, and we thought that the Countrey had been now stript, and yet GOD hath provided for them. Thus hath the Lord been pleased to furnish us with Arguments for our Faith, against we come to the next Distress: Though you should be called forth to leave your Flocks destitute, you that are my Brethren in the Ministry, and others their Families destitute, yet doubt not but GOD will provide, remember your Bonds upon all occasions. Whensoever you are in distress, remember your old Friend, remember your tried Friend.

Thirdly, Let Divne Mercy be as Oyl to the flame of your Love: *O love the Lord all ye his Saints.* Brethren, this is the Language of all GOD's dealings with you, they all call upon you to love the Lord your God with all your hearts, with all your souls, with all your strength. What hath GOD been doing ever since you came to this Prison? All that he hath been doing since you came hither, hath been to pour Oyl into the flames of your Love, thereby to increase and heighten them. GOD hath lost all these Mercies upon you, if you do not love him better then you did before. You have had Supplies, to what purpose is it unless you love GOD the more? If they that be in want love him better than you, it were better you had been in their Case. You have had health here, but if they that be in sickness love GOD better than you, it were better you had been in Sickness too: See that you love your Father, that hath been so tender of you. What hath GOD been doing, but pouring out his Love upon you? How were we mistaken? For my part, I thought that GOD took us upon his Knee to Whip us, but he took us upon his Knee to Dandle us. We thought to have felt the Strokes of his Anger, but he hath Stroked us as a Father his Children, with most dear Affection. Who can utter his loving Kindness! What (my Brethren) shall we be worse than *Publicans*? the *Publicans* will love those that love them. Will not you return Love for so much Love? Far be this from you, Brethren, you must not only exceed the *Publicans*, but the *Pharisees* too; therefore, surely you must love him that loveth you. This is my Business now to bespeak your love to GOD, to unite your hearts to him; Blessed be GOD for this Occasion, for my part I am unworthy of it. Now if I can get your Hearts nearer to GOD than they were, then happy am I, and blessed are you: Fain I would, that all these Experiences should knit our Hearts to GOD more, and endear us for ever to him. What? So much Bounty, and Kindness, and no Returns of Love? At least no further Returns? I may plead in the behalf of the Lord with you, as they did for the Centurion: *He loveth our Nation* (say they) *and hath Built us a Synagogue*. So I may say here, he hath Loved you, and poured out his Bounty upon you. How many friendly Visits from those, that you could but little expect of? Whence do you think this came? It is GOD that hath the Key of all these Hearts. He secretly turned the Cock, and caused them to pour forth Kindness upon you: There is not a motion of Love in the Heart of a Friend towards you, but it was GOD that put it in.

Fourthly, Keep your *Manna* in a Golden Pot, and forget not him that hath said so often, *Remember me*. You have had

Manna

Manna Rained plentifully about you, be sure that something of it be kept. Do not forget all the Sermons that you have heard here: O that you would Labour to Repeat them over, to Live them over! You have had such a Stock that you may live upon, and your Friends too (if you be Communicative). a great while together: If any thing have been wanting, time for the Digesting hath been wanting. See that you well Chew the Cud, and see that you especially remember *the Feasts of Love*. Do not you know who hath said to you so often, *Remember me?* How often have you heard that sweet Word since you came hither? What? Do you think it is enough to remember him for an Hour? No, but let it be a Living, and Lasting remembrance. Do not you write that Name of his in the Dust, that hath written your Names upon his Heart, Your High Priest hath your Names upon his Heart, and therewith is entered into the Holy Place, and keeps them there for a Memorial before the Lord continually. O that his Remembrance might be ever written upon your Hearts, written as with a Pen of a Diamond, upon Tables of Marble, that might never be worn out! That as *Aristotle* saith of the curious Fabrick of *Minerva*, that he had so ordered the Fabrick, that his Name was written in the midst, that if any went to take that out, the whole Fabrick was dissolved. So the Name of *Jesus* should be written upon the substance of your Souls, that they should pull all asunder, before they should be able to pull it out.

Fifthly, Let the Bonds of your Affliction, strengthen the bonds of your Affection. Brethren, GOD hath sent us hither to teach us among other things, the better to Love one another. Love is lovely, both in the sight of GOD and men, and if by your Imprisonment, you have profited in Love, then you have made an acceptable proficiency. O Brethren, look within; Are you not more indeared one to another? I bless the Lord for that Union, and Peace that hath been ever among you; but you must be sensible that we come very far short of that Love, that we owe one to another; we have not that love, that indearedness, that tenderness, that complacency, that Compassion towards each other, that we ought to have. Ministers should be more Indeared one to another, and Christians should be more dear to each other, then they

F 4 were

were before. We have Eaten and Drunk together, and Lived on our Fathers Love in one Family together; we have been Joyned together in one common Cause, and all put into one Bottom: O let the Remembrance of a Prison, and of what hath passed here, especially those Uniting Feasts, ingage you to Love one another!

Sixthly, Let present Indulgence fit you for future Hardships, and do not look that your Father should be always Dandling you on his Knee. Beloved, *GOD* hath used you like Fondlings now, rather than like Sufferers: What shall I say? I am at a loss, when I think of the tender Indulgence, and the yernings of the Bowels of our Heavenly Father upon us. But (my Brethren) do not look for such Prisons again.

Affliction doth but now Play, and Sport with you, rather than Bite you, but do you look that Affliction should hereafter fasten its Teeth on you to purpose: And do you look that that Hand that hath now gently Stroked you, may possibly Buffet you, and put your Faith hard to it, when you come to the next Tryal. This Fondness of your Heavenly Father, is to be expected only while you are young, and tender, but afterward you must look to follow your Business, and to keep your distance and to have Rebukes, and Frowns too when you need them. Bless *GOD* for what you have found here, but prepare you, this is but the beginning (shall I say the beginning of Sorrow, I cannot say so; for the Lord hath made it a place of Rejoycing) this is but the entrance of our Affliction; but you must look that when you are Trained up to better perfection, *GOD* will put your Faith to harder Exercise.

Seventhly, Cast up your Accounts at your Return, and see whether you have gone as much forward in your Souls, as you have gone backward in your Estates. I cannot be insensible but some of you are here to very great disadvantage, as to your Affairs in the World, having left your Business so rawly at Home in your Shops, Trades, and Callings, that it is like to be no little Detriment to you, upon this Account: But happy are ye if you find at your Return, that as much as your Affairs are gone backward, and behind-hand, so much your Souls have gone forward. If your Souls go forward in Grace by your Sufferings, blessed be *GOD* that hath

brought

brought you to such a place, as a Prison is.

Eighthly, Let the Snuffers of this Prison make your Light burn the brighter, and see that your Course, and Discourse be the more Savoury, Serious, and Spiritual for this present Tryal. O Brethren! Now the Voice of the Lord is to you, as it is in the Prophet *Isaiah* 60. 1. *Arise, and shine, now let your Light shine before men, that others may see your good Works, and glorifie your Father which is in Heaven.* It is said of those Preachers beyond Sea, that have been sent into *England*, and here reaped the benefit of our *English* practical Divinity: At their Return, they have Preached so much better than they had wont to do, that it hath been said of them: *Apparuit hunc fuisse in* Angliâ. So do you my Brethren, Live so much better than you had wont, that when men shall see the change in your Lives, they may say of you, *Apparuit hunc fuisse in Costodiâ.* See that your whole Course, and Discourse be more Spiritual and Heavenly then ever. See that you shine in your Families when you come Home; be you better Husbands, better Masters, better Fathers, study to do more than you have done this way, and to approve your selves better in your Family-Relations then you did before; that the savour of a Prison may be upon you in all Companys, then will you praise, and please the Lord.

Ninthly, And lastly, See that you walk *Accurately*, as those that have the Eyes of *GOD*, Angels, and Men, upon you: (my Brethren) you will be looked upon now with very Curious Eyes. *GOD* doth expect more of you then ever; for he hath done more for you, and he looketh what Fruit there will be of all this. Oh! may there be a sensible change upon your Souls, by the Showres that have fallen in Prison, as there is in the Greenness of the Earth, by the showres that have fallen lately Abroad. The Eyes of *GOD*, and Angels are upon you, and the eyes of men are upon you; now you will be *Critically* observed. Every one will be looking that you should be more Holy than others, that are called forth to this his glorious Dignity, to be the Witness of *Christ Jesus*, with the Loss of your Libertys.

By

By way of Dehortation, also I have these four things to Leave with you.

First, Revile not your Persecutors, but bless them and pray for them, as the Instruments of conveying great Mercies to you. Do not you so far forget the Rule of *Christ*, as when you come Home, to be setting your Mouths to talk against those that have Injured you. Remember the Command of your Lord; *Bless them that Curse you, Pray for them that dispitefully use you, and Persecute you.* Whatsoever they intended, yet they have been Instruments of a great deal of Mercy to us; and so we should pray for them, and bless *GOD* for the good we have received by them.

Secondly, Let not the humble acknowledgment of *GODS* Mercy, degenerate into Proud, Vain-glorious boasting, or Carnal triumph. I beseech you, see that you go Home with a great deal of Fear upon your Spirits in this respect, least Pride should get advantage of you, least instead of humble acknowledging *GODS* Mercy, there should be Carnal boasting. Beware of this I earnestly beg of you, for this will very much spoyl your Sufferings, and be very displeasing in the sight of *GOD*. But let your acknowledging of his Mercy, be ever with humble Self-abasing Thankfulness, and be careful that you do not make his Mercys to be the fuel of your Pride; which were to lose all at once.

Thirdly, Be not prodigal of your Liberty upon a conceit that the Prisons will be easie, nor fearful of adventuring your selves in the way of your Duty. Alas! I am affraid of both these Extreams, on the one hand least some among us having found a great deal of Mercy here, will now think there is no need of any Christian prudence, which is always necessary, and is a great duty. It is not Cowardise to make use of the best means to preserve our Liberty, not declining our Duty. On the otherside, there is fear least some may be fearful, and ready to decline their Duty; because they have newly tasted of a Prison for it. Far be it from you to distrust *GOD*, of whom you have had so great Experience, but be sure you hold on in your duty, whatsoever it cost you.

Fourthly, Do not Load others with Censures, whose Judgment,

ment, or Practice differs from yours, but humbly bless GOD that hath so happily directed you. You know all are not of the same mind as to the Circumstances of Suffering, and all have not gone the same way. Far be it from any of you (my Brethren) that you should so far forget your selves, as to be unmerciful to your Brethren, but bless GOD that hath directed you into a better way. Your Charity must grow higher than ever; GOD forbid that you should increase in Sensures, instead of increasing in Charity.

Having spoken to my fellow Prisoners, I have two Words to speak to you our Friends, and Brethren with us.

First, Let our Experience be your Incouragement. O love the Lord, ye our Friends, love the Lord, fear him for ever, believe in him, trust in him for ever, for our sakes; we have tasted of the Kindness of GOD.

You know how good GOD hath been to us, in Spirituals, in Temporals. Encourage your Hearts in the Lord your God, serve him the more freely, and gladly, for our sakes. You see we have tried, we have tasted how good the Lord is: Do you trust him the more, because we have tried him so much, and found him a Friend so Faithful, so Gracious, that we are utterly unable to speak his Praise. Go on and fear not in the way of your Duty: *Verily there is a Reward for the Righteous.* GOD hath given us a great Reward already, but this is but the least, we look for a Kingdom.

Secondly, And lastly, My desire is to our Friends, that they will all help us in our Praises. Our Tongues are too little to speak forth the Goodness, and the Grace of GOD, do you help us in our Praises. Love the Lord the better, Praise him the more, and what is wanting in us, let it be made good by you. O that the Praises of GOD may sound Abroad in the Country by our means, and for our sakes.

HE was prevented of going to the Waters, by his last Imprisonment; for want of which, his Distempers increased much upon him all the *winter* after, and the next *Spring* more; yet not so as to take him fully off from his Work, but he Preached, and kept many Days, and Administred the Sacrament among them frequently.

But going up to the Waters in *July*, 1667. they had a contrary

trary effect upon him, from what they had at first: For after three days taking them, he fell into a Feaver, which seised on his Spirits, and decaied his strength exceedingly, so that he seemed very near Death: But the Lord then again revoked the Sentence passed upon him, and enabled him in six Weeks to return again to his People, where he much desired to be: But finding at his return, great decay of his Strength, and a weakness in all his Limbs, he was willing to go to *Dorchester*, to advise further with Doctor *Lose*, a very Worthy and Reverend Physitian, from whom he had received many Medicines, but never conversed with him nor had seen him, which he conceived might conduce more to his full Cure.

The Doctor soon perceiving my Husbands weakness, perswaded him to continue for a Fortnight, or three Weeks there, that he might the better Advise him, and alter his Remedies, as he should see occasion; which Motion was readily yielded unto by us.

But we had not been there about five days, before the use of all his Limbs was taken away on a sudden; one day his Arms wholly failing, the next his Legs; so that he could not go, nor stand, nor move a Finger, nor turn in his Bed, but as my self and another did turn him night and day in a sheet: All means failing, he was given over by Physitians, and Friends, that saw him lying some Weeks in cold Sweats night and day, and many times for some Hours together, half his Body cold, in our apprensions, dying; receiving nothing but the best Cordials that Art could invent, and Almond Milk, or a little thin Broth once in three or four days. Thus he lay from *September*, 28. to *November*, 16. before he began to Revive, or it could be discerned that Remedies did at all prevail against his Diseases: In all this time he was still chearful, and when he did speak it was not at all complaining, but always Praising and Admiring God for his Mercies; but his Spirits were so low, that he spake seldom, and very softly. He still told us he had no pain at all, and when his Friends admired his patience, he would say; God had not yet tried him in any thing, but laying him Aside out of his Work, and keeping him out of Heaven; but through Grace he could submit to his pleasure, waiting for him: It was *Pain* he ever feared, and that he had not yet felt, so tender was his

his Father of him; and he wanted strength (as he often told us) to speak more of his Love, and to speak for God who had been, and was still so gracious to him. Being often askt by my self and others, how it was with his Spirit in all this weakness, he would Answer: He had not those *Ravishing joys* that he expected, and that some Believers did partake of; but he had a sweet Serenity of Heart, and Confidence in God, grounded on the Promises of the Gospel, and did believe it would be well with him to all Eternity.

In all this time, I never heard one Impatient word from him, nor could upon my strictest observation, discern the least discontent with his state; though he was a pitiful Object to all others that beheld him, being so consumed; besides the Loss of the use of his Limbs: Yet the Lord did support and quiet his Spirit, that he lay as if he had *indured* nothing; breaking out often most affectionately in commending the Kindness of the Lord to him, saying, Goodness and Mercy had followed him all his days.

And indeed the loving Kindness, and Care of God was singular to us in that place, which I cannot but mention to his praise.

We came Strangers thither, and being in our *Inn*, we found it very uncomfortable; yet were fearful to impose our selves on any private house: But necessity inforcing, we did enquire for a Chamber, but could not procure one; the Small Pox being very hot in most Families, and those that had them not, daily expecting them, and so could not spare Roomes, as else they might. But the Lord who saw our affliction, inclined the heart of a very good Woman (a Ministers Widdow) one Mrs. *Bartlet*, to come and Invite us to a Lodging in her House; which we readily and thankfully accepted off; where we were so accomodated as we could not have bin any where else in the Town, especially in regard of the assistance I had from four young Women who lived under the same roofe, and so were ready night and day to help me (I having no Servant, nor Friend near me;) we being so unsettled I kept none, but had alwayes tended him my self to that time: And the Ministers and Christians of that Place were very compassionate towards us, Visiting and Praying with and for us often: And Dr. *Lose* visited him twice

twice a day for twelve or fourteen Weeks, except when he was called out of Town, refusing any Fees tendered to him: The Gentry in and about the Town, and others sending to us whatever they imagined might be pleasing to him, furnishing him with all delicats that might be grateful to one so weak; So that he wanted neither Food nor Phisick, having not only for necessity, but for delight, and he did much delight himself in the consideration of the Lords kindness to him in the love he received, and would often say, *I was a Stranger and Mercy took me in; In Prison and it came to me, Sick and weak, and it Visited me.* There was also ten young Women besides the four in the house, that took their turns to watch with him constantly; for twelve Weeks space I never wanted one to help me: And the Lord was pleased to shew his power so in strengthening me, that I was every night (all these Weeks in the depth of Winter) one that helped to turn him, never lying out of the Bed one night from him, but every time he called or wanted any thing, was waking to assist her in the Chamber, though as some of them have said they did tell, that we did turn him more then 40 times a night, he seldome sleeping at all in the night, in all those Weeks; though his tender affections were such, as to have had me sometimes lain in another Room, yet mine were such to him, that I could not bear it, the thoughts of it being worse to me then the trouble or disturbance he accounted I had with him, for I feared none would do any thing about him with such ease, neither would he suffer any one all the day to touch him but me, or to give him any thing that he did receive: by which I discerned it was most grateful to him, and therefore so to me; And I never found any want of my Rest, nor did get so much as a cold all that Winter, though I do not remember that for 14 or 15 Years before, I could ever say I was one Moneth free of a most violent Cough, which if I had been molested with then, would have bin a great addition to his and my affliction; and he was not a little taken with the goodness of God to me in the time of all his sickness, but especially that VVinter, for he being not able to help himself in the least, I could not be from him night nor day, with any comfort to him, or my self.

In this condition he kept his Bed till *December* the 18th,

And

And then beyond all expectation, though in the depth of Winter, began to Revive and got out of his Bed; but he could neither stand nor go, nor yet move a finger, having *Sense* in all his Limbs, but not the least motion: As his strength did increase he learnt to go (as he would say) first by being lead by two of us, then by one; and when he could go one turn in his Chamber, though more weakly, and with more fear then the weakest Child that ever I saw, he was wonderfully taken with the Lords mercy to him: By *February* he was able with a little help to walk in the Streets; (but not to feed himself) nor to go up or down stairs without much help.

When he was deprived of the use of his Limbs, looking down on his Arms as I held him up by all the strength I had: he again lifted up his Eyes from his useless Arms to Heaven, and with a chearful countenance said: *The Lord hath given, and the Lord hath taken, and Blessed be the Name of the Lord.*

Being asked by a Freind how he could be so well contented to lye so long under such weakness, he answered.

What is God my Father, Jesus Christ my Saviour, and the Spirit my sweet Freind, my Comforter, and Sanctifier, and Heaven my Inheritance; shall I not be content without Limbs and Health? Through Grace I am fully satisfied with my Fathers pleasure.

To another that asked him the same, he Answered: *I have chosen God, and he is become mine, and I know with whom I have trusted my self, which is enough: He is an unreasonable wretch that cannot be content with a God, though he have nothing else: My interest in God is all my joy.*

His Friends (some of *Taunton*) coming to *Dorcester* to see him, he was much Revived, and would be set up in his Bed, and have all the Curtains drawn, and desired them to stand round about the Bed, and would have me take out his Hand and hold it out to them, that they might shake him, though he could not them; as he used formerly to do, when he had been absent from them: And as he was able, thus he spake to them: O how it rejoyces my Heart to see your Faces, and to hear your Voices, though I cannot speak as heretofore to you: Methinks I am now like Old *Jacob*, with all his Sons about

about him: Now you see my weak estate, thus have I been for many Weeks, since I parted with *Taunton*, but God hath been with me, and I hope with you; your Prayers have been Heard, and Answered, for me many ways; the Lord return them into your own Bosoms. My Friends, Life is mine, Death is mine, in that Covenant I was Preaching of to you, is all my Salvation, and all my desire, although my Body do not prosper, I hope through Grace my Soul doth.

I have lived a sweet Life by the Promises, and I hope through Grace can *Die* by a Promise: It is the Promises of God which are everlasting, that will stand by us: Nothing but God in them, will stead us in a day of Affliction.

My dear Friends, I feel the power of those Doctrines I Preached to you, on my Heart: Now the *Doctrines* of Faith, of Repentance, of Self-denyal, of the Covenant, of Grace, of Contentment, and the rest; O that you would live them over, now I cannot Preach to you!

It is a shame for a Believer to be cast down under Afflictions, that hath so many glorious Priviledges, Justification, Adoption, Sanctification, and eternal Glory. We shall be as the Angels of God in a little while: Nay, to say the truth, Believers are as it were little Angels already, that live in the power of Faith. O my Friends! Live like Believers, Trample this dirty World under your feet, Be not taken with its Comforts, nor disquieted with its Crosses; You will be gone out of it shortly.

When they came to take their Leaves of him, he would Pray with them as his weak state would suffer him; and in in the words of *Moses*, and of the *Apostles*, Blessed them. The same he always used after a Sacrament: *The Lord bless you and keep you, the Lord cause his Face to shine upon you, and give you Peace. And the God of Peace, that brought again from the Dead our Lord Jesus, through the Blood of the Everlasting Covenant, make you perfect in every good work to do his Will, working in you that which is well pleasing in his sight, through Jesus Christ, to whom be Glory for ever, and ever,* Amen.

And then spake thus, [Farewell, farewell my dear Freinds] Remember me to all *Taunton*; I beseech you and them, if I never see your faces more; goe Home and live over what I have

have Preached to you; and the Lord provide for you when I am gone: O! let not all my Labours, and Sufferings, let not my wasted strength, my useless Limbs, rise up in Judgement against you at the great *Day* of the *LORD*.

Another time, some coming to Visit him there, he spake thus to them: O! my Freinds, let your whole Conversation be as becomes the Gospel of Christ; whether I am present or absent, Live what I have spoken to you in the Name of the Lord; Now I cannot Preach to you, let my wasted strength, my useless Limbs be a Sermon to you; Behold me, I cannot move a finger; all this is come upon me for your sakes, and the Gospel; It is for Christ and you that I have thus spent out my self: I am afraid of you least some of you after all that I have spoken to you, should be lost in the World. There are many Professors who can pray well, and talk well, whom we shall find at the left hand of Christ another day: You have your Trades, your Estates, your Relations, be not taken with these, but with God; O live on him! For the Lords sake go home and take heed of the World, of worldly cares, worldly comforts, worldly freind, &c. Saying thus:

The Lord having given Authority to his Ministers to bless his people, accordingly I bless you in his name, using the same words as before, and so parted with them, with many other *Dear Expressions* of his Love to them, and to the Town.

And thus he was used to Converse with all that came to Visit him, as he was able, looking always chearfully upon them, and never complaining of any Affliction he was under, except it were to Excite his *Taunton* Friends to their Duties.

In *February*, he being very desirous to return among his People, he moved it to his Doctor, who consented to it; fearing that Air might be too keen for him in *March*: And hoping that it might much add to his Cure; to satisfie his mind.

In a Horse-Litter I removed him: He was much pleased at the sight of the Place, and his People, who came flocking about him; and he seemed to increase in strength, so that he was able to Feed himself the Week after he came Home: But I fearing the frequent Visits of his Friends might be prejudicial to him, perswaded him to remove to Mr. *Mallacks* House, which he was again Invited to, and most courteously Entertained.

And thus he continued increasing in strength, till the beginning of *April*, and then he began to decline again, and was taken after some days with Convulsion Fits, as he sat in his Chamber one Afternoon, and had Three or Four more fits that night: But in the use of Means, through Gods blessing, he had no more in three Weeks. One Evening being in his Chamber, he desired me to leave him a while alone, which I was very unwilling to do; but his Importunity made me to go down from him: But in less than half a quarter of an Hour, he was fallen to the Ground in one of his former Fits, and had hurt his Face; and from his Nose came much Blood, which was very clotted and corrupt, which Physitians seeing, did conclude (though it were grievous to me, that under such Weakness, he should have so sad an Accident) that the fall saved his life: For had not that Blood come from his Head, he had, so far as they could rationally judg, died in that Fit, which took away his Senses for the present; but he went to Bed and slept so well that night, as he had not in many Weeks before; so that my Self, and Friends, feared that he had been in an *Apoplexy*: But he awaked about Six in the Morning, much Refreshed, and full of the Praises of God for his Mercys to him, being very sensible how suddenly he was surprised the Evening before. After this, he Lived always expecting Death, saying often to me and his Friends, It is but a puff, and I am gone: And therefore would every Night after he had been at Prayer, bid all the Family farewell, telling them he might be dead before the Morning; and droping some holy Counsels to them, would depart to his Chamber: All the while I was Undressing of him, he would be discoursing of Spiritual things, it being all his delight; and when we lay down to Rest, his last words were usually [We shall shortly be in another Bed, therefore it is good to mind it, and provide for it apace; farewel my Dear Heart, the Lord bless thee] and so he would go to his Rest. In his Health and Sickness, his first Speeches in the Mornings would be, [Now we have one day more; here is one more for God now let us Live well this day; work hard for our Souls

Jay

lay up much Treasure in Heaven this day, for we have but a few to Live.]

After this, the strength of his Limbs which were decayed returned again, and he was beyond all expectation so far Recovered, that we had no fears of his Relapsing again: his Appetite, and Rest, and all Repaired. But about the *6th.* of *May*, he began again to find weakness in his Stomach, which in a few days so grew upon him, that he lost his Limbs again; and on the 12*th.* of *May* in the Morning, having lain some days and nights in cold Sweats, as heretofore at *Dorchester:* He was again Seised with Convulsions, first lying four Hours with his Eyes fixed to Heaven, not speaking one word, nor in the least moving himself, my self, and Friends, weeping by him, at last he spake to us with a very Audible Voice: Weep not for me, my Work is done] and seemed to be full of Matter to utter to us, but was imediately seised with a terrible Convulsion, which was sad to behold; it so altered his Countenance, and put him into such Sweats, that 'twas strange to see how the drops lay and run down his Face, and Hands, and Body: This held him two Hours or more, and ceased, but he was left by it without any Sense; and in a quarter of an Hour, or little more, fell into another, in which he Ratled, and was Cold, so that we apprehended every Breath would be his last. The Physitian who was then by him, accounted his Pulse to be gone, and that he would be Dead in a few minutes: But the Lord shewed his Power here once again in Raising him, so that many that came and saw him, that heard the next day he was Alive, would not believe till they came and saw him again: These violent Fits went off about Twelve a Clock, and he Revived, but had no Sense to Converse with us till the next day, nor did he perfectly Recover them Four days after, and then was as before, and so continued very Weak till *July*, no strength coming into his Hands, or Legs; for the most part Confined to his Bed, but still Chearful in his Spirit, and free to Discourse with any that came to Visit him, as long as he was able.

But the Lord had yet more Work for him to do: I seeing him lie so hopeless as to his Life, or Limbs, and considering the *Winter* was drawing on apace, I proposed it to the Doctors to have him to the *Bath*; some were for it, others

 against

against it; acquainting my Husband with it, he was much pleased with it, and so earnest in it, that I sent immediately to *Bath* for a Horse-Litter, and the Lord was pleased strangely to appear in strengthening him for his Journey; so that he that had not in many weeks been out of his Bed and Chamber, was able in two days, to reach near Forty Miles (but when we came to *Bath*, the Doctors there seemed to be much amazed, to behold such an Object, professing they never saw the like) much wondering how he was come Alive such a Journey, and doubted much to put him in: But he having tried all Artificial Baths, and Oyntments, and Plaisters before, he resolved against their Judgments, to adventure himself.

At his first appearing in the *Bath*, being wasted to Skin and Bone, some of the Ladies were affrighted, as if Death had been come in among them, and could not endure to look towards him.

The first time he went in, he was able to stay but a little while, but was much refreshed, and had no Symtom of his Fits, which we feared the Bath might have caused again: Through the blessing of the Lord upon this means, without any thing else, except his drinking of *Goats*-Milk; he that was not able to go nor stand, nor move a Finger, could in three Weeks time, walk about his Chamber, and Feed himself, his impaired Appetite was again Restored, and his Strength so Increased, that there seemed no doubt to the Physitians of his full Recovery, he having not the least Sign of any Inclination to his Fits, from the 12*th*. of *May*, till his Death drew nigh.

In this time of his being in *Bath*, his Soul was far more strengthened with Grace; so that my self, and all that beheld him, and conversed with him, discerned sensibly his Growth; and he was in the nights, and days, so frequently with God, and often in such Ravishments of Spirit, from the Joys and Consolations that he received from the Spirit of God, that it was oftentimes more than he could express, or his Bodily strength could bear; so that for my own part, I had less hopes of his continuance on Earth, than ever before: For I perceived plainly the Lord had spared him but to recover strength of Grace, and to make him a more evident instance

ſtance of his ſingular Love, before he took him hence.

He being now more chearful than formerly, and more exceedingly Affectionate in his Carriage to me, and to all his Friends, eſpecially with thoſe that were moſt Heavenly, the Lord was pleaſed to order it in his Providence; there were many ſuch then who came to uſe the Bath, as Mr. *Fairclough*, and his Wiſe, Mr. *How*, of *Torrington*, Mr. *Joſeph Barnard*, and his Wiſe, and ſeveral of our *Taunton* Friends, and of *Briſtol* Miniſters, and others, which was a great comfort to us, in that ſtrange and wicked place.

His parts ſeemed to be more quick in his Converſes, whatever he was put upon either by Schollars, or thoſe that were more Inferiour. He had manVisitors there, both of Strangers and Friends, who were willing to ſee him, and diſcourſe with him, having heard what a monument of Mercy he was; and he would to all of them, ſo Amplifie upon all the Paſſages of Gods dealings with him, as was very pleaſant to all that heard him; and did affect many that were ſtrangers to God, and to Religion, as well as to him.

He found much favour even among the worſt, both Gentry and others (ſuch as would make a ſcoff at Religion, or holy Diſcourſe from others) would hearken to him. Though he did often faithfully reprove many for their Oaths, and exceſs in Drinking, their Laſcivious Carriages, which he obſerved in the *Bath*; and there was none of them, but did moſt thankfully accept it from him, and ſhewed him more reſpect after, than they had done before: In which he obſerved much of Gods goodneſs to him, and would often ſay to me: O! how good is it to be faithful to God. The vileſt of theſe Perſons, as I was by ſeveral informed, ſaid of him, that he never ſpake with ſuch a man in his liſe.

His Reproofs were managed with ſo much reſpect to their Perſons, and the honourable eſteem he had of their Dignity, that they ſaid, they could not but accept his Reproofs, though very cloſe and plain; and his way was, ſometime before he intended to reprove them, he would often in the *Bath* Converſe with them, *of things that might be taking with them*; and did ſo ingage their Affections, that they would willingly every day Converſe with him: He being *furniſhed* (from his former Studys) *for any Company*, deſigning to uſe it ſtill for Holy ends; by such means hath caught many Souls.

While he was in this place, though he had many Diversions by his using the *Bath* constantly every day, and his frequent Visits, besides his Weakness, yet he kept his constant Seasons four times a day, for his holy Retirements; waking in the Morning constantly at or before five a Clock, and would not be disturbed till about seven, when he was carried to the *Bath*. Having the Curtains drawn close, he spent his time in Holy Meditation, and Prayer, and Singing, and once again before Dinner, but then he spent less time, and about half an Hour before Two in the Afternoon, just before he went Abroad.

For though he never attained to so much strength, as to be able to walk Abroad in the Streets without my leading him, or some other, yet he would be Imployed for his Lord and Master. His Chairmen that used to carry him to the *Bath*, he appointed to fetch him about Three a Clock, who carried him to Visit all the Schooles, and Alms-Houses, and the Godly Poor, especially the Widdows; to whom he would give Money, and with whom he would Pray and Converse with them, concerning their Spiritual states, according as their Necessitys required; ingaging those that were Teachers, and Governours, to Teach the *Assemblies Catechism*, buying many Dozens, and giving them to distribute to their Schollars; and many other small Books which he thought might be useful for them, and then would come and see in a Week or Fortnight, what progress they had made: He also ingaged several to send their Children once a Week to him, to be Catechised, which they did hearken to him in: And we had about Sixty or Seventy Children every Lords-day to our Lodging, and they profited much by his Instructions, till some took such offence at it, that he was forced to Desist, and the School-Master was threatned to be Cited to *Wells*, before the Bishop, and many others affrighted from it.

He also sent for all the Godly Poor he could find in that place, and entertained them at his Chamber, and gave to them every one as he was able, as a Thanks-Offering to the Lord, for his Mercy to him, and desired them, with several others to keep a day of Thanksgiving for him; Mr. *Fairclough*, Mr. *Hook*, and *Himself*, performing the Dutys of the day.

The

Thus though his Sickness had been long, and his Expences great, he thought he could never spend enough for him from whom he had received all: He constantly gave Money, or Apples, to all the Children that came to be Catechised by him, to Ingage them, besides all he gave to the Teachers, and Poor, which indeed was beyond his Ability, considering his Estate: But I am perswaded, he did foresee that his time would be but short, and having made a Competent, and Comfortable provision for me, he resolved to lay up the rest in Heaven; he did often say to me, If he Lived never so long, he would never increase his Estate, now I was provided for; he having no Children, Gods Children should have it.

But he was yet again designing what he might do before he took his leave of the World: And his next work was to send Letters to all his Relations, and intimate Friends, in most of which he urges them to observe his Counsels, for they were like to be his last to them. I always Wrote for him, for he could not by reason of his Weakness Write a Line.

At this time, he had a great desire to go to Mr. *Joseph Barnards*, which was about five Miles from *Bathe*, there to Finish his last Work for God, that ever he did on Earth; which was to Promote the Exercise of Catechising in *Sommersetshire*, and *Wiltshire*: Mr. *Barnard* having had a great Deliverance as well as himself, he proposed this to him as their Thank-Offering to God, which they would joyntly tender to him. They had ingaged one to another, to give so much for the Printing of Six Thousand of the *Assemblies Catechisms*, and among other Friends, to raise *some Money, for to send to every Minister*, that would Ingage in the *work*, and to *give to the Children for their Incouragement in Learning*: This Work was finished by Mr. *Barnard*, after my Husband was gone to his Rest.

He finding himself to decline again, apprehended it was for want of using the *Bath*, and therefore desired to return, and I being fearful he should Ride home, seeing some Symtoms of his Fits, sent for the Horse-Litter, and so carried him again to *Bath*: Where by the Doctors advise, after he had taken some things to prepare his Body, he made use of the hot *Bath* (the *Cross Bath* being then too cold) and so he did for Four days, and seemed to be Refreshed, and the

Strength that he had in his Limbs to recover, rather then abate; and two of his *Taunton* Friends coming to see him he was chearful with them: But on the Third of *November* I discerned a great Change in his countenance, and he found a great alteration in himself, but concealed it from me, as I heard after; For some Friends coming to visit him, he desired them to pray for him, for his time was very short; But desired them not to tell me of it: All that day he would not permit me to move out of the Chamber from him, except once while those Friends were with him. After we had dined he was in more then ordinary manner transported with Affections towards me; which he expressed by his returning me Thanks for all my Paines and Care for him and with him, and putting up many most Affectionate Requests for me to GOD, before he would suffer me to rise as we sate together: At Night again, at Supper before I could rise from him, he spake thus to me.

Well, now my dear Heart, my Companion in all my Tribulations and Afflictions; I thank thee for all thy pains and Labours for me, at home and abroad, in Prison, and Liberty, in Health and Sickness; reckoning up many of the Places we had bin in, in the Days of our Affliction; And with many other most endearing and affectionate Expressions, he concluded with many Holy Breathings to God for me, that he would requite me, and never forget me and fill me with all manner of Grace and Consolations, and that his Face might still shine upon me, and that I might be supported and carryed through all difficultys:

After this he desired me to see for a *Practice of Piety*, and I procuring one for him; he turned his chair from me that I might not see; and Read the *Meditations about Death* in the *later End* of that Book; which I discerning, askt of him whether he did apprehend his end was near: To which he replyed. He knew not, in a few days I would see; and so fell into other discourse, to divert me; desiring me to read two Chapters to him as I used to do every Night, and so he hasted to Bed, not being able to go to Prayer; and with his own hands did very hastily undoe his Coat, and Doublet, which he had not done in many Moneths before: As soon as he was in Bed he told me he felt some more then ordina-

ry

ry stoppage in his Head, and I brought him something to prevent the fits which I feared: But in a quarter of an hour after he fell into a very strong Convulsion: Which I being much affrighed at, called for help, and sent for the Doctors; used all former and other means, but no success the Lord was pleased to give then to any; But they continued for two Days and Nights, not ceasing one Hour.

This was most grievous to me that I saw him so like to depart, and that I should hear him speak no more to me; fearing it would harden the wicked to see him removed by such a stroak: For his fits were most terrible to behold: And I earnestly besought the Lord that if it were his Pleasure, he would so far mitigate the heavy stroak I saw was coming upon me, by causing him to utter somthing of his Heart before he took him from me; which he graciously answered me in; for he that had not spoke from Tuesday Night, did on Friday morning about Three a Clock, call for me to come to him, speaking very understandingly *between Times*, all that Day: But that Night about Nine *a Clock he brake out with* an *audible voice speaking for Sixteen Hours together* those and such like Words as you formerly had Account off, and did cease but a very little space, now and then all the Afternoon, till about six on Saterday in the Evening when he departed.

About Three in the Afternoon he had as we perceived some Conflict with *Satan*, for he uttered these Words.

Away thou foul Fiend, thou Enemy of all Man-kind, thou subtile Sophister, art thou come now to molest me! Now I am just going! Now I am so weak and Death upon me. Trouble me not for I am none of thine! I am the Lords, Christ is mine and I am his: His by Covenant; I have sworn my self to be the Lords, and his I will be: Therefore be gone. These last Words he Repeated often which I took much notice of; that *his Covenanting with God* was the means he used to expel the Devil, and all his Temptations:

The time we were in *Bath*, I had very few Hours *alone* with him, by reason of his constant using the *Bath* and Visits of Friends from all Parts thereabouts, and sometimes from *Taunton* and when they were gone he would be either retyring to GOD, or to his Rest: But what time I had with him

him he alwayes spent in Heavenly and profitable Discourse, speaking much of the Place he was going to, and his Desire to be gone: One Morning as I was dressing him, he looked up to Heaven and smiled, and I urging him to know why, he Answered me thus.

Ah my Love I was thinking of my Marriage Day it will be shortly: O what a joyful day will that be! will it not think'st thou my Dear Heart?

Another time bringing him some Broth, he said: Blessed be the Lord for these refreshments in the way home, but O how sweet will Heaven be!

Another time; I hope to be shortly where I shall need no Meat, nor Drink, nor Cloathes:

When he looked on his weak consumed Hands, he would say: These shall be changed: This vile Body shall be made like to Christs Glorious Body:

O what a Glorious Day will the Day of the Resurrection be! Methinks I see it by Faith; how will the Saints lift up their Heads and Rejoyce, and how sadly will the Wicked World look then!

O come let us make haste, our Lord will come shortly, let us prepare.

If we long to be in Heaven, let us hasten with our Work, for when that is done, away we shall be fetcht.

O this vain foolish dirty World, I wonder how reasonable Creatures can so dote upon it! What is in it worth the looking after! I care not to be in it longer then while my Master hath either doing, or Suffering Work for me, were that done farewell to Earth.

He was much in commending the Love of Christ, and from that exciting himself and me to Obedience to him, often speaking of his Sufferings and of his Glory.

Of his Love-Letters, as he called the Holy History of his Life, Death, Resurrection, Ascention, and his Second coming; The thoughts of which he seemed alwayes to be much Ravished with.

He would be frequently reckoning the Choice Tokens Christ had sent him, which I remember he would frequently reckon up, 1. The Pardon of Sin, 2. A Pattent for Heaven, 3. The Gift of the Spirit, 4. The Robe of his Righteousness,

5. The

5. The spoyles of Enemies, 6. The Charter of all Libertyes, and Priviledges, 7. The Guard of his Angels: The Consideration of this last he did frequently solace himself in; saying to me often, when we lived alone in the Prison, and divers other Places; Well my Dear, though we have not our Attendants and Servants as the Great ones, and Rich of the World have, we have the Blessed Angels of God still to wait upon us to Minister to us, and to Watch over us while we are sleeping; to be with us when journeying; and still to preserve us, from the rage of Men and Devils!

He was exceedingly affected with the three last Chapters of *Saint John's Gospel*, especially Christs parting Words, and Prayer for his Disciples. But it is time for me to set a stop to my Pen, *GOD* did pour into him, and he did pour out so much, that it was scarce possible to retain the Converses of one day, without a constant Register: His Heart, his Lips, his Life was filled up with *Grace*. In which he did shine both in Health and Sickness, Prosperity and Adversity, in Prison and at Liberty, in his own House and in the Churches of *Christ*, where ever he came: I never heard any that conversed with him but would acknowledge it was to their Advantage:

At my Husbands first coming to *Taunton*, he was entertained by Mr. *Newton*, as a Sojourner, and after he was ordained in *Taunton*, in a Publick Association Meeting, he Administered all Ordinances joyntly with him; though he were but an Assistant, Mr. *Newton* would have it so, who dearly loved him, and highly esteemed of him; and seeing him restless in his Spirit, and putting himself to many tedious Journeys to visit me (as he did once a Fortnight Twenty Five Miles) He perswaded him to marry, contrary to our purpose, we resolving to have lived much longer single. The Fourth of *October*, 1655. After a year and two Moneths acquaintance our Marriage was Consumated.

And we lived together with Mr. *Newton*, near two Years, where we were most courteously entertained, and then hopeing to be more useful in our Station, we took a House and I having been alwayes bred to work, undertook to teach a School, and had many Tablers, and Schollars, our Family being seldome less then Twenty, and many times Thirty; My School usually Fifty or Sixty of the Town and other Places:

And

And the Lord was pleased to bless us exceedingly in our endeavours: So that many were Converted in a few years that were before Strangers to God: All our Schollars called him Father: And indeed he had far more care of them then most of their Natural Parents, and was most tenderly affectionate to them, but especially to their Souls:

His Course in his Family was Prayer, and reading the Scriptures, and singing twice a day, Except when he Catechised, which was constantly once if not twice a Week: Of every Chapter that was read, he expected an Account of, and and of every Sermon, either to himself or me: He dealt with them and his Servants frequently together, and apart, about their Spiritual states, pressing them to all their Dutys, both of First, and Second Table, and calling them strictly to account, whether they did not omit them. He also gave them Books suitable to their Capacitys, and Condition, which they gave a weekly account of to him or me; but too often by Publick work was he diverted, as I was apt to think, who knew not so well what was to be preferred.

His Lords-days Work was great, for though he Preacht but once in his own Place, yet he was either desired by some of his Brethren, to Supply theirs, on any Exigency, or would go where was no Minister; and so was forced often to leave his Family to me, to my great grief and loss: In his Repetitions in publick, as well as Catechising, his own Family came all in their turns, to Answer in the Congregation, both Schollars, and Servants.

When I have pleaded with him for more of his time with my Self, and Family, he would answer me: His Ministerial Work would not permit him to be so constant as he would; for if he had Ten Bodys and Souls, he could Imploy them all, in, and about *Taunton*: And would say, Ah my Dear, I know thy Soul is safe, But how many that are Perishing, have I to look after? O that I could do more for them!

He was a Holy, Heavenly, Tenderly-Affectionate Husband, and I know nothing I could complain of, but that he was so taken up, that I could have but very little Converse with him.

His Love was expressed to me, in his great Care for me, Sick and Well; in his Provision for me; in his Delight in my Company; saying often, He could not bear to be from me, me, but when he was with God, or Imployed for Him; and that often it was hard for him to deny himself to be so long absent: It was Irksome to him, to make a Meal without me, nor would he Manage any Affair almost without Conversing with me, concealing nothing from me, that was it for me to know; being far from the Temper of those Husbands, who hide all their Concerns from their Wives, which he could not indure to hear of, especially in Good Men.

He was a faithful Reprover of any thing he saw amiss in me, which I took as a great Evidence of his real good will to my Soul; and if in any thing he gave me offence, which was but seldom, so far would he deny himself as to acknowledg it, and desire me to pass it by, professing to me he could never rest, till he had done so; and the like I was ready to do to him, as there was far more reason; by which Course, if any difference did arise, it was soon over with us.

He was a very tender Master to his Servants, every way expressing it to their Souls, and Bodies, giving them that Incouragement in their places they could desire; expecting from his whole Family that Respect, and Obedience to his Commands, which their Rule required; reproving them that were Careless, and Negligent in observing them.

He was frequent in keeping solemn days of Humiliation, especially against a Sacrament.

He was a very strict Observer of the Sabbath, the Dutys of which, he did perform with such Joy, and Alacrity of Spirit, as was most pleasant to joyn with him, both in Publick, and in the Family, when we could injoy him: And this he did much press upon Christians, to spend their Sabbaths more in Praises, and Thanksgivings, as days of holy Rejoycing in our Redeemer.

All the time of his Health, he did Rise constantly at, or before Four of the Clock, (and on the Sabbaths sooner, if he did wake) he would be much troubled if he heard any *Smiths*, or *Shoomakers*, or such Tradsmen at work at their Trades, before he was in his Dutys with God: Saying to me often, O how this Noise shames me! Doth not my Master deserve more than theirs? From Four till Eight, he spent in Prayer, Holy Contemplation, and Singing of Psalms, which he he much delighted in, and did daily practise *alone*, as well as in his Family: Having refreshed himself about half an Hour, he would call to Family-dutys, and after that to his Studys, till Eleven or Twelve a Clock, cutting out his Work for every Hour in the day. Having refreshed himself a while after Dinner, he used to retire to his Study to Prayer, and so Abroad among the Families he was to Visit, to whom he always sent the day before; going out about Two a Clock, and seldom returning till Seven in the Evening, sometimes later: He would often say, Give me a Christian that counts his time more precious than Gold. His work in his publick Ministry in *Taunton*, being to Preach but once a Sabbath, and Catechise, he devoted himself much to *private work*, and also Catechised once a Week in Publick besides, and repeated the Sermon he Preached on the Sabbath-day, on *Tuesday* in the Evening.

He found much difficulty in going from House to House, because it had not been practised a long time by any Minister in *Taunton*, nor by any others of his Brethren; and he being but a Young man, to be looked upon as *singular*, was that which called for much Self-denial, which the Lord inabled him to Exercise: For after he had Preached up in Publick, the Ministers duty to their People, and theirs to receive them when they came to them for their Spiritual advantage, he set speedily upon the Work.

In this Work, his course was to draw a Catalogue of the Names of the Families in each Street, and so to send the day or two before he intended to Visit them, that they might not be absent, and that he might understand who was willing to receive him: Those that sent slight Excuses, or did obstinately refuse his Message, he would notwithstanding go to them, and if (as some would) they did shut their Doors against him, he would speak some few Affectionate words to them; or if he saw cause, denounce the Threatnings of God against them that dispise his Ministers, and so departed; and after would send affectionate Letters to them, so full of Love and Expressions of his great desires to do their Souls good, as did overcome their Hearts; and they did many of them afterwards readily receive him into their Houses. Herein was his Compassion shewed to all Sorts, both Poor and Rich, not disdaining

daining to go into such Houses amongst the Poor, as were often very offensive to him to sit in, he being of an exact and curious Temper: Yet would he with Joy and Freedom, deny himself for the good of their Souls, and that he might fulfil his Ministry among those the Lord had given him the oversight of.

I perceiving this Work, with what he did otherwise, to be too hard for him, fearing often he would bring himself to Distempers and Diseases, as he did soon after, besought him not to go so frequently: His Answer would be, What have I strength for, but to spend for God? What is a Candle for, but to be burnt? And he would say, I was like *Peter*, still crying, *O spare thy self*: But I must not hearken to thee, no more than my Master did to him; though his Labours were so abundant, I never knew him for Nine Years together, under the *least Distemper, one quarter of an Hour.*

He was exceeding temperate in his Diet, though he had a very sharp Appetite, yet did he at every Meal deny himself, being perswaded that it did much conduce to his Health: His Converse at his Table was very profitable, and yet pleasant, never rising either at Home or Abroad, without droping something of God, according to the Rule he laid down to others. He was very much in Commending, and Admiring the Mercys of God in every Meal, and was still so pleased with his provision for him, that he would often say: He Fared deliciously every day, and lived far better than the Great ones of the World, who had their Tables far better furnished: For he injoyed God in all, and saw his Love and Bounty in what he received at every Meal: So that he would say, O Wife! I live a Voluptuous Life, but blessed be God it is upon Spiritual daintys, such as the World know not, nor taste not of.

He was much in minding the Poor, that were in want of all Things, often wondering that God should make such a difference between him and them, both for this World and that to come, and his Charity was ever beyond his Estate, As my self and many other Friends did conceive, but he would not be disswaded, alwayes saying if he were Prodigal it was for *GOD*, and not for himself, nor Sin:

There were but *few*, if any, *Poor Familyes* especially of

the

the Godly in *Taunton*, but he knew their Necessityes and did by himself or Friends relieve them: So that our Homes were seldome free of such as came to make Complaints to him. After the Times grew Dead for Trade, many of our Godly Men decaying, he would give much beyond his Ability to recover them: He would buy Pease, and Flitches, of Bacon and distribute twice a year, in the Cold and Hard Seasons. He kept several Children at School at his own Cost; bought many Books and Catechisms, and had many Thousands of *Prayers* Printed, and distributed among them! And after his Brethren were turned out, he gave Four Pounds a Year himself to a Publick Stock for them, by which he excited many others to do the same, and much more, which else would never have done it: And on any other occasions as did frequently fall in, he would give even to the offence of his Friends: So that many would grudge in the Town to give him what they had *agreed for*; because *he would give so much*. Besides all this, the Necessityes of his own Father, and many other relations, were still calling upon him, and he was open handed to them all: So that it hath been sometimes even incredible to our selves to consider how much he did, out of a *little Estate*, and therefore may seem strange to others: Moreover when he had received any more then Ordinary Mercy at the hand of *GOD*, his manner was to set a part some considerable Portion out of his Estate, and Dedicate it to the Lord, as a *Thank-Offering*, to be laid out for his *Glory* in Pious and Charitable Uses.

When I have begged him to consider himself and me; he would Answer me, he was laying up, and *GOD* would repay him: That by liberal things he should stand; when others might fall that censured him; that if he sowed sparingly he should reap so; if bountifully, he should reap bountifully.

And I must confess I did often see so much of *GOD* in his dealings with us, according to his Promises, that I have bin convinc'd and silenc't; God having often so strangely and unexpectedly provided for us: And notwithstanding al he had done, he had at last somewhat to dispose of to his Relations, and to his Brethren, besides comfortable Provision for me:

Thus his whole Life was a continual Sermon, holding forth evidently the Doctrines he Preached; Humility, Self-

denial,

denial, Patience, Meekneſs, Contentation, Faith, and holy Confidence ſhining in him with moſt dear Love to God, and his Church, and People: and where he longed and panted to be, he is now Shining in Heaven, ſinging Praiſes to God, and to the Lamb, which Work he much delighted in, whilſt here on Earth.)

A True Account (Wing W 1355A), shelfmark 132515, is reproduced by permission of the Folger Shakespeare Library. The text block of the original measures 145 × 110 mm.

Reading where the Folger copy is blotted:

9.1 was

A true Account of
ANNE WENTWORTHS
Being cruelly, unjustly, and unchristianly dealt with by some of those people called
ANABAPTISTS,
OF THE
Particular opinion, and all the cause she gave, and what she hath done.

Who would never appear in publick, but forced to declare the tender mercies of God, and cruelty of man; that will not hear truth if it were to save her life or soul, having tendred by all just and legal ways, but they reject and refuse to hear her, when so weak as a dying woman.

Also her discovering the two Spirits which are in the World, and her giving warning of what e're long will surely and suddenly come to pass.

Blessed are ye when men shall revile you, and persecute you, and say all manner of evil against you falsly for my Names sake.

Rejoyce, and be exceeding glad, for great is your reward in Heaven, for so persecuted they the Prophets which were before you, Mark 5. 11, 12.

Weeping may endure for a night, but joy cometh in the morning.

Printed in the year 1676.

An Evening-Mourning hath brought a Morning-Song of high Praises unto God alone.

HEre is a case that cannot possible be brought to an end without coming into the publick view of the World, though it is so contrary unto my nature, that I would rather suffer unto death than be seen in any publick way; but am constrained now, & thrust out by the mighty power of God, who overpowers me, that I must no longer confer with flesh and blood, and yield to my own reason of my weakness, foolishness, and fearful slavish nature, that am danted with a look of any terrible, fierce, angry man; and it is worse than death to me to see them, for it is as wounds and gores in my sides: But he who ruleth in the Heavens, and overpowreth all flesh, and can subdue Kings, and turn the hearts of all men as he doth the Rivers of water; the Lord of Life, the great *Jehovah*, he hath been stirring me up, and provoking me above this 6 months to do this, with a promise that he will go before, and allay all my enemies for me, and bids me not fear, neither be dismayed at so great a multitude, *but put on the whole armor of God, the shield of Faith, and Helmet of Salvation, and the sword of the Spirit, which is the Word of God; and being girt about with truth, fight a good fight of Faith*, with this promise, that he which overcometh shall inherit all things, and I will be his God, and he shall be my Son, which includes daughters as well as sons: Which now will be tried whether I be a daughter of the seed of *Abraham*, a true child of God, born from above, and then all the promises belong to me, as well as to all his children; *And except we be born again we cannot enter into the Kingdom of God.* Nothing of moral virtues,

virtues, or honest just dealing with men, or any thing of our own righteousness, or civil education, will give us admittance there; nor no manner of form of Religion, without the power, light and life of holiness and truth in the inward parts, without being washed in the blood of the Lamb Christ Jesus, and purged and cleansed from all our filthiness, and have that pure and undefiled Religion, we are nothing accepted with God; therefore it doth behove us to examine our hearts, and try our ways, and turn unto the Lord, and know whether God be in us of a truth, or no, and to *redeem the time, because the days are few and evil* that we have here to live: And the time is short, and eternity long, either eternal joys, or eternal flames. When we have all acted our part upon the stage, then out of the World we must be gone; and if we have not been true labourers in Christ's Vineyard, walking in truth, and making our calling and election sure here, then it will be sad with us there, where there is no returning back again, nor no remembrance of him in the grave: The living they praise thee, the dead cannot, and God will not be mocked, but whatsoever we sow, that shall we reap, and be rewarded according to the deeds in the flesh; *for God shall bring every work into judgment, with every secret thing, whether it be good, or whether it be evil*, Eccles. 12. 14. And to take up any profession of Religion, or walk in any form without the power of truth, *and speak with the tongue of men and Angels, and have not Charity, it is but as sounding Brass, or a tinkling Cymbal; and if we give all our goods to the poor, and our bodies to be burned, and have not Charity, it profiteth us nothing.* And what this gift of Charity is, all may read, in 1 *Cor.* Chap. 13. and see how far most are wanting in this excellent gift of Charity, and how few minds the Scriptures in the spiritual meaning thereof, or are able to understand them: or how can we except we have the

same

ſame Spirit to unſold them, and give us to underſtand, or elſe they are as a ſealed Book, for the Letter killeth, but the Spirit quickeneth and maketh alive, and for want of the Spirit of God, to open this Sealed Book, makes ſo many falſe interpreters of them, and many reſiſting them to their own Deſtruction; that never had the Spirit, the Anointing of the holy one, which teacheth us all things, who can inable us to do all things; and without him nothing at all as we ought, for without the Spirit of God be in us, of a truth, that teacheth us to deny all ungodlyneſs, and worldly Luſts, and Pleaſures, and Vanitys thereof, and lead us into all truth; we are Blind, Miſerable, and Naked, and the Scripture ſaith ſome may be Preachers to others, and yet themſelves caſt away, and this is ſure that all the World is in this State, either Sinners or Saints, Believers or unbelievers, in Chriſt or out of Chriſt; for betwixt theſe there is no medium or middle State, it is not minded what profeſſion we put on, and what People we walk with, but have we put on Chriſt, and walk with him, and our Garments Clean, unſpoted, from the Pollution of the World, for though there be thouſands and milions of People, and many ſorts of Profeſſors crying up, Lo here is Chriſt, and lo there, and all ready to ſay Chriſt is in us, the hope of Glory, and we are his People, the Church of Chriſt, is Chriſt divided, how can this be, when he and his Church are but one, his beloved Spouſe is Ingrafted, Knit, and Joyned unto him, all his Saints and he are one, and cannot be ſeparated or undone, and all ſorts of Religion or People whatever, yet there is but two Spirits in the World, nor never was, nor never will be, the Spirit of God, and the Spirit of the Devil, the good Spirit, and the bad, the Children of Light, & the Children of Darkneſs, & let us all profeſs what we will, yet we are one of theſe that hath either the good or evil Spirit in us, either Children of Light, or Children of

 Dark-

Darkness; and Christ saith many are called and few are chosen, and his flock is a little flock, few in number, a small remnant, and Strait is the Gate, and narrow is the way that leadeth unto Life, & few doth find it, in comparison of the great multitude that goes the broad way, yet he hath reserved unto himself many thousands that hath not bowed the knee to *Baal*; but these two Spirits that was from the beginning will remain to the end of the World, and they were always at War one with another, being set against each other, but Satan rages most when his time is short, being now upon his last Legs, and will be Chained up ere long for a time, and half a time: now he hath made war to purpose with all the Strength he can, to fight against light and truth, in a weak, Foolish, despised nothing, a worm of no might or strength, but in him who is my Lord and Master, and Law-giver, the great *Jehovah*, my King, who sees how truth is fell in the street and equity cannot enter, and it despiseth him to see men trample upon truth, and wound and bruise my heel, and now he will raise truth up more bright to break their Head, they have kicked against the Pricks, and burthened themselves with a burthensome Stone, they would not bare truth at first, but tread so hard upon it, and truth as a bed of Cammamile grows so strong to overcome them all at last, for what is so strong as truth, dying men are not, for they are rotten reeds, and shall wither as the grass, and be soon cut off, but truth liveth and abideth for ever; now they havd tryed all their strength and done all they can, they are lighter then Vanity, and will appear as they are, but dying, angry Men.

I shall give a brief and short account as possible may be, of the reason of the Publication of this, and absolute necessity for it, and could not be avoided, if it had been a thing that could possible a been ended in private, then it should never become publick by any ny will of mine, if men were not so out of all reason; as I find some not to be satisfied, with all my yielding my Body, to lay that as the ground, and as the street for them to go over, yet that will not satisfie nor content them, as now they have proved it themselves, unless my Soul bow down also unto them, which can never be done to satisfie man, I am contented to yield up my Life, but the Life of my Soul, that pretious Jewel is kept in my Fathers Hand, and it is not possible to pluck it out of my Father's hand, that to struggle and wrastle with me, to spend my Life out it is in vain, when my Soul is set upon the Rock, ar d that they can never gain, but Soul oppression is far greater then Bodily oppression, that it can be no longer born to bind the Spirit of God too hard and long, makes it at last break out into a flame: by this all may understand here is a matter of war in hand between these two Spirits, and I must confess all the cause I gave, and what I have done, and how this war begun, and how it came to rise so high, and grow so hot, that it cannot be ended or taken up in private, but must come into the open field of the World to be tryed and fought out, and all see whether truth or men be strongest, and which the Victory got. The ground and rise of all this sprung from a work that I have done, which I must confess, and never deny it, but utterly deny it to be any will of my own, but was commanded of God my Father to declare his goodness, and exalt his name alone, and make his power and Faitfulness known how he is a God gratious and Merciful, hearing the crys and Prayers of the destitute and afflicted, and all his chosen elect ones he will own, but this was not for the honour of Man, that it could not be born nor never will by any unregenerate one, that knows not what it is to be born again, but are yet in their Sin, but they have helped to purge it well and make it grow, that all the Seed of *Abraham*, the Spiritual inlightened Saints will receive

it,

it, and what Spirit it is writ with they will discern and know, the work tends only to give an account of my Faith, and the hope that is in me, to whomsoever shall ask me, and speak the way: the Lord led me in a wilderness of affliction for many years, to humble me, and prove me, and see what was in my Heart, and to do my Soul good, and declare my great and wonderful experience of the appearance of God and his Mercys to me from time to time, and to give him the Praise who is worthy of all praise. honour and glory for ever anh ever more: this is the substance of what I have suffered and been persecuted for, which may seem incr.adible at the first reading, how could any suffer for such a thing, but have but patience to read a little further, and then you will see how truth will answer you, for if truth did not stand in the gap, I durst not appear in publick, when my potent enemys and persecuting adversarys are yet alive, and may disprove me if I speak not truth, but I have nothing but truth to face them with, and can put it to all their Consciences, whether I did ever give them any cause to be angry or offended with me before this work begun, or since, but all what from it sprung, and the reason why it did so highly offend and disturb them, I could no way help, for though they could not bare truth, yet the Lord would have me speak truth, and the more they dashed at it, and beat the poor weak instrument for it, the more the Lord of Life, who was the Agent, confirms it, and in the close now gives his reasons why he would have this work done, and chose such a weak, follish, despised Woman as I, and to satisfie all strangers that may read this, why it was so great a sore to professing men, in speaking the way as the Lord led me, and declaring my experience as he taught me, and required to have recorded by me for the honour and glory of his own name, this lay in the way as the stumbling stone to give offence to man for all my afflictions, sorrow, suffering,

ing, heart-breaking grief was from my nearest Relation, and being an Anabaptist Church-member they fall upon me, and could not bear the truth to be spoke of their Brother, when the Lord knew he was that before he called and commanded me to do this work, and had took up that form of Religion before we were married to each other; and I know nothing to the contrary, but that he may be their Brother who do so freely own him, he being a moral honest, just-dealing man as any of them, and no disparagement to none to say he is an honest, just-dealing man; for is not moral honesty and formality, the top and height of most professers of Christianity: I do not say all, nor judg none, but wish the most may not be found so, and by report, all are not come up so far as my Husband is; for I know no gross sin that he is addicted too, nor never heard he was before he took up that form of Religion, to wash his body in water, the outside of the cup and platter, which stood in the least need, when his soul was never yet washed from the filth of his inbred natural corruption; but the same spirit he brought into the World with him, yet remains to this day, and he keeps that as his dellilah and pleasing delight, to satisfy himself in all his own will, without being born again; for I dare be bold to affirm that he never yet knew the new birth, the life of the new man; nor they must needs be no Saints or Christians in deed and in truth, nor know the new birth themselvess, if they take him to be one that is born again, and examine but his carriage to a Wife this 23 years, not his carriage to the World before men, for that is fair enough: but what is it in secret, that God hath seen all along, and is angry at: and all the hopes I have, that the Lord doth this out of love to his soul, because he follows him so close, seeing so stout an Oxe and strong *Leviathan*, that cannot be bended with less, no smaller cords will bind so lofty an high spirit, to put an hook in his tongue, and bore his jaw, and if the Lord should by this open his blind eyes, and soften his hard heart, and humble his proud spirit, and bring him down to the foot of God, that he may find mercy, and his soul live, and not die, then I shall not be an unfaithful wife for obeying the voice of my heavenly Husband, in answering his call, and submitting to his will, after I had spent out all my natural strength of body in obedience to satisfy the unreasonable will of my earthly Husband, and laid my body as the ground, and as the street for him to go over for 18 years together, and keep silent, for thou O Lord did'st it, and afflicted me less than I deserved, and now the Lord sees my Husband hath as much need of this as I had of his being so great a scourge and lash to me: it is as meet, and needful, and necessary for him, if he belong to God, as his natural appointed food; and I can shew no greater love to his soul than in being faithful to God and his Word, and keep his Commandments; for what love is this for his brethren to blind his eyes, and harden his heart against God and his Word, and to encourage and heighten his spirit, which needed none, and to help forward with my affliction: but I pray God to forgive them, for they have done they know not what: and I have so much love for him, that I wish his soul as well as my own, and would rather see him a convert, a new man, if I begg'd my bread with him, than to see him made Lord Mayor of *London*, and remain with this spirit; for I had better be a Coblers wife of a mild meek nature, and have the spirit of God in him, and knows the life of the new man, than to be the greatest mans wife in the world, of such a terrible spirit, and put on a form of Religion for a cloak to hide it from the world, which too many take up for a cover-slut.

I think it meet to give a short account how I come to do this work, which did occasion such a stir about me to afflict me for it, that all strangers may be made to enquire into it, and know what

what it is; after 18 years I had been my Husbands wife, and w consumed to skin and bone, a forlorn sad spectacle to be seen, unlike a woman; for my days had been spent with sighing, and my years with crying, for day and night the hand of the Lord was heavy upon me, and my moisture was turned into the drought of Summer. *When I kept silence my bones waxed old through my roaring all the day long*, having an Hectiff Fever, which came by so great oppression, and sorrow of heart; and wanting vent, and smothering it so long in my own brest, grew so hot, and burnt so strong, that I was past all cure of man, and given over by them, and lay at the point of death, being bowed together with my infirmity of 18 years, and could in no wise lift up my self: then at that inch and nick of time the great Physitian of value came, the good *Samaritan* passing by, and seeing me lye wounded, and bleeding to death, even as it were at the last gasp: then he spake as he did to the woman, *Luke* 13. 11. and said unto her, *Woman, thou art loosed from thine infirmity; and he laid his hands on her, and immediately she was made straight, and glorified God*: and I was as immediately restored as she; but men will not suffer me to glorify God, though I am commanded of God so to do: but they persecute me for it, and wound and pierce me again for making mention of his name, and oft and many a time since by their violent misusing and abusing of me, brought me to the gates of death, and laid me as one dead and slain, for bearing my witness for him: but now at their door will it lye for stopping my mouth, and quenching of the spirit, and so afflicting me, ready to dye when I should magnify the name of Jesus, that in his name, through faith in his name, yea the faith which is by him, gave me perfect soundness in the presence of you all; and this was not done in a corner, neither am I a stranger in *London*, but in and about the City an hundred that were eye-witness, that knew my body was so, but there is a greater witness in Hea-

 ven,

ven, the Father, Son, and Holy Ghost, and these three are one, who knows how all that weakness came, and why it could not be cured by man, and I was not raised up for naught by such a powerful hand, nor for this end, that my Husband and his Brethren should always afflict and oppress me, and abuse me at their pleasure, and not suffer me to speak of the things of God ; and for any other discourse, I am very slow of speech, and they binding me from that, I am as a silent woman : but how their ways have pleased God in so doing, and how he hath accepted and liked of all they have said and done in so sore afflicting me, since the time of my healing the third of *January* 1670. since which time this work begun, at which time he called me to come and follow him : and as sure as he is God, and I his little one, and as sure as he did heal and raise me up at that time, and set me to do this work without any will of my own, so sure will that same King Jesus, who was crucified upon the Cross, that poured oil into my wounds, and joy and gladness into my heart, and light and life into my soul : He it is, I say, that will bring it to light in the face of the world, he will make it known how he is angry at what he see was done, and men sheathing their swords in my bowels, and wound me so deep after he had healed up my wounds : *for there is nothing covered that shall not be revealed, neither hid that shall not be known* : and now there is no way but one, it cannot be avoided, there is no help for it, but it will come to the Worlds hearing, without you can blot out those words, *Luke* 12. 2. 3. for the decree is gone forth, and cannot be reversed, nor called back what the God of all wisdom is now resolved to do, and of his own good will hath revealed, and let such a poor unworthy despised worm as I know by going down into the deeps, and entring into the sanctuary of the Lord, and crying mightily unto my God with a loud and bitter, lamentable voice to know his end, and there he gave me to understand, that I wish all pride, cove-

tousness,

tousness, vanities, pleasures of the world, scorn and contempt, false accusing, and fierce despising might be all laid aside: and now another spirit be found that would consider and lay it to heart: and fall to mourning, and weeping, and great lamentations in City and Countreys for the great abominations that brings down judgments upon our heads, and brings to desolation, and prepare to meet the Lord in his fiery tryal, and fierce indignation, which shortly and suddenly will come, which I could tell what it is, and how I come to know what the Lord Jesus will do, and the reason why he is so highly provoked to come forth in anger; but because there is so great a despising and setting me at naught, and not at all understanding me aright, and I hasting to be as short as I can in this paper, I shall now forbear: but whoever hath any thing to accuse me of, or say against me before that time of my healing, there is none that can or will say more against me than I will confess and speak against my self; and since that time of my close retiring with the Lord, and suffering persecution, I will leave it unto him to speak for me, which in time he will make manifest unto the World, having neighbours and others can speak: I am not a woman spending my time in the pleasures and vanities of the World, and what my manner of life and conversation is, that is seen and known; and if the Lord spare my life a little longer, he will enable me to give sufficient proof to the world, that all and every word these my persecutors hath spoken against me since the beginning of this work, it all sprung from that evil spirit which is the Father of lies, and was so from the beginning: for their saying I was deceived, and deluded, and full of notions, whimsies, and self-will, and under an hour of temptation, and all this, and a great deal more they said will all be found false, and no truth in it; for they might as well accused *Abigail* for saying her Husband was a churlish *Nabal*, and folly was with him, and have reproved *Moses* for wri-

ting

ting that King *Pharaoh* was an oppressing King: what, will *Moses* disgrace a King, such great men of honour! and what, must *Joseph* speak of his brethren to dishonour them: will any discover a *Haman* that sure was a man of great parts, being so in favour with the King, and a poor *Mordecai* that wore sackcloath, and none regarded, shall he be advanced: How can any proud man upon earth bear such a thing: but let all esteem of my Husband as he is a moral honest man, full of blind zeal, and hath the gift of his tongue, a man very fit for business and employment in this World; for he will not cheat or cosen any man, but if any call him a Saint, they bring a woe upon themselves, *for woe unto them which call good evil, and evil good*: and if he be a Saint, then I am a Devil, and all as he and his brethren saith, and then all they have done is well done, and the great Judg of Heaven and Earth, who knows all hearts, he will deside this, and pass sentence which he is most pleased with, and which he most accepts of, whether my work or their words and actions, for both do not please God, but one is condemned already, and he will cast one out of his sight in the open field of the World, for that Book which I have suffered so deeply for, and was laid to my charge as a great heinous crime, to be all of my own writing, and so it is, but not at all of my own inditing, nor no mans help; and who the Author of it was hath been tried, and comes now to be seen what descent it had, and who is the Father of it, that this large compass they have fetched in going about some years tormenting and afflicting me for it, and ends nothing is now brought into so short a cut, that all is ended in two words, that is in proving whether this work was begun of God or the Devil, for one it was: and some said long ago they were sure it was begun of the Devil, and no doubt but it was of the Devil, and being he was so sure, and made no doubt of it, now must he prove what he said, or else it will be proved that it was begun of God,

and

and *Satan* hath made war against it ever since, and though it begun in much weakness, yet it will end in full strength, that the evil one shall not be able to overcome, for a child is not a man as soon as he is born, he cannot walk and talk as soon as ever he enters into the World, but gradually by degrees grows up to maturity, and at last becomes a man, so it is with a child of God that is employed in any work or service for the Lord, they do not receive all their strength at first, but gradually, as they are able to bear, for every promise of God must be fulfilled, and he saith *those that wait upon the Lord shall renew their strength, and grow stronger and stronger*; so this shall be the proof of it, whether it were begun of God or no, by the standing and growth of it, *when the rain descended, and floods came, and the winds blew, and beat hard upon it, and it fell not, for it was founded upon a rock*, and these great showers were as seasonable as rain upon new mown-grass, to make it grow effectually, for the honour, and glory, and praise of God for ever more, to exalt his name, and make his power known: But no honour to oppressing Kings, and proud *Hamans*, no honour to any formal professing men, still all this while what they strugled so hard for, they have not got their will: Now whoever reads this, you may understand here is a Book of a weak, foolish, despised womans writing, that she hath suffered and been persecuted nigh unto death oft and many a time for it, even to the Gates of death, not expecting to live, that its no less than a miracle that I am alive, or in my senses; when *Solomon* saith *oppression will make a wise man mad*, and yet such oppression above measure, so weak a worm as I must bear, that the name of God might be magnified in seeing so great a power, and keeping me close unto himself, and preserving me in my senses under so cruel oppression and great rage of man as I did appear, that whoever doth enquire into the truth of this case, and know my weakness, and how I was used, will say it was great indeed, and ad-

mire

mire the power of God when they do hear: and whoever thou art that reads this, if thou be a Christian, or desirest to be one: if thou hast any love to God at all, or desirest to love God above all: if thou desirest to forsake the Devil and all his works, the pleasures and vanities of the world, that thou mayst escape the eternal flames: if thou desirest with all thy heart to love, fear, and serve the Lord, and to be born again, and know the life of the new man, that thou mayst have eternal joys for evermore in Heaven; then do not dye unregenerate, or give thy self rest untill thou enquire and understand the true cause, the rise and bottom of all this, and come to see what the end of God is, and what he is about to do, who will act all his own pleasure, who is King of Kings, and Lord of Lords, who sitteth in the Heavens, and rules the Nations, and all men are but as a drop of a bucket before him, and that he is a God that hath all power in his hand, he will have the world know; and be not now sleety in despising me, and deceive your own selves by thinking either moral honesty, or formality, or any thing of our own righteousness, or going as far as the five foolish Virgins, just to Heavens Gate, and yet could not enter into eternal bliss. O, great is the mystery of godliness, and few considereth or layeth it to heart, though all would have Heaven at the end, yet not willing to part with earth, or any dellilah, or beloved lust, few striving to enter in at the strait gate, as if Heaven were not worth suffering or taking pains for, but might be easily got; and I fear many are split upon that rock of formal profession which they rest and content themselves in, and had better never a known, without the power of truth, light and life of holiness; for I can speak by sad experience, for 20 years being a dark, blind, formal professor, what a dry, barren soul I had; and yet thought I was as zealous, and strong, formal professor as any; and for 7 or 8 years a formal Church-member, eat up with blind zeal, and my soul starve for hunger: and

and hear hath been blind formality acted to purpose, to the top and height of it; for if they had been spiritual enlighten'd ones, they would have searched out the matter to have known whether it were truth or no I spoke, and not have fallen upon me as they have done; if they had been of that pure Religion, and undefiled, as the Apostle *James* speaks of, and have had their eye of Faith open, they would a scorned to have wronged and abused me so, had they been Christians in deed and in truth, really born from above of that holy seed, they would rather a torn their own flesh than a pierced and wounded me so deep, when I had been for 18 years such a woman of sorrow, and acquainted with grief, and from man could have no relief; but the Lord Jesus, who see all my sorrow, and heard all my cry, seeing me bleeding to death, of his own good will took pity and healed up my wounds, and would not let me dye, and when he lays his commands upon me to declare his goodness, and make his power known for the honour and glory of his own name: But because man could not have honour no more than King *Pharaoh*, they fall to wounding, piercing, and sore oppressing me again. O, was ever such a thing heard or read, that professing men should use a weak woman so, that had been spent out with sorrow, and almost dead, and give them no other cause than speaking truth, and obeying the voice of God, who knew I had been 18 years under as hard a task-master as ever the children of *Israel* were, and had cried as hard unto God as ever they did, and they were not more spent out with sorrow than I was, and may say without any offence to God, that *Pharoah*'s heart was never more hard than some that are the Anabaptist Church-members; and because the Lord brings this to light, his brethren have given me an ill reward, therefore I must enjoyn and engage all Saints that reads this, as they love God, his way and truth, and would promote the purity of the Gospel, and have *Jerusalem* become the praise of the whole earth, and *Zions* walls to be built, and light and truth ushered in, and King *Jesus* sit upon *Mount Sion*, that they will not give themselves rest until they have enquired out the truth of all this, being enough yet living to speak that knew both my Husband and me from our youth, and are no strangers to both our natural tempers: And speak now all friends and foes all the worst and every thing you know, spare not, but speak all you can that you have against me in all that time of 40 years of my life before my healing, and when you have spoke all you can, I will not justify my self in none, but confess and speak more against my self than any one else will or can when they have all done: and let now *Thomas Hicks* and *William Dix* draw up their Bill, and all the rest of my Husbands brethren what it is they have to charge me with of all they have against me in misbehaviour in life and conversation, or neglect of my duty to their Brother, in not obeying of him from the first day of my Marriage unto the day of my healing, compleat 18 years the third of *January*, 1670. For whatever any have to charge me with, must be in that time, for what hath been said or done to me since, will not help them at all, for the same *Jesus* which healed and raised me up from the grave, the same *Israel's* God, which is my Lord and my God, he will reprove them to their faces, that since that time, in all they have said and done, he doth except of none, and in that time of all my sorrow and suffering, some of these that now rise up to own my Husband for their Brother, and to abuse me, I never had heard on them before: therefore all Saints consider this, and do not neglect your duty, but know whether I speak truth or no, and be sure to answer the mind of God, to inform your selves of all the cause I gave, and of all I had done, and how it was with my soul and body, and what was my condition when my Husband brought three men to me that did fright, and amaze, and astonish me to see, knowing no cause I gave them, nor what I had done more

than

than this work to make them come and whet their tongues as sharp swords, and their teeth as spears and arrows, and distress my Soul so by speaking things so false, and laying things to my Charge, I knew not the least Sin in offending God, no more then the Child unborn, but do confess I did highly offend man, as ever did proud *Haman* when he could not bring his wicked design to pass, to destroy all the Seed of the *Jews*, and nothing they said or laid to my charge but what lay against this Work, therefore this day they came, the 13. of *February* 1673. Did the Lord cast this thing between them and me, which said truth was one, and who did the wrong, and who he was most pleased with, and how he liked of what was done, and if I be his little one he will me own, and this thing unto the World make known, for he will as soon deny himself to be God, as such a thing to hide: for there was either the truest piece of Christianity acted towards me, or else the greatest piece of Hypocrisie, Formality, and Idolatry, which was abominable in the sight of God, that he will set up standards for the World to see how his anger was kindled then, and ere long he will blow it up into a Flame, so as all Formality and Hypocrisie shall tast and feel, and for it smart, for such formal acting, to wound and pierce me so deep to the Heart, and be so blind to take the wrong side, to set against the weak Woman that could hardly Live, only strong in the Lord, and to take the part of such a man that had so high a lofty Spirit, that the Lord was angry with, and reproving him for being such a terrible oppressing King to lule so over a Wife, and bow her so low down, and then when she is called to follow God, to exalt his Name, then so many of his Bretheren fall to afflict me, and deal so unjustly, and bring me before their Church, and proceed as far against me as they can, to blind his Eyes, and harden his Heart, and double my task; to be sure that God is no more pleased at all with this, then he was with King *Pharoah*, we will let them

 know

know at last, for though I have been made drunken with affliction, but not with Wine, yet now the Lord hath taken out of mine hand the cup of trembling, even the dregs of his fury, that I shall no more drink it again, but he will put it into the hand of them that hath afflicted me, and said to my Soul, bow down, that we may go over, and was not content that I had laid my Body as the ground and as the street to them that went over, read the 3 last verses of *Isaiah* 51. And see now if any thing of scorn and contempt of me can keep of or prevent what the Lord of Life, the King of glory will do, let your Bill of charge you draw up against me, be as big as you will, if it be not made before the year 1670. then I need not fear or care; being here is a Bill of charge drawn up against all you that hath had a hand in afflicting and dealing with me since the 13 of *February* 73. that you are called to answer before the great Judge, before whom we must appear at the great Judgment day, to give an account of all the deeds done in the flesh, whether good or evil, and he is Judge whether I have wronged you, or you have wronged me; who knows every thing, even the thoughts of the Heart, he doth see; and here is a charge he writes against you, the want of the gift of Charity, and since *February* 73. Charges you with Labouring with all your might and strength to force my Conscience, and would make a rape of my Soul, to have it bow down to you, and is unsatisfied as the horsleach with all my Bodily sufferings, that doth not content you to see that lost, but still saith give, you would have my Soul lost also: you must throw me into so deep a Pit, that the Lord might bring me with double advantage out of it, you must make the Fiery Furnace seven times more hot to Purge a way all filth and dross, and make more pure Gold for others to see no hurt my Soul got, for the Son of God hath been with me all this while, that Men and Devils cannot my Soul beguile, you must shut me up in Prison' in a Lions Den, that I might

have

have all my food sent down from Heaven, and now I have for 6 Moneths been hid as one out of the World, and with *Manna* feed, and seen such wonders in the deep, that I must no more return into the World again, but close unto God keep, and forbid any coming at me, but such as come in Love, and are comfortable refreshing Company, for uncomfortable ones I have had enough, and desire no more knowledg of their ways, but shake off the dust of my feet against them, and my peace shall return to me again, and let me not see no more of the Faces of my Persecuting Enemys, but let them labour all to get to Heaven through that strait and narrow gate which leadeth to Life, but come no more at me, they having left such a sting of the Serpent behind, and made my wounds so deep, that I must carry them to my Grave, then blame me not because I cannot them see, and let them but stay away until they have broken down that wall of defence, which is set as walls and bulwarks for to defend me from them that hath fought so hard against me without a cause, let them now break that down which made all this stir, and wholly destroy it root and branch, from the beginning to the ending, by proveing it not to be of God, and when they have done so, they shall not need to come to me, but I will make hast to go to them, to learn the way to Heaven; and in the mean time trouble me no more, but keep their Brother, and in their form make much one of another, until the Lord comes forth with a Shout of his Voice, to give their forms such a shake as will break them all to Pieces, and set them to War one with another, Oh all Nations, fear and dread this great God of Heaven, who can quickly send his Judgments down upon our heads, and except ye return and repent he will quickly come to do such a thing as never yet was done, all may be satisfied that I have no counsel of Man or any Creature upon Earth, for I know no Man that is willing that God should Plead my cause, or that the Lord should discover

Proud,

Proud, Impious, hard hearted Men, and lay open Hypocrisie and formality, and look upon a poor weak despised Woman, that is trampled under the feet of men, rather then God should do such a thing to own a Woman and disgrace a Man, they would rather have her Soul and Body lost and damned to all Eternity, as they have proved it themselves in what they have done to me: If all Professors had been Saints, then such a work could never a been, nor if there were no dark formal ones, there would have been none to a warred against that which is for the Honour of God, but not for the honour of Man, to exalt the name of God, and abase proud man to stain the glory of all Flesh, for he will not give his glory unto another, and this is for the honour of God to declare his goodness, and make his power and faithfulness known, that he hath pleaded the cause of a poor desolate, despised woman against Men and Devels, he hath prevailed with the high and mighty one that saw all her sorrows, and heard her Crys when men was mad, and against her railed, who pleads the cause of his own elect, that cry unto him day and night, he hath accepted her mourning, and heard the voice of her roaring, and her prayers, sighs, and groans ascended up to heaven for a memorial before him, Oh all Saints be glad and rejoyce with me, when you hear how the great *Jehovah* hath turned my mourning into singing, Hallelujah, all honour, glory, and praise, might, & dominion, be for ever and ever more unto him given, not unto man, but unto God alone, for ever more, *Amen*.

What the God of all wisdom will do, for now it is too late when the decree is gone forth and cannot be reversed, that no railing or searce despising, or any more hard usage of me will not prevent, no nor all the men in the world cannot hinder or stop what the God of Heaven, the great and mighty Judge of Heaven and Earth is purposed to do, and of his own good will hath revealed, & let such an unworthy poor despised worme as I know,

and

and do not now deceive your selves, to suppose that he is coming to give peace on earth, for I tell you nay, but rather division, for he saith, I am come to send fire on the earth, and what will I if it be already kindled, *Luke* 12 49. It is already kindled, but how will you bear his hottest wrath, if you be not prepared with your loins girded about with truth, and your lights burning, and ye your selves like unto men that wait for the Lord when he will return from the Wedding, that when he commeth, and knocketh, ye may open unto him immediately, for blessed are those servants whom the Lord when he cometh shall find watching, verily I say unto you, that he shall gird himself, and make them to sit down to meat, and will come forth, and serve them; and if he shall come in the second watch, or come in the third watch, and find them so, blessed are those servants, *Luke* 12. 36, 37, 38. Be ye therefore ready, for the Son of man cometh at an hour when we think not on, as a thief in the night, and no man knoweth the day and hour but the Father only; but he will come in an hour when we are not aware of, therefore let us all prepare to meet the Lord, lest he cut us in sunder, and appoint us our portion with the unbelievers, where there will be weeping, and wailing, and gnashing of teeth: Let us rather sell all, and part with our own righteousness, and all our own wisdom, and become a fool for Christ, and be nothing in our own eyes, but poor, empty, hungry beggers, that so he may fill us with that hid treasure in the Heavens, that faileth not, where no thief approcheth, neither moth corrupteth, *for where our treasure is, there will our hearts be also*; a portion in heaven is worth ten thousand worlds, to have a stock of grace there in that heavenly Country, is better than the richest Merchant here, if he have not laid up indurable riches there which never fadeth away, but abideth for ever: this doth not come to the view of the World with eloquence of speech, nor any artificial dress, but in plainness.

ness of speech, in its own Mothers tongue, not set forth and adorned with the wisdom of men, for I have no help of any creature to advise me herein, no none but the great Creator for my Counsellor and Teacher, being willing to spend and be spent for Christ, so he may be but all in all, and I nothing at all, if he be honoured, and I abased, he alone exalted, and all flesh laid low and abased before him, who is King of all the Saints, and that light, and truth, and purity of the Gospel may break forth and shine yet more and more abundantly, until *Jerusalem* become the praise of the whole earth, and he sit upon *Mount Sion*, and rule the Nations as with a rod of Iron, so he gain, though I lose, if his Kingdom increase, and Satans Kingdom decrease, I have my end, who am given up as a thank-offering unto him, to walk in his Laws, and keep his Statutes, and to abide in his Courts for ever and evermore, *Amen.*

ANNE WENTWORTH.

From the house of my abode this ten years in *Kings-Head Court* in *White-Cross-street* neer *Cripple-Gate*. Writ and ended in my retirements between God and my self all alone, *June* 26. 1676.

THE END.

A Vindication (Wing W 1356), shelfmark T. 370(2), is reproduced by permission of The British Library. The text block of the original measures 166 × 111 mm.

A

VINDICATION

OF

Anne Wentworth,

TENDING

To the better preparing of all People for Her *Larger Teſtimony*, which is making ready for Publick View. Publiſhed according to the *Will of God*, and *Direction of Charity*.

By *Anne Wentworth*.

Be ſtill and know that I am God. I will be exalted among the Heathen: I will be exalted in the Earth. The Lord of Hoſt is with us, the God of Jacob *is our Refuge.* Pſal. 46. 10. 11.

To which is annexed

A Letter written by an eminent Chriſtian, concerning the ſaid *Anne Wentworth*, and directed to the ſeveral Congregations of the *Anabaptiſts*, and their reſpective Paſtors.

As alſo a Song of Tryumph by the ſaid *Anne Wentworth*, a Daughter of *Sion*, newly delivered from the Captivity of *Babylon*, &c.

How ſhould we Sing the Lords Song in a ſtrange Land? Pſal. 137. 1. 2. 3. 4.
Where is God my Maker that giveth Songs in the Night? Job 35. 10.
Let the Saints be joyful in Glory, let them Sing upon their Beds, Pſal. 149. 5.

Printed in the Year 1677.

THe Great Searcher of hearts has seen, neither is it unknown to several Christians in and about this City of *London*, or to the Consciences of my very Enemies, what Severe and Cruel persecutions I have sustained for the space of Eighteen years, from the unspeakable Tyrannies of an *Hard-hearted Yoak-Fellow*: and since, from the bitter zeal of several eminent professors of Religion, commonly call'd *Baptists*, VVho have most unjustly and unchristian-like caused all their pretended Church power to wait upon and serve the wrath of my oppressors; and who not being able truly to charge me with any sin committed against God that call'd for such a proceeding, have declared me an *Heathen*, and a *Publican* for *matters of Conscience*, in which I was faithful to the Teachings of God, according to the Scriptures of Truth, and obey'd the voyce of the Lord, who called me out from amongst them, that I might not partake of those Terrible Plagues, and dreadful judgments which are coming upon all *Formalists*, *Hypocrites*, and *profane Persons*, who are all of them the Inhabitants of this Earth; and who (however separated from one another *now*, by outward forms, and observations, or inward notions and opinions, in that *particular* and *great day* of the Lord, which is coming upon this Nation, will be found to be in *one Spirit*, and *Principle*.

My *cause* in this respect, being committed to Almighty God, the Righteous Judge of all, unto whom I have *appealed*, and who has accepted my *appeal*, and is speedily arising on my behalf, I will say nothing of *it* here. But only acquaint thee, whoever thou art, that readest these few lines, that it has pleased my most gratious God and Father (*who abounds towards his Children in all wisdome and prudence of Love*) to turn all the fierce wrath of man, which has been against me, into his own praise: And to change all the evil mine Enemies have thought and done against me, into a sweet designe for good; making all

A my

my *unspeakable sufferings* from man, my *wonderful supports* and *deliverances from God*, a *figure* of his *intended dispensations* towards his *Enemies*, and *people* in this Nation: Revealing to me how *Babilon* the Mother of Fornications is in her inward principle and Spirit, as also in her outward practices and pollutions, spread over the whole face of the Christian world; and every where found among the litteral and outward Churches: How her delusions, sorceries, and fornications are *here* most bewitching and dangerous, because she *here* comes forth as the *mystery of iniquity*, dressing and adorning her self in all the forms and notions of the heavenly things, sitting, and showing her self in the *Temple of God*: As also revealing to me, that the judgments which are determin'd to come upon her, should begin at the *House of God*, the *Formal Carnal Notional* Christians, the worshipers in the *outward Court*: And that the flood of the Divine vengeance having swep't away what is to be destroyed *there*, the Rod of Gods anger should be thrown into unquenchable fire, and the indignation of the Lord should end in the utter desolation, Ruine and confusion of the *Prophane world* and *grosser Babylon*. And that these things are at the *very door*, and ready to enter upon us as an *Armed Man*.

And because the mouth of iniquity is opened against me, and I bear the reproaches of the *mighty ones* wherewith they have reproached, the foot-steps of the Lord and his deallings with me; representing me as a *Proud*, *Passionate*, *Revengful*, *Discontented*, and *Mad* VVoman, and as one that has unduly published things to the prejudice and scandal of my Husband; and that have wickedly left him: designing (according to the craftiness and subtlety of the old Serpent in all Ages) by Marring my face, to darken and disappoint my Testimonie from the Lord, which I am with all convenient speed making ready for publick view. In great tenderness to all people concern'd in my Testimony, and that they may be the better prepared to receive the same when it shall be layd before them; I do in the presence of the most *holy* and *Jealous* God, who is *our God*, and yet a *consuming fire*; and in a deep sence of the manifold weaknesses, infirmities, and passions I am subject too, hereby *solemnly declare*.

That I am not conscious to my self of any *spiritual pride* in this matter, nor in the least desirous to have any appearance, or to make any noise in this VVorld. Nor durst I for ten thousand worlds pretend to come in the Name of God, or in the pride and forwardness of my own Spirit put my self into this work, without his express command concerning it, and his Spirit and presence with me in it; having learnt what unprofitable things the *Staff* and *Mantle* are, without the *God* of the *Prophets*: how dangerous and desperate an attempt it is, to put the *Commission* and *Authority* of God upon the *Dreams* and *Visions* of my own heart. I am well assured, if spiritual pride, the eagerness of my own spirit, any worldly designe, or any other delusion whatsoever has engaged me in my present Testimony, the holy God will discover me herein, and take open vengeance on all my *Inventions*, my *Idols*, and *strange Gods*; and that this matter will prove unto me like the waters of *Jealousie* unto the suspected person. And I have also through the tender mercies of God, the riches of an assurance, that my *God* who has been so many years *Emptying* me from Vessel to Vessel, *breaking* me all to peices in my self, and making me to become as *nothing* before him; and who has by many and great Tribulations been *bowing* my own will, and fitting me for his service, and who having taught me to tremble at his *word*, has thereby call'd and commanded me into this work, when I was as a thing that *is not* in my own eyes, and pleaded with him to be excused, I have I say, the *riches of an assurance*, that this *God* will be with me; and however the Spirit of prophecy in a poor weak VVoman shall be dispised by the wise and prudent of this world, yet *Wisdome is justified of her Children*; and that *God* who has commanded me to go forth in his *Name*, will by a *Divine power* go before me, making way for me, and subduing the Spirits before me which I am to deal with, and will also by a *Divine presence*, support me in the midst of all those sufferings his work can bring me into. *Out of the mouth of Babes and Sucklings God has ordained strength, because of his Enemies, that he might quell the Enemy and the avenger*, Psal. 8. 2.

And I declare, I have no wrath, discontent or revenge in my Spirit against the person of my Husband, or of any of his abetters;

but

but am taught by the forgiveness of *God*, freely to forgive all the Injuries he has done me; and my hearts desire and prayer to *God* (who can alone change the heart) is, that he may be converted, and saved; and I bow my Soul to the Father of lights, that the Eyes of all my persecutors may be opened; some of which I judge to be the Lords People, however acted in this matter by a *Zeal without knowledg. God is love, and he that dwells in love, dwells in God, and God in him.*

And however I am censured and reproached by persons who judge onely according to *outward appearance*, but not *Righteous judgment*, that I have unduly left my Husband; I do for the satisfaction of all plain hearted ones that may be offended at their reports herein, Declare, *first*, That it would be very easie for me, from the great Law of *self-preservation* to justifie my present absence from my Earthly Husband to all persons who have learn't to judg of *Good* and *Evil*, not onely according to the *outward Act*, but the *inward Spirit* and *Principle*; and who have *tenderness* enough, duly to weigh the various Tempers of minds, and the different circumstances of Bodies: Forasmuch as the Natural constitution of my mind and Body, being both considered, *He* has in his barbarous actions towards me, a many times over-done such things, as not only in the *Spirit* of them will be one day judged a murdering of, but had long since *really* proved so, if God had not wonderfully supported, and preserved me. But my natural life, through the springing up of a *better*, not being otherwise considerable, then as it is my duty to preserve it in a subierviency to the will and service of that God, whose I am in *Spirit*, *Soul*, and *Body*. I will not urge any thing of this nature as my defence upon this occasion, having learnt through the mercy of God, not to be affraid of him, who can only kill the *Body*, but can do no more. I do therefore *secondly*, in the fear of him who can kill both *Soul* and *Body*, further declare, That I was forced to fly to preserve a life more pretious than this natural one; and that it was necessary to the peace of my Soul, to absent my self from my earthly Husband, in obedience to my Heavenly Bridegroom, who call'd and commanded me (in a way too terrible, too powerful to be denyed) to undertake and finish a work, which my

earthly

earthly husband in a most cruel manner hindered me from performing, seizing, and running away with my Writings. And however man judges me in this action, yet I am satisfied, that I have been obedient to the *Heavenly Vision* herein, not *consulting with flesh and blood*. All the clouds of afflictions, troubles, sorrows, and deaths, upon the outward man, are nothing, compared with those of the inward man; when the life of our Souls is angry, and withdraws himself, cutting off the sweet beams of a spiritual communion between himself and us. This was my case, and I am not afraid or ashamed to say my Soul's beloved has abundantly owned me in this matter: and whilst men have done all they can to break my heart, he has bound up my Soul in the bundle of *Life* and *Love*, and he pleads my cause, and takes my part, and has spoken by his Word, with power and authority from Heaven, saying, *I shall abide with him, and he will abide with me, and come and Supp with me, and never leave me, nor forsake me:* And he bids me take no thought what I shall eat, what I shall drink, or wherewith I shall be cloathed, but cast all my care upon him, for he careth for me. And I am enabled in his power to role my self upon him; and my heart is fixed, trusting in him; and comforted with his word, in which he has caused me to hope, having no confidence in the Arm of Flesh, knowing that the Earth is the Lords, and the fulness thereof; and that he knows all my weaknesses, and wants, and my willingness to work, so far as he inables me, that my own hands may administer to my necessity, that I may not be burdensome to any. And he has assured me, that the man of the earth shall oppress no more; no more shall I return to be under the hands of the hard-hearted Persecutors, unless he become a new-man, a changed man, a man sensible of the wrong he has done me, with his fierce looks, bitter words, sharp tongue, and cruel usage. And I do further declare, That in the true reason of the case, I have not left my Husband, but he me. That I do own every *Law* and *Command* of God in the letter of his word, to be *right* and *true*; and do submit to every *rule* given forth by the Spirit of God, to govern the relation of Man and Wife *in the Lord*. And that I always stand ready to return to my Husband, or to welcome him to me: (and have signified so much to him by several Christian friends) provided I may have my *just* and *necessary* liberty to attend a more then ordinary call and command of God to publish the things which concern the *peace of my own Soul*, and *of the whole Nation*. In which work, I stand not in my own will, but in the will of him who has *sent*, and *sealed* me; as the *day* will very quickly declare, and decide this matter between me, and my Husband, and all his abettors. To which *day* I do here appeal for my justification, not doubting but that God to whom I have committed my cause will speedily arise, and cause my *Innocency* to break forth as the *Noon day*. For I do hereby declare in the presence of the most holy God, that I have no revengful, worldly or sinister end in this matter, but am against my own natural will, obeying God herein: And I do in all tenderness admonish and caution all my Enemies, and all persons whatsoever to whom these Papers shall come, that they take heed least they *hurt themselves*, in *reproaching me*; and that they do not set themselves to *justifie* by the *letter* that *Spirit* that is to be *condemned*, or to *condemn* that *Spirit* which it ownes and allows. And that they take heed least they urge the *letter* of any command against the *Spirit* of it, and so come to condemn *themselves* in the *Person* and *case* of another. The *Spirit* and the *letter* are no-where *contrary*, but thou mayst think them so; and by not duly attending upon the *Spirit* in the *letter* mayst unnaturally set the *letter* to oppose the *Spirit* from whence it comes, to which it testifies, and whither it tends. I beg of you all that read these lines for your *own sakes*, that you will remember still how the *Jewes* did of old, vilifie, reproach, condemn, and execute our Saviour, and justified themselves herein by the *letter* of the Law of God; with the *breach* of which Law they were continually charging *him* throughout his whole life, yet was it exactly according to their own Law, and in those very cases about which they were so much offended at him. Nor has it fared otherwise with the *whole seed* of Christ and all the spiritual manifestations of him in all ages. The best of Men, and Principles, have still been challeng'd for their *Non-conformity* to the *letter* and *outward rule*, although they have been most agreeable thereunto. As the Apostle speaks, *not without Law to God, but under the Law to Christ*.

And

And I do further declare, that the things I have published and written, and which are such an offence to my Husband, and indeed the cause of all the Persecutions I have suffered from others, were written sorely against my own natural *mind* and *will*; That I often beg'd of God I might rather die, then do it. That I was commanded of God to record them. That my own natural temper was so greatly averse to it, that for eleven months together I withstood the Lord, till by an Angel from Heaven he threatned to *kill me*, and took away my sleep from me: And then the *terrors of the Lord* forced me to obey the command. And indeed, the writings that man was so displeased with, were in themselves very warrantable, if I had not had any such command of God, for I only wrote the *way* he lead me in a wilderness of affliction for 18 years, to do me good; and declared my *experiences*, my *great* and *wonderful deliverances*, my many *answers* of Prayers in difficult cases from time to time: but most true it is, I did not speak of these things, nor set Pen to paper (for several reasons) till the Lord *commanded* and by his word and Spirit constrained me so to do at 18 years end, after I was consumed with grief, sorrow, oppression of heart, and long travail in the wilderness, and brought even to the gates of Death, and when past the Cure of all men, was raised up by the immediate and mighty hand of God. And being thus *healed*, I was commanded to write, and give glory to him who had so miraculously raised me up from the grave. And I do further declare, the things I have written are *true*, and *no lye*: and that what is so distasteful in them to man, are such things as I could not leave out, without *prejudice* to the Truth, and *disobedience* to God. And what ever censures I now undergo from *mans day* and *judgment* for this plain dealing in matters which concern so near a Relation in the flesh, I am well assured my faithfulness to God herein, will be owned in the *day* of his *impartial* and *righteous judgment*. And yet I must declare, it would have been much more agreeable to my Spirit, to have concealed the miscarriages of my Husband, then to have exposed them, if I had not been under a *command* herein not to be *disputed*: and it was not without great *resistings* that I was at length made *obedient*, *having tasted of that love, which both covers, and teaches us to cover a multitude of sinnes*: And yet I am fully perswaded, that my duty to *God* in this matter, will be found not only most *reasonable* and *necessary* on my part, but *exceeding beautiful in its season*, and to have been mannaged in some measure of the Spirit of that *God*, who is still *Love*, and *in whom* there is *no fury*, however he *marches against*, *goes through the Bryars and Thorns, and burns them together when they are set against him in Battle*. And whereas my Enemies have represented me as one *distracted*, and *beside my self*; in answer to such wicked proceedings against not only *me*, but the *truth*, I do for the Truths sake further say, *First*, That I judge my *Enemies* who have raised this false report of *me*, to be *themselves* most highly concerned, that this their *Report* should be found a *Lie*; for as much as if it were otherwise, the *cause* and *occasion* of my distraction might justly be laid at their own doors; for as the *Preacher* says, *Eccles.* 7. *Oppression makes a Wise man Mad*. *Secondly*, And yet I also judge it is the *mistaken* and *rotten Interest* of my Adversaries, not only to *report*, but to *believe* me a person beside my self: for if I be found in a *right mind*, how *Mad* must they be discovered to have been, in their blind rage and fury against *me* and *my Testimony*. *Thirdly*, I do with great chearfulness receive the *reproach* of this *report*; and all the *humiliation* that goes along with it; as a further *measure* of my *conformity* to my *Saviour*, and *fellowship with him in his Sufferings*. For thus has *he* throughout all ages been *blasphemed* in his *Prophets*, his *Messengers*, and in *himself*. Thus when *Elisha* sent a *young Prophet* with instructions to anoint *Jehu*, his Fellow-servants askt him; *Wherefore came this Mad fellow to thee?* 2 *King*. 9. Thus we read in *Mark*. 3. That *the Kindred of our Lord went out to lay hold on him; for they said, he is beside himself*. And again, in *Joh*. 10. *Many of the Jews said, he has a Devil, and is mad*. *Fourthly*, I do with great pleasure acknowledg, that in this great work (*in which I am set for a sign and a wonder*) I have *no wit*, *no wisdom*, *no understanding*, *no will* of *my own*. And if this be to be *mad*, I confess my self to be *beside my self to God*; whose Love *constrains me*, and whose Spirit has in this matter after an irresistable, but sweetest manner, *Captivated* my proper understanding, will and affections, to his Divine wisdom and will. And *Lastly*, I am well assured, that it will *speedily*, *very speedily* be known, that I am not *mad*, as my Enemies have

have reported, but have *spoken forth the words of truth and soberness.* I have not *run* before I was *sent*; but the word of the Lord is, *Come unto me*, and his *Spirit is upon me.* And he will perform every *Iota* and *title* of his own word, to overthrow *Babylon* with such an overturning, as never was, nor never will be again. The beginnings of this overturning will within a few days be seen upon her more refined parts, and the severity of the wrath shall afterwards come upon her Walls. Although man is so confident I am deceived, and has loaden me and my Testimony with all manner of reproach, yet the God whom I serve and obey, and who has spoken by me, will speedily turn the flood of scorn, contempt, bitter railing, false accusations, scandalous papers, and lying Pamphlets upon them, by whom they have been poured out against me. *The Lord frustreth the tokens of the Liars, and maketh Diviners mad; he turneth wise men backwards, and maketh their knowledge foolish: but he confirmeth the word of his servant, and performeth the Counsel of his Messengers*, Isa. 44.

And now in this *Faith* and *assurance* I do shut up this my *Vindication* and *preparitory Testimony*, *Declaring* unto all people whom it may concern, That it is the Lord has mooved me, and his Spirit which has stirred me up. My heavenly Bridegroom is come, and has given me courage, with an humble boldness, and holy confidence to speak the truth in all faithfulness, and to fear no man, but God alone, in whose strength I stand to encounter with all discouragements from my own understanding, will, affections, former thoughts and principles within; and with all opposition from difficulties, dangers, temptations of friends, and conspiracies of enemies without; I am sensible any of these things would be too strong for me, a worm of no might or strength; but I have renounced my self, and laid down my own wisdom and will in this work, and am given up to all the will of God herein; standing upon my watch, and having in his power *put on the whole Armor of God; the Shield of Faith, the Brestplate of Righteousness, with my Loyns girt about with truth, and my feet shod with the Preparation of the Gospel of peace, having taken the Helmet of Salvation, and the sword of the Spirit, which is the word of God, Praying alwaies with all prayer*

 and

and suplication in the Spirit, and watching thereunto with all perseverance, and supplication for all Saints. In this spiritual warfare, and combate I am called to wrestle not only against *flesh and blood, but against Principalities, and Powers, against the Rulers of the darkness of this world, and against spiritual wickedness in high places:* and must have no respect of persons because of advantage, but be faithful to God and his Word, sparing neither Friend nor Brother in matter of Truth, nor calling *good evil,* or *evil good*; nor putting *light* for *darkness*, or *darkness* for *light*; but obeying God, and not Man; loving him above all, keeping his Commandments, and pleasing him, although the whole world should be displeased. Man has made my Cup very bitter, and my Cross very heavy for obeying *God*, but my *God* has sweetned my Cup, and caused it to overflow with draughts of Love; my *God* has made my Yoak easie, and my Burthen light, because he bears me and them; he draws me, and *binds me with Cords to the Altar, his left hand is under my Head, his right Hand doth Embrace me, and his Banner over me is Love. I must not, I will not* be affraid to make my boast of my *God*, by whose Almighty Power I have been hitherto helped, and upheld, or else I had perished in my afflictions. When the compassion and bowels of man were shut up, the tender mercies of *God* were opened. When it was come to *Mordecay*'s pinch, *Israel*'s distress, *Paul*'s streight, God appeared. My extremity was his opportunity; he beheld my affliction, the sorrows and Agonies of my Soul; my groans, my prayers, my cries, my appeals ascended up for a memorial before him, and were had in remembrance with him. And he will arise, and that right speedily, he will make haste and not tarry, but send relief from Heaven, and save me, and all the poor of his Flock who hear the voice of their own Shepheard, and follow him, but a stranger they will not follow. He will smite the Rocky heart, he will convince the Consciences of men, he will bring down all them that glory in appearance, in face, and not in heart; he will make a speedy decision, he will turn the stream and flood of scorn and contempt cast upon me, and his poor despised ones in me; *he will arise to our joy, and they shall be ashamed that have hated us without a*

cause,

cause, and cast us out for his Name's sake, saying, *Let the Lord be glorified*. I have committed my way unto the Lord who judgeth righteously, who will not suffer the guilty always to go undiscovered and unpunished. He will take the Cup of trembling out of my hands, and put it into the hands of them who have afflicted me, who have said unto my Soul, *Bow down that we may go over*: and he will make their own *Tongues to fall upon themselves*, and *will measure out unto them again, the measure they have meeted.* The Lord has said it, and he will perform it. The Lord will plead my cause, and the cause of all his meek ones: but his anger is kindled against all *Formality*, *Hypocrisie*, *Idolatry*, and *Prophaneness*. He knows the secrets of all hearts, we are all open and naked in his sight: there is no dissembling in his sight, no mocking before him, no outward Form, no empty Opinion can shelter from his wrath. Upon the 13. of the Twelfth Month 1673. The Lord wonderfully discovered to me the unprofitableness of the best outward forms of Religion without the Power: and what a great deal of blindness, injustice, false accusations, barbarous usage, bitter and cruel zeal, with all manner of wickedness, has at this day taken Sanctuary in the exactest Forms according to the Letter, which are without the Spirit, yea, in enmity against it: It was the time four eminent Professors of the people called *Baptists*, did in a most rough and severe manner come to deal with me, to accuse me falsly, and blindly, and bitterly to rebuke me, although I was then in a very weak and dangerous condition of body. And I mention it here, because it is a time in remembrance with the Lord, and *God* was in that very season pleased to open mine eyes, to show me where *Babylon* was, what Spirit she was built upon, and how the Lord would begin to strike at her, and throw her down, and then it was he called me out from her, that I might escape the anger I then saw was kindled against her. And however they are now justifying themselves, and their proceedings against me, and have condemned the Innocent; yet an appeal has been made to *God*, and accepted by him, and he will search out this matter, and make a true and manifest judgment of it, for there is nothing *hid* from him, and this matter is now become a *publick figure.* Yes, I am satisfied God will speedily arise, and decide this controversie, and he has shown me when I have been thinking his Chariot wheels move slowly, that then his motion has been swiftest: And that whatever seems to hinder, and work against me, does indeed help on, and work things to a more full and perfect end. And although I should be surrounded, and beset on every side, and left alone in the midst of all discouragements from *within*, and *without*, yet can I believingly call to all that fear the Lord to come and behold the wonders of the Lord for my deliverance. I cry'd unto him when there was none to help me, and in a deep sense of my own unworthyness and nothingness, my Soul was humbled, and laid low at his foot, and my heart was lifted up to him. and he raised me from the Grave, and took fast hold of me at that very time when he so wonderfully healed me, which was the 3d of the 11 month, 1670. Then was the full communion between Christ and my Soul, the Love knot, the comly bands of Marriage; then did he espouse me unto himself for ever, and enable me to follow him, and give up my self as a thank-offering unto him, no more to be my own but the Lords, subjecting my self to all his will as a chast Virgin, holy in lip and life, pure and undefiled in heart. Then did the Lord my God say unto me, *I even, I am he that comforteth thee; who art thou that thou shouldest be affraid of a man that shall die, and of the Son of Man which shall be made as Grass.* And again he said, he was come to *Judge the Fatherless and the opressed, that the Man of the earth may no more oppress.* And many more pretious Promises did the Lord make to me, when he first called me to write what man has been so offended with; and his word was, and is my support, and he has comforted me therewith, assuring me as soon as I had done his will, I should receive the promises. And he afterwards revealed to me, (what I did not then know) that my *oppressions* and *deliverance* had a *Publick Ministry* and *meaning* wrapt up in them, that it must be seven years before I could perfect that writing, and the Lord would bring forth his end in all this, and give an open Testimony to the world that he had chosen and called me to write to glorifie him. And now I have done his will, my deli-

verer

veter is come to make good his word, and set me free from the oppression of Man, and to bear witness against him that has wounded and oppressed me for 18 years, and more severely is his anger kindled against them who have so deeply wounded me since the time of my healing, and who have made me an Heathen and a Publican for no other cause, but obeying the word of the Lord, and following him. And as near as *New-Years day is*, before that day the Lord will begin to cast a cloud of his anger upon all them that have done me so great wrong, and persecuted me without a cause; and stroak after stroak will follow, until all Hypocrisie be discovered and formality thrown down, and whole Babylon sinck like a stone never to rise up any more: and let not the minds of any be lifted up to scorn me, because I have said, God will begin to appear in my behalf within so short a time: for my God has a many times over made that *Season of the year* eminently signal to me in the dispensations of his grace and providence towards me. Then was I enter'd into my aflictions, then was I in an extraordinary manner healed, and chosen and call'd to write what has occasion'd so many persecutions to me from formal and literal professors; and now it will be compleatly 7 years since my healing; and the Lord has made known the end of all his dispensations to me, and has revealed to me, that I shall now receive the promises, having done his will, and be made partaker of his blessing: for he will fulfil his word, *to bind up the Broaken hearted, and proclaim liberty to the Captive, and open the Prison doors*; and I shall no more be under the oppression of man; and he has also revealed to me what wrath shall fall upon the *same spirit* throughout the Nation, which every where oppresses the true seed, as I have been oppressed by it; and the deliverance which is drawing nigh through terrible things in righteousness, to all his *poor* and *meek ones*. A more full accompt of which things, and how the Lord has lead me into this ministry and witness, I am with all convenient speed preparing for the Press, and had before this been made publick, had not my Enemies hindred, by seizing and destroying my writings. And in the mean time I beg of all Persons to whom this paper shall come, that they will for their own sakes lay a side all prejudice,

and

and try *me*, *my Spirit* and *Testimony* according to the word of God, and wait patiently upon the Lord to know his mind in this thing; and in love to themselves, take heed how they rashly reproach and condemn me and my witness, least they should in so doing run against that *Hiding of power* the Prophet *Habakuk* mentions, *chap* 3. 4. and that they be watchful over themselves, that they be not found *dispising Prophecy* and *quenching the Spirit*, because of the *contemptibleness* of the *messenger*: alwaies remembring, that *God will destroy the Wisdome of the Wise, and bring to nothing the understanding of the prudent*; that *he chooses the foolish*, the *weak*, the *base* and *dispised things of the World*, yea, and *things which are not*, *to bring to nought things that are*. In a word, let all Persons so far take the Alarm, as to look well to their own Souls, where they stand; Whither they are founded upon that Rock against which the Gates of Hell shall not prevail; whither they are interested in that Covenant of Grace which is ordered in all things and sure, and which is *all our Salvation in a day of desolation*. Whether they be in the number of those that are *Eating and Drinking with the Drunken*, and *beating their Fellow Servants*; or of the Family of the *true Noah* who shall be taken into the Ark, and preserved in the day of that Flood of the Divine vengence, which is ready to overflow the inhabitants of the Earth.

What I have here published is according to the word of truth which must be fulfiled in its time. It is but a very little while and this matter will be cleared, made manifest, and determined. In the mean while I declare to all the world I am at rest in the will of my God who has not left me without his *witness*, *presence*, and *seal* in this work, and who ever thou art, that canst not yet see a Divine Charactar, either upon *me* or *it*, my advice to thee is, that thou perplex not thy selfe concerning me, but wait patiently upon God, and quietly expect the discovery which the *day* will make herein.

The

To the Congregations of the Anabaptists *and their respective Pastors.*

THese verses contain the summons, complaint, and appeal of a despised and oppressed Christian, once a member of one of your Churches, now by your unjust and unchristian abuse of her, made a spectacle to God, Angels, and Men, yea, a gazeing stock to this great City, and a *by-word* to the common Rabble. Beloved, have you so learned Christ? Doth the Gospel teach you to defame you neighbour in Coffee-Houses, Ale Houses? will not that word spoken by the Holy Ghost to the Apostle *James* restrain you, 1 *James* 26. If any man among you seems to be religious, and bridle not his Tongue, but deceiveth his own heart, that mans Religion is vain. You may sooner hinder the Sun from shining, then the truth of God from displaying it self in such manner, and by such instruments as he is pleased to chuse, who is the Holy one of *Israel*, who will not suffer himself to be limited by man; the great God hath put the word of truth in her mouth, and dare you forbid her to declare it? can your scorn and contempt of the weak instrument, frustrate the purposes and Counsels of God? no, his foolishness is wiser then your imaginary wisdom, and his weakness stronger then all your conjoyned power. Can you prove that God hath not spoken to her and by her? No, you dare not produce that Book of hers (in your custody:) you too well know

it

it would demonstrate her to be in the Truth, and your selves shameless Lyars. Pray consider, if one of your Preachers should be silenced, you would presently cry out of Persecution; and dare you attempt to silence the Word of God, whose sound is gone forth to the ends of the Earth? Take heed of resisting, deriding a Message sent from Heaven, (though by a weak Instrument) lest you be found guilty of Blasphemies against the Spirit of God; but rather to day, while you hear his Voice, harden not your hearts, lest he swear in his wrath, that you shall never enter into his Rest. It is heard and received by such who love the Truth, and submit to the Power of it; but if you persist in your Rebellion against it, you will find and feel to your cost, that Truth is stronger than all. Consider these things Brethren, and the Lord give you understanding to judge aright.

The 5th of the 10th Month, 1677.

The Lord *Awaked* me in the *Night-Season*, and by his Spirit taught me thus in *Verse*, and made me Sing unto him a Triumphant Victorious Song over my Enemies, with a command from God to send it forth into the World, to be answered by the same Spirit of Love, Meekness, Gentleness, Goodness, Plainness, Lamb-like, lowly and Humble, for such is the Spirit of Gods Teachings.

Let us be followers of our Head, Christ Jesus, as dear Children, whom we have for our Example, Ephes. 5. 1, 2. *For he that overcometh, shall Inherit all things, and I will be his God, and ye shall be my Sons and Daughters: The Promise belongs either to Sons or Daughters walking in the Truth,* Revel. 21. 7.

I Am commanded by the King of Kings, to send this in the same manner and method he taught it me ; Let none despise the Spirits teaching, quench not the Spirit, despise not Prophesie ; There hath been too much despising and disdaining of me already, I pray God forgive them for all their hard speeches, and cruel usage of me, for they have done they know not what ; The Lord help us to remember our Creator in the days of our youth, and declining years, for when we have done all we can to please our selves, yet the end of all is death ; for pride, passion, self-will, bitterness, wrath, envy, malice, will yield no comfort at the Judgment Seat, where we must give an account of all the deeds done in the flesh, whether they be good or evil, *Eccles*. 12. 14.

Who hath believed our report, (hath been the cry of old) *and to whom is the Arm of the Lord revealed*, Esa. 53. 1. *For they have not at all obeyed the Gospel*, Rom. 10. 16.

To *England* sweet, my Native soyl,
This summons now I send,
Her speedy answer I require,
Before this Year doth end.
In four and twenty years, Declare
What evil have I done,
VVhat all this time they have against
My Conversation.
VVhat cause gave I to make your wrath
So hot to burn at me ?
Speak as you'l answer it to God,
And let all hear and see.
In Coffee-House and Ale-House now
VVhy do you me Defame ?
VVhy doth your Church, a Heathen me,
And Publican proclaim.
Speak out and spare not what's my sin,
Speak truth in his presence ;
Else God a bitter Cup will give
You, as your recompence.
If he who judgeth Heaven and Earth,
Disowneth what you have done ;

Then to curb you, and set me free
He's now most surely come.
You'l punish me, and think for me
No Prison is too ill;
But whether you or I offend
most, he determine will.
I'm falsly slandered, and opprest,
By men that have no Love:
But I commit my cause to him,
who sees, and sits above;
And from his Sanctuary looks,
and roars out of *Sion*,
To shew my Foes, he is my God,
and I his little one.
He sees my griefs so great, the weight
I can no longer bear,
That now he comes to be my Judge,
The Innocent to clear:
To testifie he is my Spouse,
and Husband of my Soul;
Whom I must serve, and keep his Laws,
though proud men would controul.
I give no other cause, but in
the Worship of my God;
If clean from sin, I'm in his sight,
my Foes will feel his Rod.
The same measure of wrath which they
do pour forth upon me,
According to his word, he'l pour
On them, as they will see.
They can't excuse themselves before
God, for what they have done:
They hate me, 'cause I in Gods word
and ways of Truth do run.
Full eighteen years with grief consum'd,
and to the Grave bow'd down,
Because the Lord have rais'd me up,
to make his power known;

And bad me shew his wondrous works,
and glorifie his Name!
This only, nothing else but this,
a great offence became.
They rage, they Persecute to Death,
a Woman weak and wan,
For giving all glory unto God,
and not to wretched man.
Now Country-men, if I the Truth
do not make to appear,
Disprove me plainly if you can,
Before the next New Year.
For after that, great wrath expect,
which on those will burn as fuel,
Who to their fellow creature were
Not merciful, but cruel.
And have no Love to God, his way,
His Truth, and holy word,
But only love themselves, as he
hath seen, and much abhor'd.
For taking up this heavy Cross
to follow the Lord my God,
Wormwood and *gall* they give, and scourge
me with their sharpest Rod.
O God arise, make hast to judge
between my Foes and me,
O stop their mouths, clear me, and let
not guilty ones go free.
Now strike at *Babylon*, thou said'st
This year thou would'st begin
To pour thy Plagues on that great *Whore
Babylon*, for her Sin.
Give Testimony, speak aloud
O Lord, and make them hear,
To let them know, I speak from God,
And only him do fear.
Thou knowest, O Lord, I have no end,
Doing and suffering this.

But that thy will obeying I,
May gain Eternal bliss.
If King and subjects cannot me
disprove, in what I say,
If truth I speak, O Lord, let them
'Not take my life away.
That will not quench the wrath denounc'd
For what's already done;
Nor can prevent the pouring forth,
That wrath which is begun.
What he hath purpos'd and decreed,
on *Babylon* to do.
Shall suddenly in one day come,
Her Judgment, Plagues, and wo.
As he revealed hath unto
his faithful Servant *John*.
Such as ne're was, nor e're again,
the world shall fall upon.
That for my Native soyl and folks,
I now could weep and mourn,
Though they unkind to me, no thanks,
But Grief and Scorn return.
Only some of the little flock
Of Christ I late have seen,
VVho have to me, distrest and left
Alone, a comfort been.
Blest be his power, who helpt, and saith,
He will my sorrows end,
I hope he will my foes convince,
That they their lives may mend.
Take me O Lord from strife of Tongues,
as thou hast promis'd me,
Give rest and peace, if so thou please,
O take me home to thee.
Let me no longer bear this Yoak,
And in this vile world stay.
Think on thy promise Lord, and free
me, before *New-Years Day*.

The Ninth of the same month the Lord taught me this Song in the Night.

IF all Men can't disprove what by me God hath said,
Then with all *England* it will be very sad.
VVhat ye do, do quickly, before *New-Years Day*,
Least after that, all your lives be swept away.
Wo, wo, to *England*, for what she hath done,
For woes upon *England* will certainly come.
Because she doth not love God with all her heart,
Nor stretch up her self to take his Childrens part.
Shall I yet doubt when God upholds me then,
Fear mortal Men, who've done the worst they can.
No, lift up thy Head, and now rejoyce,
That God for thee made such a choice.

A. W.

My Maker is my Husband, the Holy one of *Israel*, my Redeemer, the Eternal, ever living God, my Father, in obedience to his reveiled will do I suffer, in obeying his strict commands I offend; their are several of his Children that are sufferers with me, and are not ashamed of me in my bonds (which are) for doing the will of Christ. Now, as they have owned me so, God will own them, and bless them, but for such as are ashamed of me, under my reproaches for Christ, they in time may be more ashamed for their Neglect, in not owning me in the work of the Lord. O my God, fulfil thy word, and deliver me, for thou knowest I have suffered as much Tiranny and Cruelty under a formal profession of Religion, as I could have done amongst Turks, Heathens, and Infidels, and if so, then what need is it that my Country-men should so highly scorn me as they do, for if I live to see *New-Years Day* over, I shall be able to speak to them, and ask them how they do, and rejoyce when they will have cause to mourn; and I now know my friends from my foes, and if I out of this world be taken, it will be my greater mercy to be singing *Halalujah* in Heaven.

FINIS.

'Mary Penington her Testimony', excerpted from *The Works of the Long-Mournful and Sorely Distressed Isaac Penington* (Wing P 1149), shelfmark RB 223624, is reproduced by permission of The Huntington Library, San Marino, California. The text block of the original measures 140 × 235 mm.

THE WORKS OF THE LONG-MOURNFUL AND SORELY-DISTRESSED Isaac Penington,

Whom the Lord in his Tender Mercy, at length Visited and Relieved by the Ministry of that Despised People,

CALLED

QUAKERS;

And in the Springings of that Light, Life and Holy Power in him, which they had Truly and Faithfully Testified of, and Directed his mind to, were these things Written, and are now Published as a thankful Testimony of the goodness of the Lord unto him, and for the Benefit of others.

In Two Parts.

They also that erred in Spirit shall know Understanding, and they that murmured, shall learn Doctrine, Isa. 29. 24.

LONDON:
Printed, and Sold by *Benjamin Clark* Bookseller in *George-yard* in *Lombard-street*. 1681.

Mary Penington her

TESTIMONY

Concerning her Dear Husband.

WHilst I keep silent touching Thee, O Thou blessed of the LORD and his People, my heart burneth within me. I must make mention of thee, for thou wast a most pleasant Plant of renown, planted by the right hand of the Lord, and *thou took'st deep rooting downwards, and sprang upward.* The dew of Heaven fell on thee, and made thee fruitful, and thy fruit was of a fragrant smell, and most delightfull. O! where shall I begin to recount the Lord's remarkable dealings with thee? He set his love on thee, O thou one of the Lord's peculiar choice, to place his Name on! Wast not thou sanctified in the womb? Thy very babish dayes declared of what stock and lineage thou wert. Thou desired'st after *the sincere Milk of the Word, as a new-born babe*, even in the bud of thy age. O! who can declare how thou hast travelled towards the *holy Land* in thy very infancy as to dayes? O, who can tell what thy Soul hath felt in thy travel? O, thou wast gotten to be in the *mount with the Lord* and his spiritual *Moses*, when the Princes and Elders saw but his *back-parts*, and feared and quaked to hear the *terrible Thundrings* in mount *Sinai*. The breast of Consolation was held out to thee early, and thou sucked'st thy fill, till the vessel could not longer contain, for thou couldst not in that fulness *see God and live* in this tabernacle, so that thou besoughtst the Lord to abate this exceeding *excellent glory*, and give thee such a measure as was *food convenient*. O, the heavenly, bright, living openings that were given to thee many years past: His *Light* shone round about thee, and the book of the Creatures was opened to thee, and his Mysteries made known to holy men of old, who spoke them forth as they were *inspired by the Holy Ghost*, were made known to thee to discern. Such a state as I have never known any in, in that day, have I heard thee declare of. O, this did it please the Lord to withdraw and shut up as in one day, and so leave thee desolate and mourning many a day, weary of the night and of the day; poor and naked; sad, distressed and bowed down. Thou refused'st to be comforted, because it was a time of night and not day; and because he that was gone, was not come. His time of manifesting his Love was not at hand, but he was as a stranger, or one gone into a far countrey, not

ready

ready to return, & thou would'st accept of no *beloved* in his absence, but testified'st, that he thy Soul longed for, was not in this or that *observation*, nay nor opening; but thy Beloved, when he came, would sit as a *Refiner's fire*, and would come with *his fan in his hand, and throughly purge his floor*. No likeness, or appearance, or taking sound of words, or visions, or revelations would'st thou take up with in stead of him that was *Life indeed*. O! the many years thou put'st thy mouth in the dust, and went'st softly, and bowed down, and hadst anguish of soul, weeping and groaning, panting and sighing! O! who can tell the one half of the bitterness of thy soul, because Substance was in thy eye, all shaddows did fly away from before thee; thou could'st not feed on that which was not bread from heaven! In this state I married thee, and my love was drawn to thee, because I found thou sawest the deceit of all notions, and lay as one that *refused to be comforted* by any thing that had the appearance of Religion, till he came to his Temple, who is *Truth and no ly:* for all those shows of Religion were very manifest to thee, so that thou wert sick and weary of them all. And in this my heart cleft to thee, and a desire was *in* me to be serviceable to thee, in this *desolate condition*; for thou wast *alone* and *miserable* in this world, and I gave up much to be a *companion* to thee in this thy suffering. O! my sense, my sense of thee and thy state in that day even makes me as one *dumb*; for the greatness of it is beyond my capacity to utter.

This little testimony to thy *hidden life*, my dear and precious one, in a day and time, when none of the Lord's gathered People knew thy face, nor were in any measure acquainted with thy many sorrows, & deep wounds and distresses have I stammered out, that it might not be forgotten that thou wast in the *land of the living*, and *thy fresh springs were in God*, and *Light* was on thy *Goshen*, when thick darkness covered the people. But now, that *the day is broken forth*, and thou wert so eminently gathered into it, and a *faithfull Publisher* of it, I leave this bright state of thine, to be declared of by the *Sons of the Morning*, who have been witnesses of the rising of that *bright Star of Righteousness in thee*, and its guiding thee to the Saviour, even Jesus *the first and the last*; They, I I say, who are *strong, and have overcome the evil one*, and are *fathers* in *Israel*, have declared of thy life in God, and have published it in many testimonies here, to the glorious, saving *Truth*, that thou wert partaker of, lived'st and passed'st hence in, as in a *fiery chariot*, into the eternal habitation with the Holy Saints, Prophets and Apostles of Jesus.

Ah me, he is gone! he that none exceeded in kindness, in tenderness, in love inexpressible to the relation as a wife. Next to the love of God in Christ Jesus to my soul, was his love precious and delightfull to me. My bosom one that was as my guide and counsellour, my pleasant companion, my tender sympathizing friend, as near to the sense of my pain, sorrow, grief and trouble as it was possible. Yet this great help and benefit is gone, and I, a poor worm, a very little one to him, *compassed about with many infirmitys*, through mercy let him go without an unadvised word of discontent, or inordinate grief: Nay further, such was the great Kindness of the Lord shewed to me in that hour, that my spirit ascended with him, in that very moment that his spirit left his body, and I saw him safe in his own mansion, and rejoyced with him, and was at that instant gladder of it, than ever I was of enjoying him in the body. And from this sight my spirit returned again to perform my duty to his outward Tabernacle, to the answer of a good Conscience.

This was written at my house at *Woodside*, the 27. of the 2. month 1680. between 12 and 1 at night, while I was watching with my sick child.

This Testimony to dear I. P. is from the greatest loser of all that had a share in his life.

MARY PENINGTON.

A True History (Wing R 2094), shelfmark RB 12477, is reproduced by permission of The Huntington Library, San Marino, California. The text block of the original measures 120 × 175 mm.

Readings where the Huntington Library copy is obscure:

35.26	turn that
40.24	vvays
40.25	to
40.27	see
40.31	of
40.32	pati
40.38	sharp
42. catchword	neration
45.43	not hear
40.41	the
40.42	us
40.43	their

A TRUE HISTORY OF THE Captivity & Restoration OF Mrs. *MARY ROWLANDSON*, A Minister's Wife in *New-England*.

Wherein is set forth, The Cruel and Inhumane Usage she underwent amongst the *Heathens*, for Eleven Weeks time: And her Deliverance from them.

Written by her own Hand, for her Private Use: And now made Publick at the earnest Desire of some Friends, for the Benefit of the Afflicted.

Whereunto is annexed,

A Sermon of *the Possibility of God's Forsaking a People that have been near and dear to him.*

Preached by Mr. *Joseph Rowlandson*, Husband to the said Mrs. *Rowlandson*: It being his Last Sermon.

Printed first at *New-England*: And Re-printed at *London*, and sold by *Joseph Poole*, at the *Blue Bowl* in the *Long-Walk*, by *Christs-Church* Hospital. 1682.

The PREFACE to the READER.

IT was on Tueſday Feb. 1. 1675. in the afternoon, when the Narrhaganſets Quarters (in or toward the Nipmug Country, whither they were now retired for fear of the English Army lying in their own Country) were the ſecond time beaten up by the Forces of the United Colonies; who thereupon ſoon betook themſelves to flight, and were all the next day purſued by the English, ſome overtaken and deſtroyed. But on Thurſday Feb. 3. the English having now been ſix days on their March, from their Head-quarters at Wickford, in the Narrhaganſet Country, toward, and after the Enemy, and Proviſion grown exceeding ſhort; inſomuch that they were fain to kill ſome Horſes for the ſupply, eſpecially of their Indian Friends, they were neceſſitated to conſider what was beſt to be done; and about noon (having hitherto followed the Chaſe as hard as they might) a Council was called, and though ſome few were of another mind, yet it was concluded by far the greater part of the Council of War, that the Army ſhould deſiſt the purſuit, and retire: The Forces of Plimouth and the Bay to the next Town of the Bay, and Connecticut Forces to their own next Towns: which determination was immediately put in execution. The conſequent whereof, as it was not difficult to be foreſeen by thoſe that knew the cauſleſs enmity of theſe Barbarians againſt the English, and the malicious and revengeful ſpirit of theſe Heathen; ſo it ſoon proved diſmal.

The Narrhaganſets were now driven quite from their own Country, and all their Proviſions there hoarded up, to which they durſt not at preſent return, and being ſo numerous as they were, ſoon devoured thoſe to whom they went, whereby both the one and the other were now reduced to extream ſtraits, and ſo neceſſitated to take the firſt and beſt opportunity for ſupply, and very glad no doubt of ſuch an opportunity as this, to provide for themſelves, and make ſpoile of the English at once; and ſeeing themſelves thus diſcharged of their purſuers, and a little refreſhed after their flight, the very next week on Thurſday Feb. 10. they fell with mighty force and fury upon Lancaſter: which ſmall Town, remote from aid of others, and not being Garriſon'd as it might, the Army being now come in, and as the time indeed required (the deſign of the Indians againſt that place being known to the English ſome time before) was not able to make effectual reſiſtance; but notwithſtanding the utmoſt endeavour of the Inhabitants, moſt of the buildings were turned into aſhes; many People (Men, Women and Children) ſlain, and others captivated. The moſt ſolemn and remarkable part of this Tragedy, may that juſtly be reputed, which fell upon the Family of that Reverend Servant of God, Mr. Joſeph Rowlandſon, the faithful Paſtor of the Church of Chriſt in that place, who being gon down to the Council of the Maſſachuſets, to ſeek aid for the defence of the place; at his return found the Town in flames, or ſmoke, his own houſe being ſet on fire by the Enemy, through the diſadvantage of a defective Fortification, and all in it conſumed: His precious yoke-fellow, and dear Children, wounded and captivated (as the iſſue evidenced, and following Narrative declares) by theſe cruel and barbarous Salvages. A ſad Cataſtrophe! Thus all things come alike to all: None knows either *love or hatred by all that is before him. 'Tis no new thing for Gods precious ones to drink as deep as others, of the Cup of common Calamity: take just* Lot *(yet captivated) for instance, beside others. But it is not my business to dilate on these things, but only in few words introductively to preface to the following script, which is a Narrative of the wonderfully awful, wise, holy, powerful, and gracious providence of God, toward that worthy and precious Gentlewoman, the dear Consort of the said Reverend Mr.* Rowlandson, *and her Children with her, as in casting of her into such a waterless pit, so in preserving, supporting, and carrying through so many such extream hazards, unspeakable difficulties and disconsolateness, and at last delivering her out of them all, and her surviving Children also. It was a strange and amazing dispensation, that the Lord should so afflict his precious Servant, and Hand-maid: It was as strange, if not more, that he should so bear up the spirits of his Servant under such bereavements, and of his Hand-maid under such Captivity, travels, and hardships (much too hard for flesh and blood) as he did, and at length deliver and restore. But he was their Savior, who hath said,* When thou passest through the Waters, I will be with thee, and through the Rivers, they shall not overflow thee: when thou walkest through the Fire, thou shalt not be burnt, nor shall the flame kindle upon thee, *Isai. 43. Ver. 3. and again,* He woundeth, and his hands make whole, He shall deliver thee in six troubles, yea in seven there shall no evil touch thee: In Famine he shall redeem thee from death; and in War from the power of the sword, *Job. 5. 18, 19, 20. Methinks this dispensation doth bear some resemblance to those of* Joseph, David *and* Daniel, *yea and of the three Children too, the stories whereof do represent us with the excellent textures of divine providence, curious pieces of divine work: And truly so doth this, and therefore not to be forgotten, but worthy to be exhibited to, and viewed, and pondered by all, that disdain not to consider the operation of his hands.*

The works of the Lord (not only of Creation, but of Providence also, especially those that do more peculiarly concern his dear ones, that are as the apple of his eye, as the signet upon his hand, the delight of his eyes, and the object of his tenderest care) are great, sought out of all those that have pleasure therein. And of these, verily this is none of the least.

This Narrative was Penned by this Gentlewoman her self, to be to her a Memorandum *of Gods dealing with her, that she might never forget, but remember the same, and the several circumstances thereof, all the daies of her life. A pious scope, which deserves both commendation and imitation. Some Friends having obtained a sight of it, could not but be so much affected with the many passages of working providence discovered therein, as to judge it worthy of publick view, and altogether unmeet that such works of God should be hid from present and future Generation: and therefore though this Gentlewomans modesty would not thrust it into the Press, yet her gratitude unto God, made her not hardly perswadable to let it pass, that God might have his due glory, and others benefit by it as well as her selfe.*

I hope by this time none will cast any reflection upon this Gentlewoman, on the score of this publication of her Affliction and Deliverance. If any should, doubtless they

may

may be reckoned with the nine Lepers, of whom it is said, Were there not ten cleansed, where are the nine? *but one returning to give God thanks. Let such further know, that this was a dispensation of publick note, and of Universal concernment; and so much the more, by how much the nearer this Gentlewoman stood related to that faithful Servant of God whose capacity and employment was publick, in the House of God, and his Name on that account of a very sweet savour in the Churches of Christ. Who is there of a true Christian Spirit, that did not look upon himself much concerned in this bereavement, this Captivity in the time thereof, and in this deliverance when it came, yea more than in many others? and how many are there to whom, so concerned, it will doubtless be a very acceptable thing, to see the way of God with this Gentlewoman in the aforesaid dispensation, thus laid out and pourtrayed before their eyes.*

To conclude, Whatever any coy phantasies may deem, yet it highly concerns those that have so deeply tasted how good the Lord is, to enquire with David, What shall I render to the Lord for all his benefits to me? *Psal. 116. 12. He thinks nothing too great: yea, being sensible of his own disproportion to the due praises of God, he calls in help;* O magnifie the Lord with me, let us exalt his Name together, Psal. 34. 3. *And it is but reason, that our praises should hold proportion with our prayers; and that as many have helped together by prayer for the obtaining of this mercy, so praises should be returned by many on this behalf; and forasmuch as not the general but particular knowledge of things makes deepest impression upon the affections, this Narrative particularizing the several passages of this providence, will not a little conduce thereunto: and therefore holy* David, *in order to the attainment of that end, accounts himself concerned to declare what God had done for his Soul,* Psal. 66. 16. Come and hear, all ye that fear God, and I will declare what God hath done for my Soul, *i. e.* for his Life: *See Ver.* 9, 10. He holdeth our soul in life, and suffers not our feet to be moved; for thou our God hast proved us: thou hast tried us, as silver is tried. *Life-mercies are heart-affecting-mercies; of great impression and force, to enlarge pious hearts in the praises of God, so that such know not how but to talk of Gods acts, and to speak of and publish his wonderful works. Deep troubles, when the waters come in unto the Soul, are wont to produce vows: Vows must be paid,* It is better not vow, than to vow and not pay. *I may say, that as none knows what it is to fight and pursue such an enemy as this, but they that have fought and pursued them: so none can imagine, what it is to be captivated, and enslaved to such Atheistical, proud, wild, cruel, barbarous, brutish, (in one word) diabolical Creatures as these, the worst of the heathen; nor what difficulties, hardships, hazards, sorrows, anxieties, and perplexities, do unavoidably wait upon such a condition, but those that have tried it. No serious spirit then (especially knowing any thing of this Gentlewomans Piety) can imagine but that the vows of God are upon her. Excuse her then if she come thus into the publick, to pay those Vows. Come and hear what she hath to say.*

I am

I am confident that no Friend of divine Providence, will ever repent his time and pains spent in reading over these sheets; but will judge them worth perusing again and again.

Here Reader, *you may see an instance of the Soveraignty of God, who doth what he will with his own as well as others; and who may say to him,* what dost thou? *here you may see an instance of the Faith and Patience of the Saints, under the most heart-sinking Tryals: here you may see, the Promises are breasts full of Consolation, when all the World besides is empty, and gives nothing but sorrow. That God is indeed the supream Lord of the World: ruling the most unruly, weakening the most cruel and salvage: granting his People mercy in the sight of the most unmerciful: curbing the lusts of the most filthy, holding the hands of the violent, delivering the prey from the mighty, and gathering together the out-casts of Israel. Once and again, you have heard, but here you may see, that power belongeth unto God: that our God is the God of Salvation: and to him belong the issues from Death. That our God is in the Heavens, and doth what ever pleases him. Here you have* Samsons *Riddle exemplified, and that great promise,* Rom. 8. 28. *verified:* Out of the Eater comes forth meat, and sweetness out of the strong; *The worst of evils working together for the best good. How evident is it that the Lord hath made this Gentlewoman a gainer by all this Affliction, that she can say, 'tis good for her, yea better that she hath been, than she should not have been, thus afflicted.*

Oh how doth God shine forth in such things as these!

Reader, *if thou gettest no good by such a Declaration as this, the fault must needs be thine own. Read therefore, peruse, ponder, and from hence lay up something from the experience of another, against thine own turn comes: that so thou also through patience and consolation of the Scripture mayest have hope,*

PER AMICUM.

A Nar-

A Narrative of the Captivity and Restoration of Mrs. *Mary Rowlandson.*

ON the tenth of *February*, 1675. came the *Indians* with great numbers upon *Lancaster*. Their first coming was about Sunrising. Hearing the noise of some Guns, we looked out; several Houses were burning, and the Smoke ascending to Heaven. There were five Persons taken in one House, the Father, and the Mother, and a sucking Child they knock'd on the head; the other two they took, and carried away alive. There were two others, who being out of their Garrison upon some occasion, were set upon; one was knock'd on the head, the other escaped. Another there was who running along was shot and wounded, and fell down; he begged of them his Life, promising them Money (as they told me); but they would not hearken to him, but knock'd him on the head, stripped him naked, and split open his Bowels. Another seeing many of the *Indians* about his Barn, ventured and went out, but was quickly shot down. There were three others belonging to the same Garrison, who were killed. The *Indians* getting up upon the Roof of the Barn, had advantage to shoot down upon them over their Fortification. Thus these murtherous Wretches went on, burning and destroying before them.

At length they came and beset our own House, and quickly it was the dolefullest day that ever mine eyes saw. The House stood upon the edge of a Hill; some of the *Indians* got behind the Hill, others into the Barn, and others behind any thing that would shelter them: from all which Places they shot against the House, so that the Bullets seemed to fly like Hail: and quickly they wounded one Man among us, then another, and then a third. About two Hours (according to my observation in that amazing time) they had been about the House, before they could prevail to fire it, (which they did with Flax and Hemp which they brought out of the Barn, and there being no Defence about the House, onely two Flankers, at two opposite Corners, and one of them not finished.) They fired it once, and one ventured out and quenched it; but they quickly fired it again, and that took. Now is that dreadful Hour come, that I have often heard of, (in the time of the War, as it was the Case of others) but now mine Eyes see it. Some in our House were fighting for their Lives, others wallowing in their Blood; the House on fire over our Heads, and the bloody Heathen ready to knock us on the Head if we stirred out. Now might we hear Mothers and Children crying out for themselves, and one another, *Lord, what shall we do!* Then I took my Children (and one of my Sisters, hers) to go forth and leave the

House:

Houſe: But as ſoon as we came to the Door and appeared, the *Indians* ſhot ſo thick; that the Bullets ratled againſt the Houſe, as if one had taken an handful of Stones and threw them; ſo that we were fain to give back. We had ſix ſtout Dogs belonging to our Garriſon, but none of them would ſtir, though another time, if an *Indian* had come to the Door, they were ready to fly upon him, and tear him down. The Lord hereby would make us the more to acknowledge his Hand, and to ſee that our Help is always in him. But out we muſt go, the Fire increaſing, and coming along behind us roaring, and the *Indians* gaping before us with their Guns, Spears, and Hatchets, to devour us. No ſooner were we out of the Houſe, but my Brother-in-Law (being before wounded (in defending the Houſe) in or near the Throat) fell down dead, whereat the *Indians* ſcornfully ſhouted, and hallowed, and were preſently upon him, ſtripping off his Clothes. The Bullets flying thick, one went thorow my Side, and the ſame (as would ſeem) thorow the Bowels and Hand of my dear Child in my Arms. One of my elder Siſters Children (named *William*) had then his Leg broken, which the *Indians* perceiving, they knock'd him on the head. Thus were we butchered by thoſe mercileſs Heathen, ſtanding amazed, with the Blood running down to our Heels. My elder Siſter being yet in the Houſe, and ſeeing thoſe woſul Sights, the Infidels haling Mothers one way, and Children another, and ſome wallowing in their Blood, and her elder Son telling her that (her Son) *William* was dead, and my ſelf was wounded; ſhe ſaid, And *Lord, let me die with them*: Which was no ſooner ſaid, but ſhe was ſtruck with a Bullet, and fell down dead over the Threſhold. I hope ſhe is reaping the Fruit of her good Labours, being faithful to the Service of God in her Place. In her younger years ſhe lay under much trouble upon Spiritual accounts, till it pleaſed God to make that precious Scripture take hold of her Heart, 2 *Cor.* 12. 9. *And he ſaid unto me, My grace is ſufficient for thee.* More than twenty years after I have heard her tell, how ſweet and comfortable that Place was to her. But to return: The *Indians* laid hold of us, pulling me one way, and the Children another, and ſaid, *Come, go along with us*: I told them, they would kill me: They anſwered, *If I were willing to go along with them, they would not hurt me.*

O the doleful Sight that now was to behold at this Houſe! *Come, behold the Works of the Lord, what deſolation he has made in the Earth.* Of thirty ſeven Perſons who were in this one Houſe, none eſcaped either preſent Death, or a bitter Captivity, ſave onely one, who might ſay as he, *Job* 1. 15. *And I onely am eſcaped alone to tell the News.* There were twelve killed, ſome ſhot, ſome ſtabb'd with their Spears, ſome knock'd down with their Hatchets. When we are in proſperity, Oh the Little that we think of ſuch dreadful Sights, and to ſee our dear Friends and Relations lie bleeding out their Heart-blood upon the Ground! There was one who was chopp'd into the Head with a Hatchet, and ſtripp'd naked, and yet was crawling up and down. It is a ſolemn Sight to ſee ſo many Chriſtians lying in their Blood, ſome

some here, and some there, like a company of Sheep torn by Wolves. All of them stript naked by a company of hell-hounds, roaring, singing, ranting and insulting, as if they would have torn our very hearts out, yet the Lord by his Almighty power, preserved a number of us from death, for there were twenty four of us taken alive: and carried Captive.

I had often before this said, that if the *Indians* should come, I should chuse rather to be killed by them, than taken alive: but when it came to the trial my mind changed; their glittering Weapons so daunted my Spirit, that I chose rather to go along with those (as I may say) ravenous Bears, than that moment to end my daies. And that I may the better declare what happened to me during that grievous Captivity, I shall particularly speak of the several Removes we had up and down the Wilderness.

The first Remove. Now away we must go with those Barbarous Creatures, with our bodies wounded and bleeding, and our hearts no less than our bodies. About a mile we went that night; up upon a hill within sight of the Town where they intended to lodge. There was hard by a vacant house (deserted by the English before, for fear of the *Indians*) I asked them whether I might not lodge in the house that night? to which they answered, what will you love *English-men* still? this was the dolefullest night that ever my eyes saw. Oh the roaring, and singing, and dancing, and yelling of those black creatures in the night, which made the place a lively resemblance of hell: And as miserable was the waste that was there made, of Horses, Cattle, Sheep, Swine, Calves, Lambs, Roasting Pigs, and Fowls (which they had plundered in the Town) some roasting, some lying and burning, and some boyling, to feed our merciless Enemies; who were joyful enough though we were disconsolate. To add to the dolefulness of the former day, and the dismalness of the present night, my thoughts ran upon my losses and sad bereaved condition. All was gone, my Husband gone (at least separated from me, he being in the Bay; and to add my grief, the *Indians* told me they would kill him as he came homeward) my Children gone, my Relations and Friends gone, our house and home, and all our comforts within door, and without, all was gone (except my life) and I knew not but the next moment that might go too.

There remained nothing to me but one poor wounded Babe, and it seemed at present worse than death, that it was in such a pitiful condition, bespeaking Compassion, and I had no refreshing for it, nor suitable things to revive it. Little do many think, what is the savageness and bruitishness of this barbarous Enemy! even those that seem to profess more than others among them, when the *English* have fallen into their hands.

Those seven that were killed at *Lancaster* the summer before upon a Sabbath day, and the one that was afterward killed upon a week day, were slain and mangled in a barbarous manner, by one-ey'd *John*, and *Marlberough's* Praying *Indians*, which Capt. *Mosely* brought to *Boston*, as the *Indians* told me.

The second Remove But now (the next morning) I must turn my back upon the Town, and travel with them into the vast and desolate Wilderness, I know not whither. It is not my tongue, or pen can express the sorrows of my heart, and bitterness of my spirit, that I had at this departure: But God was with me, in a wonderful manner, carrying me along, and bearing up my Spirit, that it did not quite fail. One of the *Indians* carried my poor wounded Babe upon a horse: it went moaning all along, I shall die, I shall die. I went on foot after it, with sorrow that cannot be exprest. At length I took it off the Horse, and carried it in my arms, till my strength failed, and *I* fell down with it. Then they set me upon a horse, with my wounded Child in my lap, and there being no Furniture upon the horse back; as we were going down a steep hill, we both fell over the horses head, at which they like inhuman creatures laught, and rejoiced to see it, though I thought we should there have ended our dayes, as overcome with so many difficulties. But the Lord renewed my strength still, and carried me along, that I might see more of his power, yea, so much that *I* could never have thought of, had *I* not experienced it.

After this it quickly began to Snow, and when night came on, they stopt: and now down I must sit in the Snow, (by a little fire, and a few boughs behind me) with my sick Child in my lap; and calling much for water, being now (thorough the wound) fallen into a violent Fever. (My own wound also growing so stiff, that I could scarce sit down or rise up) yet so it must be, that I must sit all this cold winter night, upon the cold snowy ground, with my sick Child in my arms, looking that every hour would be the last of its life; and having no Christian Friend near me, either to comfort or help me. Oh I may see the wonderful power of God, that my Spirit did not utterly sink under my affliction; still the Lord upheld me with his gracious and merciful Spirit, and we were both alive to see the light of the next morning.

The third Remove. The morning being come, they prepared to go on their way: one of the *Indians* got up upon a horse, and they set me up behind him with my poor sick Babe in my lap. A very wearisome and tedious day I had of it; what with my own wound, and my Childs being so exceeding sick, and in a lamentable Condition with her wound. It may easily be judged what a poor feeble condition we were in, there being not the least crumb of refreshing that came within either of our mouths, from Wednesday night to Satturday night, except only a little cold water. This day in the afternoon, about an hour by Sun, we came to the place where they intended, *viz.* an *Indian Town* called *Wenimesset*, Northward of *Quabaug*. When we were come, Oh the Number of *Pagans* (now merciless Enemies) that there came about me, that I may say as *David*, Psal. 27. 13. *I had fainted, unless I had believed*, &c. The next day was the Sabbath: I then remembred how careless I had been of Gods holy time: how many Sabbaths I had lost and mispent, and how evilly I had walked in Gods sight; which lay so close upon my Spirit, that it was easie for me to see how righteous it was with God to cut off the threed of my life, and cast me out of his presence for ever. Yet the Lord still shewed mercy to me, and upheld me; and as he wounded me with one hand, so he healed me with the other. This day there came to me one *Robert Pepper* (a Man belonging to *Roxbury*,) who was taken in Capt. *Beers* his fight; and had been now a considerable time with the *Indians*; and up with them almost as far as *Albany* to see King *Philip*, as he told me, and was now very lately come with them into these parts. Hearing I say that I was in this *Indian* Town he obtained leave to come and see me. He told me he himself was wounded in the Leg at Capt. *Beers* his fight; and was not able sometime to go, but as they carried him, and that he took oaken leaves and laid to his wound, and through the blessing of God, he was able to travel again. Then I took Oaken leaves and laid to my side, and with the blessing of God it cured me also; yet before the cure was wrought, I may say as it is in *Psal.* 38. 5, 6. *My wounds stink and are corrupt, I am troubled, I am bowed down greatly, I go mourning all the day long.* I sate much alone with a poor wounded Child in my lap, which moaned night and day, having nothing to revive the body, or chear the Spirits of her: but instead of that, sometimes one Indian would come and tell me, one hour, and your Master will knock your Child in the head, and then a second, and then a third, your Master will quickly knock your child in the head.

This was the Comfort I had from them; miserable comforters are ye all, as he said. Thus nine dayes I sat upon my knees, with my babe in my lap, till my flesh was raw again: my child being even ready to depart this sorrowful world, they bad me carry it out, to another Wigwam: (I suppose because they would not be troubled with such spectacles.) Whither I went with a very heavy heart, and down I sate with the picture of death in my lap. About two hours in the Night, my sweet Babe like a Lamb departed this life, on *Feb.* 18. 1675. it being about six years and five months old. It was nine dayes (from the first wounding) in this Miserable condition, without any refreshing of one nature or other, except a little cold water. I cannot but take notice, how at another time I could not bear to be in the room where any dead person was, but now the case is changed: I must and could lye down by my dead Babe, side by side, all the night after. I have thought since of the wonderful goodness of God to me, in preserving me so in the use of my reason and senses, in that distressed time, that I did not use wicked and violent means to end my own miserable life. In the morning, when they understood that my child was dead, they sent for me home to my Masters Wigwam: (by my Master in this writing must be understood *Quannopin*, who was a Saggamore and married King *Philips* wives Sister; not that he first took me, but I was sold to him by another *Narrhaganset Indian*, who took me when first I came out of the Garrison) I went to take up my dead Child in my arms to carry it with me, but they bid me let it alone: there was no resisting, but go

I must and leave it. When I had been a while at my Masters wigwam, I took the first opportunity I could get, to go look after my dead child: when *I* came I asked them what they had done with it? they told me it was upon the hill: then they went and shewed me where it was, where I saw the ground was newly digged, and there they told me they had buried it; there I left that child in the Wilderness, and must commit it, and my self also in this Wilderness condition, to him who is above all. God having taken away this dear child, I went to see my daughter *Mary*, who was at this same *Indian Town*, at a Wigwam not very far off, though we had little liberty or opportunity to see one another: she was about ten years old, and taken from the door at first by a Praying *Indian*, and afterward sold for a gun. When *I* came in sight she would fall a weeping; at which they were provoked, and would not let me come near her, but bade me be gone: which was a heart-cutting word to me. *I* had one child dead, another in the wilderness, *I* knew not where, the third they would not let me come near to: *Me* (as he said) *have ye bereaved of my Children, Joseph is not, and Simeon is not, and ye will take Benjamin also, all these things are against me.* *I* could not sit still in this condition, but kept walking from one place to another. And as *I* was going along, my heart was even overwhelmed with the thoughts of my condition, and that *I* should have Children, and a Nation which *I* knew not ruled over them. Whereupon *I* earnestly intreated the Lord, that he would consider my low estate, and shew me a token for good, and if it were his blessed will, some sign and hope of some relief. And indeed quickly the Lord answered, in some measure, my poor Prayer: For as *I* was going up and down mourning and lamenting my condition, my Son came to me, and asked me how *I* did? *I* had not seen him before, since the destruction of the Town: and *I* knew not where he was, till *I* was informed by himself, that he was amongst a smaller parcel of *Indians*, whose place was about six miles off, with tears in his eyes, he asked me whether his Sister *Sarah* was dead? and told me he had seen his Sister *Mary*; and prayed me, that *I* would not be troubled in reference to himself. The occasion of his coming to see me at this time was this: There was, as *I* said, about six miles from us, a small Plantation of *Indians*, where it seems he had been during his Captivity: and at this time, there were some Forces of the *Indians* gathered out of our company, and some also from them (amongst whom was my Sons Master) to go to assault and burn *Medfield*: in this time of the absence of his Master, his Dame brought him to see me. *I* took this to be some gracious Answer, to my earnest and unfeigned desire. The next day, *viz.* to this, the *Indians* returned from *Medfield*: (all the Company, for those that belonged to the other smaller company, came thorow the Town that now we were at) But before they came to us, Oh the outragious roaring and hooping that there was! They began their din about a mile before they came to us. By their noise and hooping they signified how many they had destroyed: (which was at that time twenty three) Those that were with us at home, were gathered

together

together as soon as they heard the hooping, and every time that the other went over their number, these at home gave a shout, that the very Earth rang again. And thus they continued till those that had been upon the expedition were come up to the Saggamores Wigwam; and then Oh the hideous insulting and triumphing that there was over some *English-mens* Scalps, that they had taken (as their manner is) and brought with them. *I* cannot but take notice of the wonderful mercy of God to me in those afflictions, in sending me a Bible: one of the *Indians* that came from *Medfield* fight and had brought some plunder; came to me, and asked me, if I would have a Bible, he had got one in his Basket, I was glad of it, and asked him, whether he thought the *Indians* would let me read? he answered yes: so I took the Bible, and in that melancholly time, it came into my mind to read first the 28 *Chapter* of *Deuteronomie*, which I did, and when I had read it, my dark heart wrought on this manner, that there was no mercy for me, that the blessings were gone, and the curses came in their room, and that I had lost my opportunity. But the Lord helped me still to go on reading, till I came to *Chap*. 30. the seven first verses: where I found there was mercy promised again, if we would return to him, by repentance: and though we were scattered from one end of the earth to the other, yet the Lord would gather us together, and turn all those curses upon our Enemies. I do not desire to live to forget this Scripture, and what comfort it was to me.

Now the *Indians* began to talk of removing from this place, some one way, and some another. There were now besides my self nine *English* Captives in this place (all of them Children, except one Woman) I got an opportunity to go and take my leave of them; they being to go one way, and I another. I asked them whether they were earnest with God for deliverance; they all told me, they did as they were able; and it was some comfort to me, that the Lord stirred up Children to look to him. The Woman, *viz*. Goodwife *Joslin* told me, she should never see me again, and that she could find in her heart to run away: I wisht her not to run away by any means, for we were near thirty miles from any *English* Town, and she very big with Child and had but one week to reckon: and another Childe, in her Arms, two years old, and bad rivers there were to go over, and we were feeble with our poor and course entertainment. I had my Bible with me, I pulled it out, and asked her, whether she would read; we opened the Bible, and lighted on *Psal*. 27. in which Psalm we especially took notice of that, *ver. ult. Wait on the Lord, be of good courage, and he shall strengthen thine Heart, wait I say on the Lord.*

The fourth Remove. And now must I part with that little company that I had. Here I parted from my daughter *Mary*, (whom I never saw again till I saw her in *Dorchester*, returned from Captivity) and from four little Cousins and Neighbours, some of which *I* never saw afterward, the Lord only knows the end of them. Amongst them also was that poor woman before mentioned, who came to a sad end, as some of the company told me in my travel:

she

she having much grief upon her Spirit, about her miserable condition, being so near her time, she would be often asking the *Indians* to let her go home; they not being willing to that, and yet vexed with her importunity, gathered a great company together about her, and stript her naked, and set her in the midst of them: and when they had sung and danced about her (in their hellish manner) as long as they pleased: they knockt her on the head, and the child in her arms with her: when they had done that, they ma dea fire and put them both into it: and told the other Children that were with them, that if they attempted to go home they would serve them in like manner: The Children said she did not shed one tear, but prayed all the while. But to return to my own Journey: we travelled about half a day or a little more, and came to a desolate place in the Wilderness; where there were no Wigwams or Inhabitants before: we came about the middle of the afternoon to this place; cold, and wet, and snowy, and hungry, and weary, and no refreshing (for man) but the cold ground to sit on, and our poor *Indian cheer*.

Heart-aking thoughts here I had about my poor Children, who were scattered up and down amongst the wild Beasts of the Forest: my head was light and dizzy (either through hunger, or hard lodging, or trouble, or all together) my knees feeble, my body raw by sitting double night and day, that *I* cannot express to man the affliction that lay upon my Spirit, but the Lord helped me at that time to express it to himself. I opened my Bible to read, and the Lord brought that precious Scripture to me, *Jer.* 31. 16. *Thus saith the Lord, refrain thy voice from weeping, and thine eyes from tears, for thy work shall be rewarded, and they shall come again from the land of the Enemy.* This was a sweet Cordial to me, when *I* was ready to faint; many and many a time, have *I* sate down, and wept swetely over this Scripture. At this place we continued about four days.

The fifth Remove. The occasion (as I thought) of their moving at this time, was, the *English Army* its being near and following them: For they went as if they had gone for their lives, for some considerable way; and then they made a stop, and chose out some of their stoutest men, and sent them back to hold the *English* Army in play whilst the rest escaped; and then like *Jehu* they marched on furiously, with their old, and with their young: some carried their old decrepit Mothers, some carried one, and some another. Four of them carried a great *Indian* upon a Bier: but going through a thick Wood with him they were hindered, and could make no haste; whereupon they took him upon their backs, and carried him, one at a time, till we came to *Bacquaug* River. Upon a Fryday a little after noon we came to this River. When all the Company was come up, and were gathered together, I thought to count the number of them, but they were so many, and being somewhat in motion, it was beyond my skill. *In* this Travel, because of my wound, *I* was somewhat favoured in my load; I carried only my knitting-work, and two quarts of parched Meal: Being very faint I asked my Mistress, to give me me one spoonful of the Meal, but she would not give me a taste. They quickly fell to cutting dry trees, to make rafts to carry them over the River: and soon my turn came to go over: By the advantage of some brush which they had laid upon the Raft to sit on; I did not wet my foot, (when many of themselves at the other end were mid-leg-deep) which cannot but be acknowledged as a favour of God to my weakned body, it being a very cold time. I was not before acquainted with such kind of doings or dangers. *When thou passest through the waters I will be with thee, and through the rivers they shall not overflow thee.* Isai 43. 2. A certain number of us got over the river that night, but it was the night after the Sabbath before all the company was got over. On the Saturday they boyled an old Horses leg (which they had got) and so we drank of the broth; as soon as they thought it was ready, and when it was almost all gone, they filled it up again.

The first week of my being among them, *I* hardly ate any thing: the second week I found my stomach grow very faint for want of something; and yet 'twas very hard to get down their filthy trash: but the third week (though I could think how formerly my stomach would turn against this or that, and *I* could starve and die before *I* could eat such things, yet) they were pleasant and savoury to my taste. *I* was at this time knitting a pair of white Cotton Stockins for my Mistriss: and *I* had not yet wrought upon the Sabbath day: when the Sabbath came they bad me go to work; *I* told them it was Sabbath-day, and desired them to let me rest, and told them *I* would do as much more to morrow: to which they answered me, they would break my face. And here I cannot but take notice of the strange providence of God in preserving the Heathen: They were many hundreds, old and young, some sick and some lame, many had *Papooses* at their backs, the greatest number (at this time with us) were *Squaws*: and they travelled with all they had, bag and baggage, and yet they got over this River aforesaid: and on Monday they set their Wigwams on fire, and away they went: on that very day came the *English* Army after them to this River, and saw the smoke of their Wigwams; and yet this River put a stop to them. God did not give them courage or activity to go over after us: we were not ready for so great a mercy as victory and deliverance: if we had been, God would have found out a way for the *English* to have passed this River, as well as for the *Indians* with their *Squaws* and *Children*, and all their *Luggage*. *Oh that my people had hearkened to me, and Israel had walked in my wayes, I should soon have subdued their Enemies, and turned my hand against their Adversaries,* Psal. 81. 13, 14.

The sixth Romove. On Monday (as I said) they set their Wigwams on fire, and went away. It was a cold morning; and before us there was a great Brook with Ice on it: some waded through it, up to the knees and higher: but others went till they came to a Beaver-Dam, and I amongst them, where thorough the good providence of God, I did not wet my foot. I went along that day, mourning and lamenting, leaving farther my own Countrey,

Countrey, and travelling into the vast and howling Wilderness; and I understood something of *Lots* Wife's Temptation, when she looked back: we came that day to a great Swamp; by the side of which we took up our lodging that night. When I came to the brow of the hill, that looked toward the Swamp, I thought we had been come to a great *Indian Town*, (though there were none but our own Company) the *Indians* were as thick as the Trees; it seemed as if there had been a thousand Hatchets going at once: if one looked before one, there was nothing but *Indians*, and behind one, nothing but *Indians*, and so on either hand: I my self in the midst, and no Christian Soul near me, and yet how hath the Lord preserved me in safety! Oh the experience that I have had of the goodness of God, to me and mine!

The seventh Remove. After a restless and hungry night there, we had a wearisome time of it the next day. The Swamp by which we lay, was as it were, a deep Dungeon, and an exceeding high and steep hill before it. Before I got to the top of the hill, I thought my heart and legs and all would have broken, and failed me. What through faintness and soreness of Body, it was a grievous day of Travel to me. As we went along, I saw a place where *English* Cattle had been: that was a comfort to me, such as it was: quickly after that we came to an *English* path, which so took with me, that I thought I could there have freely lyen down and died. That day, a little after noon, we came to *Squaukheag*; where the *Indians* quickly spread themselves over the deserted *English* Fields, gleaning what they could find; some pickt up Ears of Wheat, that were crickled down; some found ears of *Indian Corn*; some found Ground-nuts, and others sheaves of Wheat, that were frozen together in the Shock, and went to threshing of them out. My self got two Ears of *Indian Corn*, and whilst I did but turn my back, one of them was stollen from me, which much troubled me. There came an *Indian* to them at that time, with a Basket of *Horse-liver*: I asked him to give me a piece: what (sayes he) can you eat Horse-liver? I told him, I would try, if he would give a piece; which he did: and I laid it on the coals to rost; but before it was half ready, they got half of it away from me; so that I was fain to take the rest and eat it as it was with the blood about my mouth, and yet a savoury bit it was to me: For to the hungry Soul every bitter thing is sweet. A solemn sight methought it was, to see whole fields of Wheat, and Indian Corn forsaken and spoiled: and the remanders of them to be food for our merciless Enemies. That night we had a mess of Wheat for our supper.

The eighth Remove. On the morrow morning we must go over the River, *i.e. Connecticot*, to meet with King *Philip*, two Cannoos full, they had carried over, the next turn I my self was to go; but as my foot was upon the Cannoo to step in, there was a sudden outcry among them, and I must step back: and instead of going over the River, I must go four or five miles up the River farther northward. Some of the *Indians* ran one way, and some another. The cause of this rout was as I thought their espying some *English* Scouts, who were thereabout.

In

In this travel up the River; about noon the Company made a stop, and sate down; some to eat, and others to rest them. As I sate amongst them, musing of things past, my Son *Joseph* unexpectedly came to me: we asked of each others welfare; bemoaning our doleful condition, and the change that had come upon us: we had Husband and Father, and Children and Sisters, and Friends and Relations, and House, and Home, and many Comforts of this life: but now we might say as *Job*, *Naked came I out of my mothers womb, and naked shall I return, The Lord gave, and the Lord hath taken away, blessed be the Name of the Lord.* I asked him whether he would read? he told me, he earnestly desired it. I gave him my Bible, and he lighted upon that comfortable Scripture, *Psal.* 118. 17, 18. *I shall not die but live, and declare the works of the Lord: The Lord hath chastened me sore, yet he hath not given me over to death.* Look here *Mother*, (sayes he) did you read this? And here I may take occasion to mention one principal ground of my setting forth these few Lines; even as the Psalmist sayes, To declare the works of the Lord, and his wonderful power in carrying us along, preserving us in the Wilderness, while under the Enemies hand, and returning of us in safety again. And his goodness in bringing to my hand so many comfortable and suitable Scriptures in my distress. But to Return; We travelled on till night; and in the morning we must go over the River to *Philip*'s Crew. When I was in the Cannoo, I could not but be amazed at the numerous Crew of Pagans, that were on the Bank on the other side. When I came ashore, they gathered all about me, I sitting alone in the midst: I observed they asked one another Questions, and laughed, and rejoyced over their Gains and Victories. Then my heart began to faile: and I fell a weeping; which was the first time to my remembrance, that I wept before them. Although I had met with so much Affliction, and my heart was many times ready to break, yet could I not shed one tear in their sight; but rather had been all this while in a maze, and like one astonished; but now I may say, as *Psal.* 137. 1. *By the Rivers of* Babylon, *there we sate down, yea, we wept when we remembred Zion.* There one of them asked me, why I wept; I could hardly tell what to say; yet I answered, they would kill me: No, said he, none will hurt you. Then came one of them, and gave me two spoonfuls of Meal (to comfort me) and another gave me half a pint of Pease, which was more worth than many Bushels at another time. Then I went to see King *Philip*; he bade me come in, and sit down, and asked me whether I would smoak it (an usual Complement now a days amongst Saints and Sinners.) But this no way suited me. For though I had formerly used Tobacco, yet I had left it ever since I was first taken. *It seems to be a Bait the Devil layes to make men lose their precious time*: I remember with shame, how formerly, when I had taken two or three Pipes, I was presently ready for another, such a bewitching thing it is: But I thank God, he has now given me power over it; surely there are many who may be better imployed, than to lye sucking a stinking Tobacco-pipe.

Now the *Indians* gather their Forces to go against *North-hampton*: over night one went about yelling and hooting to give notice of the design. Whereupon they fell to boyling of Ground Nuts, and parching of Corn, (as many as had it) for their Provision: and in the morning away they went. During my abode in this place *Philip* spake to me to make a shirt for his Boy, which I did; for which he gave me a shilling; I offered the money to my Master, but he bade me keep it: and with it I bought a piece of Horse-flesh. Afterwards I made a Cap for his Boy, for which he invited me to Dinner: I went, and he gave me a Pancake, about as big as two fingers; it was made of parched Wheat, beaten and fryed in Bears-grease, but I thought I never tasted pleasanter meat in my life. There was a Squaw who spake to me to make a shirt for her Sannup; for which she gave me a piece of Bear. Another asked me to knit a pair of Stockins, for which she gave me a quart of Pease. I Boyled my Pease and Bear together, and invited my Master and Mistress to Dinner: but the proud Gossip, because I served them both in one Dish, would eat nothing, except one bit that he gave her upon the point of his Knife. Hearing that my Son was come to this place, I went to see him, and found him lying flat upon the ground: I asked him how he could sleep so? he answered me, that he was not asleep, but at Prayer; and lay so, that they might not observe what he was doing. I pray God, he may remember these things now he is returned in safety. At this place (the Sun now getting higher) what with the beams and heat of the Sun, and the smoak of the Wigwams, I thought I should have been blind: I could scarce discern one Wigwam from another. There was here one *Mary Thurston* of *Medfield*, who seeing how it was with me, lent me a Hat to wear; but as soon as I was gone, the Squaw (who owned that *Mary Thurston*) came running after me, and got it away again. Here there was a Squaw who gave me one spoonful of Meal, I put it in my Pocket to keep it safe: yet notwithstanding some body stole it, but put five *Indian Corns* in the room of it: which Corns were the greatest Provision I had in my travel for one day.

The *Indians* returning from *North-hampton*, brought with them some Horses and Sheep, and other things which they had taken; I desired them, that they would carry me to *Albany* upon one of those Horses, and sell me for Powder; for so they had sometimes discoursed. I was utterly hopeless of getting home on foot, the way that I came. I could hardly bear to think of the many weary steps I had taken, to come to this place.

The ninth Remove: But instead of going either to *Albany* or homeward we must go five miles up the River, and then go over it. Here we abode a while. Here lived a sorry *Indian*, who spake to me to make him a shirt, when I had done it, he would pay me nothing. But he living by the River side, where I often went to fetch water, I would often be putting him in mind, and calling for my pay: at last, he told me, if I would make another shirt, for a Papoos

not

not yet born, he would give me a knife, which he did, when I had done it. I carried the knife in, and my Master asked me to give it him, and I was not a little glad that I had any thing that they would accept of, and be pleased with. When we were at this place my Masters Maid came home, she had been gone three Weeks into the *Narrhaganset Country*, to fetch Corn, where they had stored up some in the ground: she brought home about a peck and half of Corn. This was about the time that their great Captain (*Naananto*) was killed in the *Narrhaganset* Country.

My Son being now about a mile from me, I asked liberty to go and see him, they bade me go, and away I went; but quickly lost my self, travelling over Hills and through Swamps, and could not find the way to him. And I cannot but admire at the wonderful power and goodness of God to me, in that though I was gone from home, and met with all sorts of *Indians*, and those I had no knowledge of, and there being no *Christian Soul* near me; yet not one of them offered the least imaginable miscarriage to me. I turned homeward again, and met with my Master; he shewed me the way to my Son. When I came to him I found him not well; and withal he had a Boyl on his side, which much troubled him: we bemoaned one another a while, as the Lord helped us, and then I returned again. When I was returned, I found my self as unsatisfied as I was before. I went up and down moaning and lamenting: and my spirit was ready to sink, with the thoughts of my poor Children: my Son was ill, and I could not but think of his mournful looks: and no *Christian Friend* was near him, to do any office of love for him, either for Soul or Body. And my poor Girl, I knew not where she was, nor whether she was sick, or well, or alive, or dead. I repaired under these thoughts to my Bible (my great comforter in that time) and that Scripture came to my hand, *Cast thy burden upon the Lord and he shall sustain thee*, Psal. 55. 22.

But I was fain to go and look after something to satisfie my hunger: and going among the Wigwams, I went into one, and there found a Squaw who shewed her self very kind to me, and gave me a piece of Bear. I put it into my pocket, and came home; but could not find an opportunity to broil it, for fear they would get it from me, and there it lay all that day and night in my stinking pocket. In the morning I went again to the same Squaw, who had a Kettle of Ground-nuts boyling: I asked her to let me boyle my piece of Bear in her Kettle, which she did, and gave me some Ground-nuts to eat with it, and I cannot but think how pleasant it was to me. I have seen Bear baked very handsomly amongst the *English*, and some liked it, but the thoughts that it was Bear, made me tremble: but now that was savoury to me that one would think was enough to turn the stomach of a bruit-Creature.

One bitter cold day, I could find no room to sit down before the fire: I went out, and could not tell what to do, but I went into another Wigwam where they were also sitting round the fire: but the Squaw laid a skin for me, and bid me sit down; and gave me some Ground-nuts, and bade me come again; and told me they would buy me if they were able; and yet theſe were Strangers to me that I never knew before.

The tenth Remove. That day a ſmall part of the Company removed about three quarters of a mile, intending farther the next day. When they came to the place where they intended to lodge, and had pitched their Wigwams; being hungry, *I* went again back to the place we were before at, to get ſomething to eat: being incouraged by the Squaws kindneſs, who bade me come again; vvhen I was there, there came an *Indian* to look after me: vvho vvhen he had found me, kickt me all along: I went home and found Veniſon roaſting that night, but they would not give me one bit of it. Sometimes I met with Favour, and ſometimes with nothing but Frovvns.

The eleventh Remove. The next day in the morning they took their Travel, intending a dayes journey up the River, I took my load at my back, and quickly we came to vvade over a River: and paſſed over tireſome and vveariſome Hills. One Hill vvas ſo ſteep, that I vvas fain to creep up, upon my knees: and to hold by the tvvigs and buſhes to keep my ſelf from falling backvvard. My head alſo vvas ſo light, that I uſually reeled as I vvent, but I hope all thoſe vveariſome ſteps that I have taken, are but a forvvarding of me to the Heavenly reſt. *I know, O Lord, that thy Judgments are right, and that thou in faithfulneſs haſt afflicted me,* Pſal. 119.75.

The twelfth Remove. It vvas upon a Sabbath day morning, that they prepared for their Travel. This morning, I asked my Maſter vvhether he vvould ſell me to my Husband? he anſvvered *Nux*; vvhich did much rejoyce my ſpirit. My Miſtriſs, before vve vvent, vvas gone to the burial of a *Papoos*; and returning, ſhe found me ſitting, and reading in my Bible: ſhe ſnatched it haſtily out of my hand, and threvv it out of doors; I ran out, and catcht it up, and put it into my pocket, and never let her ſee it afterward. Then they packed up their things to be gone, and gave me my load, I complained it vvas too heavy, vvhereupon ſhe gave me a ſlap in the face, and bade me go: *I* lifted up my heart to God, hoping that Redemption vvas not far off: and the rather becauſe their inſolency grevv vvorſe and vvorſe.

But the thoughts of my going homevvard (for ſo vve bent our courſe) much cheared my Spirit, and made my burden ſeem light, and almoſt nothing at all. But (to my amazement and great perplexity) the ſcale vvas ſoon turned: for vvhen vve had gone a little vvay, on a ſudden my Miſtriſs gives out, ſhe vvould go no further, but turn back again, and ſaid *I* muſt go back again vvith her, and ſhe called her Sannup, and vvould have had him gone back alſo, but he vvould not, but ſaid, he vvould go on, and come to us again in three dayes. My Spirit vvas upon this (*I* confeſs) very impatient and almoſt outragious. *I* thought *I* could as vvell have died as vvent back. *I* cannot declare the trouble that *I* vvas in about it: but yet back again *I* muſt go. As ſoon as *I* had an opportunity, *I* took my Bible to read,

and

and that quieting Scripture came to my hand, *Psal.* 46. 10. *Be still, and know that I am God*; which stilled my spirit for the present: but a sore time of trial I concluded I had to go through. My Master being gone, who seemed to me the best Friend that I had of an *Indian*, both in cold and hunger, and quickly so it proved. Down I sat, with my Heart as full as it could hold, and yet so hungry that I could not sit neither: but going out to see what I could find, and walking among the Trees, I found six Acorns and two Chesnuts, which were some refreshment to me. Towards night I gathered me some sticks for my own comfort, that I might not lye a Cold: but when we came to lye down, they bade me go out, and lye somewhere else, for they had company (they said) come in more than their own: I told them I could not tell where to go; they bade me go look: I told them, if I went to another *Wigwam* they would be angry, and send me home again. Then one of the Company drew his Sword, and told me he would run me through if I did not go presently. Then was I fain to stoop to this rude fellow, and to go out in the Night, I knew not whither. Mine eyes have seen that Fellow afterwards walking up and down in *Boston*, under the appearance of a *Friend-Indian*: and several others of the like Cut. I went to one *Wigwam*, and they told me they had no room. Then I went to another, and they said the same: at last an old *Indian* bade me come to him, and his Squaw gave me some Ground-nuts: she gave me also something to lay under my Head, and a good Fire we had: and through the good Providence of God, I had a comfortable lodging that Night. In the morning another *Indian* bade me come at night, and he would give me six Ground-nuts, which I did. We were at this place and time about two miles from *Connecticut River*. We went in the morning (to gather Ground-nuts) to the River, and went back again at Night. I went with a great load at my back (for they when they went, though but a little way, would carry all their trumpery with them) I told them the skin was off my back, but I had no other comforting answer from them than this, that it vvould be no matter if my Head vvere off too.

The thirteenth Remove. Instead of going toward the Bay (which was that I desired) I must go with them five or six miles down the River, into a mighty Thicket of Brush: where we abode almost a fortnight. Here one asked me to make a shirt for her Papoos, for which she gave me a mess of Broth, which was thickened with meal made of the Bark of a Tree: and to make it the better she had put into it about a handful of Pease, and a few rosted Ground-nuts. I had not seen my Son a pretty while, and here was an *Indian* of whom I made inquiry after him, and asked him when he saw him? he answered me that such a time his Master roasted him; and that himself did eat a piece of him, as big as his two fingers, and that he was very good meat: but the Lord upheld my Spirit, under his discouragement; and I considered their horrible addictedness to lying, and that there is not one of them that makes the least conscience of speaking the truth. In this place on a cold night

as

as I lay by the fire, I removed a stick which kept the heat from me, a Squaw moved it down again; at which I lookt up, and she threw an handful of ashes in my eyes; I thought I should have been quite blinded and have never seen more: but lying down, the Water run out of my eyes, and carried the dirt with it, that by the morning, I recovered my sight again. Yet upon this, and the like occasions, I hope it is not too much to say with *Job*, *Have pity upon me, have pity upon me, Oh ye my Friends, for the hand of the Lord has touched me.* And here I cannot but remember how many times sitting in their Wigwams, and musing on things past, I should suddenly leap up and run out, as if I had been at home, forgetting where I was, and what my condition was: But when I was without, and saw nothing but Wilderness, and Woods, and a company of barbarous Heathen; my mind quickly returned to me, which made me think of that, spoken concerning *Sampson*, who said, *I will go out and shake my self as at other times, but he wist not that the Lord was departed from him.* About this time, I began to think that all my hopes of Restoration would come to nothing. I thought of the *English* Army, and hoped for their coming, and being retaken by them, but that failed. I hoped to be carried to *Albany*, as the *Indians* had discoursed, but that failed also. I thought of being sold to my Husband, as my Master spake; but instead of that, my Master himself was gone, and I left behind; so that my spirit was now quite ready to sink. *I* asked them to let me go out, and pick up some sticks, that *I* might get alone, and pour out my heart unto the Lord. Then also *I* took my Bible to read, but *I* found no comfort here neither: yet *I* can say, that in all my sorrows and afflictions, God did not leave me to have my impatience work towards himself, as if his ways were unrighteous; but *I* knew that he laid upon me less then *I* deserved. Afterward, before this doleful time ended with me, I was turning the leaves of my Bible, and the Lord brought to me some Scriptures, which did a little revive me, as that *Isai.* 55. 8. *For my thoughts are not your thoughts, neither are your ways my ways, saith the Lord.* And also that, *Psal.* 37. 5. *Commit thy way unto the Lord, trust also in him, and he shall bring it to pass.*

About this time they came yelping from *Hadly*, having there killed three *English-men*, and brought one Captive with them, *viz. Thomas Read.* They all gathered about the poor Man, asking him many Questions. I desired also to go and see him; and when I came he was crying bitterly: supposing they would quickly kill him. Whereupon I asked one of them, whether they intended to kill him? he answered me, they would not: He being a little cheared with that, *I* asked him about the welfare of my Husband, he told me he saw him such a time in the *Bay*, and he was well, but very Melancholly. By which I certainly understood (though I suspected it before) that whatsoever the *Indians* told me respecting him, was vanity and lies. Some of them told me, he was dead, and they had killed him: some said he was Married again, and that the Governour wished him to Marry; and told him he should have his choice, and that all perswaded him I was dead. So like

were

were these barbarous creatures to him who was a liar from the beginning.

As *I* was sitting once in the Wigwam here, *Philips* Maid came in with the Child in her arms, and asked me to give her a piece of my Apron, to make a flap for it, *I* told her *I* would not: then my Mistress bad me give it, but still *I* said no. The Maid told me, if *I* would not give her a piece, she would tear a piece off it: I told her I would tear her Coat then: with that my Mistress rises up: and takes up a stick big enough to have killed me, and struck at me with it, but *I* stept out, and she struck the stick into the Mat of the Wigwam. But while she was pulling of it out, *I* ran to the Maid and gave her all my Apron, and so that storm went over.

Hearing that my Son was come to this place, I went to see him, and told him his Father was well, but very melancholly: he told me he was as much grieved for his Father as for himself; I wondred at his speech, for I thought I had enough upon my spirit in reference to my self, to make me mindless of my Husband and every one else: they being safe among their Friends. He told me also, that a while before, his Master (together with other *Indians*) were going to the *French* for Powder; but by the way the *Mohawks* met with them, and killed four of their Company, which made the rest turn back again: for which I desire that my self and he may bless the Lord; for it might have been worse with him, had he been sold to the *French*, than it proved to be in his remaining with the *Indians*.

I went to see an *English* Youth in this place, one *John Gilberd* of *Springfield*. I found him lying without doors, upon the ground; I asked him how he did? he told me was very sick of a flux, with eating so much blood. They had turned him out of the Wigwam, and with him an *Indian Papoos*, almost dead (whose Parents had been killed) in a bitter cold day, without fire or clothes: the young man himself had nothing on, but his shirt and wastcoat. This sight was enough to melt a heart of flint. There they lay quivering in the Cold, the youth round like a dog; the *Papoos* stretcht out, with his eyes, and nose, and mouth full of dirt, and yet alive, and groaning. I advised *John* to go and get to some fire: he told me he could not stand, but I perswaded him still, lest he should ly there and die. And with much ado I got him to a fire, and went my self home. As soon as I was got home, his Masters Daughter came after me, to know what I had done with the *English-man*? I told her I had got him to a fire in such a place. Now had I need to pray *Pauls* Prayer, 2 *Thess*. 3. 2. *That we may be delivered from unreasonable and wicked men*. For her satisfaction I went along with her, and brought her to him; but before I got home again, it was noised about, that I was running away, and getting the *English* youth along with me: that as soon as I came in, they began to rant and domineer: asking me where I had been? and what I had been doing? and saying they would knock me in the head: I told them, I had been seeing the *English Youth*: and that I would not run away: they told me I lied, and taking up a Hatchet, they came to me, and said, they would knock me down

if

if I stirred out again: and so confined me to the Wigwam. Now may I say with *David*, 2 *Sam*. 24. 14. *I am in a great strait*. If I keep in, I must dye with hunger, and if I go out, I must be knockt in the head. This distressed condition held that day, and half the next; and then the Lord remembred me, whose mercies are great. Then came an *Indian* to me, with a pair of Stockins which were too big for him; and he would have me ravel them out, and knit them fit for him. I shewed my self willing, and bid him ask my Mistress, if I might go along with him a little way: She said yes, I might, but I was not a little refresht with that news, that I had my liberty again. Then I went along with him, and he gave me some roasted Ground-nuts, which did again revive my feeble stomach.

Being got out of her sight, I had time and liberty again to look into my Bible: which was my guide by day, and my Pillow by night. Now that comfortable Scripture presented it self to me, *Isai*. 54. 7. *For a small moment have I forsaken thee: but with great mercies will I gather thee.* Thus the Lord carried me along from one time to another: and made good to me this precious promise, and many others. Then my Son came to see me, and I asked his Master to let him stay a while with me: that I might comb his head, and look over him for he was almost overcome with lice. He told me, when I had done, that he was very hungry, but I had nothing to relieve him; but bid him go into the Wigwams as he went along, and see if he could get any thing among them. Which he did, and (it seems) tarried a little too long; for his Master was angry with him, and beat him, and then sold him. Then he came running to tell me he had a new Master, and that he had given him some Ground-nuts already. Then I went along with him to his new Master, who told me he loved him: and he should not want. So his Master carried him away, and I never saw him afterward: till I saw him at *Pascataqua* in *Portsmouth*.

That night they bad me go out of the Wigwam again: my Mistresses *Papoos* was sick, and it died that night; and there was one benefit in it, that there was more room. I went to a Wigwam, and they bad me come in, and gave me a skin to lye upon, and a mess of Venison and Ground-nuts; which was a choice Dish among them. On the morrow they buried the *Papoos*; and afterward, both morning and evening, there came a company to mourn and howl with her: though I confess, I could not much condole with them. Many sorrowful days I had in this place: often getting alone; *like a Crane or a Swallow so did I chatter; I did mourn as a Dove, mine eyes fail with looking upward. Oh Lord I am oppressed, undertake for me*, Isai. 38. 14. I could tell the Lord, as *Hezekiah*, ver. 3. *Remember now, O Lord, I beseech thee, how I have walked before thee in truth.* Now had I time to examine all my wayes: my Conscience did not accuse me of unrighteousness toward one or other: yet I saw how in my walk with God, I had been a careless creature. As *David* said, *Against thee thee only have I sinned*: and I might say with the poor Publican, *God be merciful*

ciful unto me a sinner. On the Sabbath days I could look upon the Sun, and think how People were going to the house of God, to have their Souls refresht; and then home, and their Bodies also: but I was destitute of both; and might say as the poor Prodigal, *he would fain have filled his belly with the husks that the Swine did eat, and no man gave unto him,* Luke 15. 16. For I must say with him, *Father I have sinned against Heaven, and in thy sight,* ver. 21. I remembred how on the night before and after the Sabbath, when my Family was about me, and Relations and Neighbours with us, we could pray and sing, and then refresh our bodies with the good creatures of God: and then have a comfortable Bed to ly down on: but instead of all this, I had only a little Swill for the body, and then like a Swine, must ly down on the Ground: I cannot express to man the sorrow that lay upon my Spirit, the Lord knows it. Yet that comfortable Scripture would often come to my mind, *For a small moment have I forsaken thee, but with great mercies I will gather thee.*

The fourteenth Remove. Now must we pack up and be gone from this Thicket, bending our course towards the Bay-Towns. I having nothing to eat by the way this day, but a few crumbs of Cake, that an *Indian* gave my Girl, the same day we were taken. She gave it me, and I put it into my pocket; there it lay till it was so mouldy (for want of good baking) that one could not tell what it was made of; it fell all to crumbs, and grew so dry and hard, that it was like little flints; and this refreshed me many times, when I was ready to faint. It was in my thoughts when I put it into my mouth, that if ever I returned, I would tell the World, what a blessing the Lord gave to such mean food. As we went along, they killed a *Deer,* with a young one in her: they gave me a piece of the *Fawn,* and it was so young and tender, that one might eat the bones as well as the flesh, and yet I thought it very good. When night came on we sate down; it rained, but they quickly got up a Bark Wig-wam, where I lay dry that night. I looked out in the morning, and many of them had lain in the rain all night, I saw by their Reeking. Thus the Lord dealt mercifully with me many times; and I fared better than many of them. In the morning they took the blood of the *Deer,* and put it into the Paunch, and so boiled it. I could eat nothing of that, though they ate it sweetly. And yet they were so nice in other things, that when I had fetcht water, and had put the Dish I dipt the water with, into the Kittle of water which I brought, they would say, they would knock me down; for they said, it was a sluttish trick.

The fifteenth Remove. We went on our travel. I having got one handful of Ground-nuts, for my support that day: they gave me my load, and I went on cheerfully (with the thoughts of going homeward) having my burden more on my back than my spirit: we came to *Baquaug* River again that day, near which we abode a few days. Sometimes one of them would give me a Pipe, another a little Tobacco, another a little Salt: which I would change for a little Victuals. I cannot but think what a Wolvish appetite persons have in a starving condition: for many times when they gave me that which was hot, I was so greedy, that I should burn my mouth, that it would trouble me hours after; and yet I should quickly do the same again. And after I was throughly hungry, I was never again satisfied. For though sometimes it fell out, that I got enough, and did eat till I could eat no more, yet I was as unsatisfied as I was when I began. And now could I see that Scripture verified (there being many Scriptures which we do not take notice of, or understand till we are afflicted) *Mic.* 6. 14. *Thou shalt eat and not be satisfied.* Now might I see more than ever before, the miseries that sin hath brought upon us. Many times I should be ready to run out against the Heathen, but that Scripture would quiet me again, *Amos* 3. 6. *Shall there be evil in the City, and the Lord hath not done it?* The Lord help me to make a right improvement of his word, and that I might learn that great lesson, *Mic.* 6. 8, 9. *He hath shewed thee, O Man, what is good; and what doth the Lord require of thee, but to do justly, and love mercy, and walk humbly with thy God? Hear ye the rod, and who hath appointed it.*

The sixteenth Remove. We began this Remove with wading over *Baquaug* River. The Water was up to the knees, and the stream very swift, and so cold that I thought it would have cut me in sunder. I was so week and feeble, that I reeled as I went along, and thought there I must end my days at last, after my bearing and getting through so many difficulties. The *Indians* stood laughing to see me staggering along, but in my distress the Lord gave me experience of the truth and goodness of that promise, *Isai.* 43. 2. *When thou passest thorough the waters, I will be with thee, and thorough the Rivers, they shall not overflow thee.* Then I sate down to put on my stockins and shoes, with the tears running down my eyes, and many sorrowful thoughts in my heart: but I gat up to go along with them. Quickly there came up to us an *Indian*, who informed them, that I must go to *Wachuset* to my Master, for there was a Letter come from the Council to the *Saggamores*, about redeeming the Captives, and that there would be another in fourteen days, and that I must be there ready. My heart was so heavy before that I could scarce speak, or go in the path; and yet now so light, that I could run. My strength seemed to come again, and to recruit my feeble knees, and aking heart: yet it pleased them to go but one mile that night, and there we stayed two days. In that time came a company of *Indians* to us, near thirty, all on Horse back. My heart skipt within me, thinking they had been *English-men* at the first sight of them: for they were dressed in *English* Apparel, with Hats, white Neckcloths, and Sashes about their wasts, and Ribbons upon their shoulders: but when they came near, there was a vast difference between the lovely Faces of *Christians*, and the foul looks of those *Heathens*; which much damped my spirit again.

The seventeenth Remove. A comfortable Remove it was to me, because of my hopes. They gave me my pack, and along we went cheerfully: but quickly my Will proved more than my strength; having little or no refreshing

freshing my strength failed, and my spirits were almost quite gone. Now may I say as *David*, *Psal.* 109. 22, 23, 24. *I am poor and needy, and my heart is wounded within me. I am gone like the shadow when it declineth: I am tossed up and down like the Locust: my knees are weak through fasting, and my flesh faileth of fatness.* At night we came to an *Indian Town*, and the *Indians* sate down by a Wigwam discoursing, but I was almost spent, and could scarce speak. I laid down my load, and went into the Wigwam, and there sate an *Indian* boiling of *Horses feet*: (they being wont to eat the flesh first, and when the feet were old and dried, and they had nothing else, they would cut off the feet and use them) I asked him to give me a little of his Broth, or Water they were boiling in: he took a Dish, and gave me one spoonful of Samp, and bid me take as much of the Broth as I would. Then I put some of the hot water to the Samp, and drank it up, and my spirit came again. He gave me also a piece of the Ruffe or Ridding of the small Guts, and I broiled it on the coals; and now may I say with *Jonathan*, *See I pray you, how mine eyes have been enlightened, because I tasted a little of this honey*, 1 *Sam.* 14. 29. Now is my Spirit revived again: though means be never so inconsiderable, yet if the Lord bestow his blessing upon them, they shall refresh both Soul and Body.

The eighteenth Remove. We took up our packs, and along we went. But a wearisome day I had of it. As we went along, I saw an *Englishman* stript naked, and lying dead upon the ground, but knew not who it was. Then we came to another *Indian Town*, where we stayed all night. In this Town there were four *English Children*, Captives: and one of them my own Sisters. I went to see how she did, and she was well, considering her Captive condition. I would have tarried that night with her, but they that owned her would not suffer it. Then I went to another Wigwam, where they were boiling Corn and Beans, which was a lovely sight to see, but I could not get a taste thereof. Then I went into another Wigwam, where there were two of the *English Children*: The Squaw was boiling horses feet, then she cut me off a little piece, and gave one of the *English Children* a piece also. Being very hungry, I had quickly eat up mine: but the Child could not bite it, it was so tough and sinewy, but lay sucking, gnawing, chewing, and slobbering it in the Mouth and Hand, then I took it of the Child, and eat it my self; and savoury it was to my taste.

That I may say as *Job*, *Chap.* 6. 7. *The things that my Soul refused to touch, are as my sorrowful meat.* Thus the Lord made that pleasant and refreshing, which another time would have been an Abomination. Then I went home to my Mistresses Wigwam: and they told me I disgraced My Master with begging: and if I did so any more, they would knock me on the Head: I told them, they had as good knock me on the Head, as starve me to death.

The nineteenth Remove. They said, when we went out, that we must travel to *Wachuset* this day. But a bitter weary day I had of it; travelling now three dayes together, without resting any day between. At last, after many weary steps, I saw *Wachuset* hills, but many miles off. Then we came to a great Swamp, through which we travelled up to the knees in mud and water, which was heavy going to one tried before. Being almost spent, I thought I should have sunk down at last, and never got out; but I may say, as in *Psal.* 94. 18. *When my foot slipped, thy mercy, O Lord, held me up.* Going along, having indeed my life, but little Spirit, *Philip*, (who was in the Company) came up, and took me by the hand, and said, *Two weeks more, and you shall be Mistriss again.* I asked him if he speak true? he answered, Yes, and quickly you shall come to your Master again: who had been gone from us three weeks. After many weary steps we came to *Wachuset*, where he was; and glad I was to see him. He asked me, when I washt me? I told him not this moneth; then he fetch me some water himself, and bid me wash, and gave me the Glass to see how I lookt, and bid his Squaw give me something to eat. So she gave me a mess of Beans and meat, and a little Ground-nut Cake. I was wonderfully revived with this favour shewed me, *Psal.* 106. 46. *He made them also to be pitied of all those that carried them Captives.*

My Master had three Squaws: living sometimes with one, and sometimes with another. One, this old Squaw at whose Wigwam I was, and with whom my Master had been those three weeks. Another was *Wettimore*, with whom I had lived and served all this while. A severe and proud Dame she was, bestowing every day in dressing her self near as much time as any of the Gentry of the land: powdering her hair and painting her face, going with her Neck-laces, with Jewels in her ears, and bracelets upon her hands. When she had dressed her self, her Work was to make Girdles of Wampom and Beads. The third Squaw was a younger one, by whom he had two Papooses. By that time I was refresht by the old Squaw, with whom my Master was, *Wettimores* Maid came to call me home, at which I fell a weeping; then the old Squaw told me, to encourage me, that if I wanted victuals, I should come to her, and that I should lye there in her Wigwam. Then I went with the Maid, and quickly came again and lodged there. The Squaw laid a Mat under me, and a good Rugg over me; the first time I had any such Kindness shewed me. I understood that *Wettimore* thought, that if she should let me go and serve with the old Squaw, she would be in danger to lose not only my service but the redemption-pay also. And I was not a little glad to hear this; being by it raised in my hopes, that in Gods due time there would be an end of this sorrowful hour. Then came an *Indian*, and asked me to knit him three pair of Stockins, for which I had a Hat, and a silk Handker chief. Then another asked me to make her a shift, for which she gave me an Apron.

Then came *Tom* and *Peter*, with the second Letter from the Council, about the Captives. Though they were *Indians*, I gat them by the hand, and burst out into Tears; my heart was so full that I could not speak to them: but recovering my self, I asked them how my Husband did? and all my Friends and Acquaintance? they said, they were well, but very Melancholy. They

brought

brought me two Biskets, and a pound of Tobacco. The Tobacco I quickly gave away: when it was all gone, one asked me to give him a pipe of Tobacco, I told him all was gone; then began he to rant and threaten; I told him when my Husband came, I would give him some: Hang him Rogue (says he) I will knock out his brains, if he comes here. And then again in the same breath, they would say, that if there should come an hundred without Guns, they would do them no hurt. So unstable and like mad men they were. So that fearing the worst, I durst not send to my Husband; though there were some thoughts of his coming to Redeem and fetch me, not knowing what might follow; for there was little more trust to them than to the Master they served. When the Letter was come, the Saggamores met to consult about the Captives, and called me to them to enquire how much my Husband would give to redeem me: When I came, I sate down among them, as I was wont to do, as their manner is: Then they bade me stand up, and said, they were the *General Court*. They bid me speak what I thought he would give. Now knowing that all we had was destroyed by the *Indians*, I was in a great strait. I thought if I should speak of but a little, it would be slighted, and hinder the matter; if of a great Sum, I knew not where it would be procured: yet at a venture, I said *Twenty pounds*, yet desired them to take less; but they would not hear of that, but sent that message to *Boston*, that for *twenty pounds* I should be redeemed. It was a Praying *Indian* that wrote their Letter for them. There was another Praying *Indian*, who told me, that he had a Brother, that would not eat Horse; his Conscience was so tender and scrupulous, (though as large as Hell, for the destruction of poor *Christians*) Then he said, he read that Scripture to him, 2 *King.* 6. 25. *There was a Famine in* Samaria, *and behold they besieged it, until an Asses head was sold for fourscore pieces of silver, and the fourth part of a Kab of Doves dung, for five pieces of silver*. He expounded this place to his Brother, and shewed him that it was lawful to eat that in a Famine, which is not at another time. And now, says he, he will eat Horse with any *Indian* of them all. There was another Praying *Indian*, who when he had done all the Mischief that he could, betrayed his own Father into the *Englishes* hands, thereby to purchase his own Life. Another Praying *Indian* was at *Sudbury* Fight, though, as he deserved, he was afterward hanged for it. There was another Praying *Indian*, so wicked and cruel, as to wear a string about his neck, strung with *Christian* Fingers. Another Praying *Indian*, when they went to *Sudbury* Fight, went with them, and his Squaw also with him, with her Papoos at her back: before they went to that Fight, they got a company together to *Powaw*: the manner was as followeth. There was one that kneeled upon a *Deer-skin*, with the Company round him in a Ring, who kneeled, striking upon the Ground with their hands, and with sticks, and muttering or humming with their Mouths. Besides him who kneeled in the Ring, there also stood one with a Gun in his hand: Then he on the Deer-skin made a speech, and all manifested assent to

it;

it; and so they did many times together. Then they bade him with the Gun go out of the Ring, which he did; but when he was out they called him in again; but he seemed to make a stand; then they called the more earnestly, till he returned again. Then they all sang. Then they gave him two Guns, in either hand one. And so he on the Deer-skin began again; and at the end of every Sentence in his speaking, they all assented, humming or muttering with their Mouthes, and striking upon the Ground with their Hands. Then they bade him with the two Guns go out of the Ring again: which he did a little way. Then they called him in again, but he made a stand, so they called him with greater earnestness: but he stood reeling and wavering, as if he knew not whether he should stand or fall, or which way to go. Then they called him with exceeding great vehemency, all of them, one and another: after a little while, he turned in, staggering as he went, with his Arms stretched out; in either hand a Gun. As soon as he came in, they all sang and rejoyced exceedingly a while. And then he upon the Deer-skin, made another speech, unto which they all assented in a rejoycing manner: and so they ended their business, and forthwith went to *Sudbury* Fight. To my thinking they went without any scruple but that they should prosper and gain the Victory. And they went out not so rejoycing, but that they came home with as great a Victory. For they said they had killed two Captains, and almost an hundred men. One *Englishman* they brought alive with them; and he said it was too true, for they had made sad work at *Sudbury*; as indeed it proved. Yet they came home without that rejoycing and triumphing over their Victory, which they were wont to shew at other times; but rather like Dogs, (as they say) which have lost their Ears. Yet I could not perceive that it was for their own loss of Men: they said, they had not lost above five or six: and I missed none, except in one Wigwam. When they went, they acted as if the Devil had told them that they should gain the Victory; and now they acted, as if the Devil had told them that they should have a fall. Whether it were so or no, I cannot tell, but so it proved: for quickly they began to fall, and so held on that Summer, till they came to utter ruine. They came home on a Sabbath day, and the Powaw that kneeled upon the Deer-skin, came home (I may say without any abuse) as black as the Devil. When my Master came home, he came to me and bid me make a shirt for his Papoos, of a Holland laced Pillowbeer. About that time there came an *Indian* to me, and bade me come to his *Wigwam* at night, and he would give me some Pork and Ground-nuts. Which I did, and as I was eating, another *Indian* said to me, he seems to be your good Friend, but he killed two *English-men* at *Sudbury*, and there lye their Cloaths behind you: I looked behind me, and there I saw bloody Cloathes, with Bullet-holes in them; yet the Lord suffered not this Wretch to do me any hurt. Yea, instead of that, he many times refresht me: five or six times did he and his Squaw refresh my feeble Carcass. If I went to their *Wigwam* at any time, they would always

give

give me something, and yet they were strangers that I never saw before. Another *Squaw* gave me a piece of fresh Pork, and a little Salt with it, and lent me her Frying-pan to fry it in; and I cannot but remember what a sweet, pleasant and delightful relish that bit had to me, to this day. So little do we prize common mercies, when we have them to the full.

The Twentieth Remove. It was their usual manner to remove, when they had done any mischief, lest they should be found out; and so they did at this time. We went about three or four miles, and there they built a great *Wigwam*, big enough to hold an hundred *Indians*, which they did in preparation to a great day of Dancing. They would say now amongst themselves, that the *Governour* would be so angry for his loss at *Sudbury*, that he would send no more about the Captives, which made me grieve and tremble. My Sister being not far from the place where we now were, and hearing that I was here, desired her Master to let her come and see me, and he was willing to it, and would go with her; but she being ready before him, told him she would go before, and was come within a Mile or two of the place. Then he overtook her, and began to rant as if he had been mad; and made her go back again in the Rain; so that I never saw her till I saw her in *Charlstown*. But the Lord requited many of their ill-doings, for this *Indian* her Master, was hanged afterward at *Boston*. The *Indians* now began to come from all quarters, against their merry dancing day. Among some of them came one Goodwife *Kettle*: I told her that my Heart was so heavy that it was ready to break: so is mine too, said she; but yet said, *I* hope we shall hear some good news shortly. I could hear how earnestly my Sister desired to see me, and *I* as earnestly desired to see her: and yet neither of us could get an opportunity. My Daughter was also now but about a Mile off, and I had not seen her in nine or ten Weeks, as I had not seen my Sister, since our first taking. *I* earnestly desired them to let me go and see them; yea, *I* intreated, begged, and perswaded them, but to let me see my Daughter; and yet so hard-hearted were they, that they would not suffer it. They made use of their Tyrannical Power whilst they had it; but through the Lord's wonderful mercy, their time was now but short.

On a Sabbath-day, the Sun being about an hour high, in the Afternoon, came Mr. *John Hoar* (the Council permitting him, and his own forward spirit inclining him) together with the two forementioned *Indians*, *Tom* and *Peter*, with the third Letter from the Council. When they came near, I was abroad; though I saw them not, they presently called me in, and bade me sit down, and not stir. Then they catched up their Guns, and away they ran, as if an Enemy had been at hand; and the Guns went off apace. I manifested some great trouble, and they asked me what was the matter? I told them *I* thought they had killed the *Englishman* (for they had in the mean time informed me that an *Englishman* was come) they said No; they shot over his Horse, and under, and before his Horse, and they pusht him this way and that way, at their pleasure, shewing what they could do: Then they let them come to their Wigwams. I begged of them to to let me see the *English-man*, but they would not. But there was I fain to sit their pleasure. When they had talked their fill with him, they suffered me to go to him. We asked each other of our welfare, and how my Husband did? and all my Friends? He told me they were all well, and would be glad to see me. Amongst other things which my Husband sent me, there came a pound of *Tobacco*: which I sold for nine shillings in Money: for many of the *Indians* for want of *Tobacco*, smoked *Hemlock*, and *Ground-Ivy*. It was a great mistake in any, who thought I sent for *Tobacco*: for through the favour of God, that desire was overcome. I now asked them, whether I should go home with Mr. *Hoar*? they answered No, one and another of them: and it being Night, we lay down with that Answer: in the Morning Mr. *Hoar* invited the *Saggamores* to Dinner: but when we went to get it ready, we found that they had stollen the greatest part of the Provision Mr. *Hoar* had brought out of his Bags in the Night. And we may see the wonderful power of God, in that one passage, in that when there was such a great number of the *Indians* together, and so greedy of a little good Food; and no *English* there, but Mr. *Hoar*, and my self: that there they did not knock us in the Head, and take what we had: there being not only some Provision, but also Trading Cloth, a part of the twenty pounds agreed upon: But instead of doing us any mischief, they seemed to be ashamed of the Fact, and said, it were some *Matchit Indians* that did it. O that we could believe that there is nothing too hard for God! God shewed his power over the Heathen in this, as he did over the hungry Lions when *Daniel* was cast into the Den. Mr. *Hoar* called them betime to Dinner; but they ate very little, they being so busie in dressing themselves, and getting ready for their Dance: which was carried on by eight of them; four Men and four Squaws: my Master and Mistriss being two. He was dressed in his Holland Shirt, with great Laces sewed at the tail of it; he had his silver Buttons, his white Stockings, his Garters were hung round with Shillings, and he had Girdles of Wampon upon his Head and Shoulders. She had a Kersoy Coat, and covered with Girdles of Wampom from the Loins and upward. Her Arms from her Elbows to her Hands were covered with Bracelets; there were handfuls of Neck-laces about her Neck, and several sorts of Jewels in her Ears. She had fine red Stockins, and white Shoos, her Hair powdered, and her Face painted Red, that was always before Black. And all the Dancers were after the same manner. There were two other singing and knocking on a Kettle for their Musick. They kept hopping up and down one after another, with a Kettle of Water in the midst, standing warm upon some Embers, to drink of when they were a dry. They held on, till it was almost night, throwing out Wampom to the standers by. At night I asked them again, if I should go home? they all as one said no, except my Husband would come for me. When we were lain down, my Master went out of the Wigwam, and by and by sent in an *Indian*, called *James*, the PRINTER, who told Mr. *Hoar*, [illegible] that

that my Master would let me go home to morrow, if he would let him have one pint of *Liquors*. Then Mr. *Hoar* called his own *Indians*, *Tom* and *Peter*: and bid them all go, and see whether he vvould promise it before them three: and if he would, he should have it; which he did, and had it. Then *Philip* smelling the business, called me to him, and asked me what I would give him, to tell me some good news, and to speak a good word for me, that I might go home to morrow? I told him I could not tell what to give him; I would give any thing I had, and asked him what he would have? He said two Coats, and twenty shillings in Money, and half a bushel of Seed-Corn, and some Tobacco. I thanked him for his love: but I knew the good nevvs as well as that crafty Fox. My Master, after he had had his Drink, quickly came ranting into the Wigwam again, and called for Mr. *Hoar*, drinking to him, and saying he was a good man; and then again he would say, Hang him Rogue. Being almost drunk, he would drink to him, and yet presently say he should be hanged. Then he called for me; I trembled to hear him, yet I was fain to go to him; and he drunk to me, shewing no incivility. He was the first *Indian*, I saw drunk all the vvhile that I was amongst them. At last his Squaw ran out, and he after her, round the Wigwam, with his money gingling at his knees: but she escaped him; but having an old Squaw, he ran to her: and so through the Lords mercy, we were no more troubled with him that night. Yet I had not a comfortable nights rest: for I think I can say, I did not sleep for three nights together. The night before the Letter came from the Council, I could not rest, I was so full of fears and troubles, (God many times leaving us most in the dark, when deliverance is nearest) yea at this time I could not rest night nor day. The next night I was over-joyed, Mr. *Hoar* being come, and that with such good Tydings. The third night I was even swallovved up vvith the thoughts of things; *viz.* that ever I should go home again: and that I must go, leaving my Children behind me in the Wilderness; so that sleep vvas novv almost departed from mine eyes.

On *Tuesday* morning they called their General Court (as they stiled it) to consult and determine, vvhether I should go home or no: And they all as one man did seemingly consent to it, that I should go home: except *Philip*, vvho vvould not come among them.

But before I go any further, I would take leave to mention a few remarkable passages of Providence; which I took special notice of in my afflicted time.

1. Of the fair opportunity lost in the long March, a little after the Fort-fight, when our *English* Army was so numerous, and in pursuit of the Enemy; and so near as to overtake several, and destroy them: and the Enemy in such distress for Food, that our men might track them by their rooting in the Earth for Ground-nuts, whilst they were flying for their lives: I say, that then our Army should want Provision, and be forced to leave their pur-

suit, and return homeward: and the very next week the Enemy came upon our Town, like Bears bereft of their whelps, or so many ravenous Wolves, rending us and our Lambs to death. But what shall I say? God seemed to leave his People to themselves, and ordered all things for his own holy ends. *Shall there be evil in the City and the Lord hath not done it? They are not grieved for the affliction of Joseph, therefore they shall go Captive, with the first that go Captive. It is the Lords doing, and it should be marvelous in our Eyes.*

2. I cannot but remember, how the *Indians* derided the slowness, and dulness of the *English* Army, in its setting out. For after the desolations at *Lancaster* and *Medfield*, as I went along with them, they asked me when I thought the *English* Army would come after them? I told them I could not tell: it may be they will come in *May*, said they. Thus did they scoffe at us, as if the *English* would be a quarter of a Year getting ready.

3. Which also I have hinted before, when the *English* Army with new supplies were sent forth to pursue after the Enemy, and they understanding it; fled before them till they came to *Baquang River*, where they forthwith went over safely: that that River should be impassable to the *English*. I cannot but admire to see the wonderful providence of God in preserving the Heathen for farther affliction to our poor Country. They could go in great numbers over, but the *English* must stop: God had an over-ruling hand in all those things.

4. It was thought, if their Corn were cut down, they would starve and die with hunger: and all their Corn that could be found, was destroyed, and they driven from that little they had in store, into the Woods in the midst of Winter; and yet how to admiration did the Lord preserve them for his holy ends, and the destruction of many still amongst the *English*! strangely did the Lord provide for them: that I did not see (all the time I was among them) one Man, or Woman, or Child, die with Hunger.

Though many times they would eat that, that a Hog or a Dog would hardly touch; yet by that God strengthened them to be a scourge to his People.

Their chief and commonest food was Ground-nuts: they eat also Nuts, and Acorns, Hartychoaks, Lilly-roots, Ground-beans, and several other weeds and roots that I know not.

They would pick up old bones, and cut them in pieces at the joynts, and if they were full of worms and magots, they would scald them over the fire to make the vermine come out; and then boyle them, and drink up the Liquor, and then beat the great ends of them in a Morter, and so eat them. They would eat Horses guts and ears, and all sorts of wild birds which they could catch: Also Bear, Venison, Beavers, Tortois, Frogs, Squirils, Dogs, Skunks, Rattle-snakes: yea, the very Barks of Trees; besides

ſides all ſorts of Creatures, and proviſion which they plundered from the *Engliſh.* I cannot but ſtand in admiration to ſee the wonderful power of God, in providing for ſuch a vaſt number of our Enemies in the Wilderneſs, where there was nothing to be ſeen, but from hand to mouth. Many times in the morning, the generality of them, would eat up all they had, and yet have ſome farther ſupply againſt they wanted. It is ſaid, *Pſal.* 81. 13. 14. *Oh that my people had hearkened to me, and Iſrael had walked in my wayes; I ſhould ſoon have ſubdued their Enemies, and turned my hand againſt their adverſaries.* But now our perverſe and evil carriages in the ſight of the Lord, have ſo offended him; that inſtead of turning his hand againſt them, the Lord feeds and nouriſhes them up to be a ſcourge to the whole Land.

5. Another thing that I would obſerve, is, the ſtrange providence of God in turning things about when the *Indians were at the higheſt,* and the *Engliſh at the loweſt.* I was with the Enemy eleven weeks and five days; and not one Week paſſed without the fury of the Enemy, and ſome deſolation by fire and ſword upon one place or other. They mourned (with their black faces) for their own loſſes: yet triumphed and rejoyced in their inhumane, (and many times devilliſh cruelty) to the *Engliſh.* They would boaſt much of their Victories; ſaying, that in two hours time, they had deſtroyed ſuch a Captain, and his Company, in ſuch a place; and ſuch a Captain, and his Company, in ſuch a place; and ſuch a Captain, and his Company, in ſuch a place: and boaſt how many Towns they had deſtroyed, and then ſcoff, and ſay, they had done them a good turn, to ſend them to Heaven ſo ſoon. Again they would ſay, this Summer they would knock all the Rogues in the head, or drive them into the Sea, or make them flie the Country: thinking ſurely, *Agag-like, The bitterneſs of Death is paſt.* Now the *Heathen* begin to think that all is their own, and the poor *Chriſtians* hopes to fail (as to man) and now their eyes are more to God, and their hearts ſigh heaven-ward: and to ſay in good earneſt, *Help Lord, or we periſh*; when the Lord had brought his People to this, that they ſaw no help in any thing but himſelf; then he takes the quarrel into his own hand: and though they had made a pit (in their own imaginations) as deep as hell for the *Chriſtians* that Summer; yet the Lord hurll'd themſelves into it. And the Lord had not ſo many wayes before, to preſerve them, but now he hath as many to deſtroy them.

But to return again to my going home: where we may ſee a remarkable change of providence: at firſt they were all againſt it, except my Husband would come for me; but afterwards they aſſented to it, and ſeemed much to rejoyce in it: ſome asking me to ſend them ſome Bread, others ſome Tobacco, others ſhaking me by the hand, offering me a Hood and Scarf to ride in: not one moving hand or tongue againſt it. Thus hath the Lord anſwered my poor deſires, and the many earneſt requeſts of others put up unto God for me. In my Travels an *Indian* came to me, and told me, if I were willing, he and his Squaw would run away, and go home along with me. I told him, No, I was not willing to run away, but desired to wait Gods time, that I might go home quietly, and without fear. And now God hath granted me my desire. O the wonderful power of God that I have seen, and the experiences that I have had! I have been in the midst of those roaring Lions, and Salvage Bears, that feared neither God, nor Man, nor the Devil, by night and day, alone and in company, sleeping all sorts together; and yet not one of them ever offered the least abuse of unchastity to me, in word or action. Though some are ready to say, I speak it for my own credit; but I speak it in the presence of God, and to his Glory. Gods power is as great now, and as sufficient to save, as when he preserved *Daniel* in the Lions Den, or the three Children in the Fiery Furnace. I may well say, as he, *Psal.* 107. 1,2. *Oh give thanks unto the Lord, for he is good, for his mercy endureth for ever. Let the Redeemed of the Lord say so, whom he hath redeemed from the hand of the Enemy*; especially that I should come away in the midst of so many hundreds of Enemies, quietly and peaceably, and not a Dog moving his tongue. So I took my leave of them, and in coming along my heart melted into Tears, more than all the while I was with them, and I was almost swallowed up with the thoughts that ever I should go home again. About the Suns going down, Mr. *Hoar*, and my self, and the two *Indians* came to *Lancaster*, and a solemn sight it was to me, There had I lived many comfortable years amongst my Relations and Neighbours; and now not one *Christian* to be seen, nor one House left standing. We went on to a Farm-house that was yet standing, where we lay all night; and a comfortable lodging we had, though nothing but straw to lye on. The Lord preserved us in safety that night, and raised us up again in the morning, and carried us along, that before noon we came to *Concord*. Now was I full of joy, and yet not without sorrow: joy, to see such a lovely sight, so many *Christians* together, and some of them my Neighbours: There I met with my Brother, and my Brother in Law, who asked me, if I knew where his Wife was? poor heart! he had helped to bury her, and knew it not; she being shot down by the house, was partly burnt: so that those who were at *Boston* at the desolation of the Town, and came back afterward, and buried the dead, did not know her. Yet I was not without sorrow, to think how many were looking and longing, and my own Children amongst the rest, to enjoy that deliverance that I had now received; and I did not know whether ever I should see them again. Being recruited with Food and Raiment, we went to *Boston* that day: where I met with my dear Husband, but the thoughts of our dear Children, one being dead, and the other we could not tell where, abated our comfort each in other. I was not before so much hem'd in with the merciless and cruel *Heathen*, but now as much with pitiful, tender-hearted, and compassionate *Christians*. In that poor, and distressed, and beggarly condition, I

was

was received in, I was kindly entertained in several houses: so much love I received from several, (some of whom I knew, and others I knew not) that I am not capable to declare it. But the Lord knows them all by name: the Lord reward them seven-fold into their bosoms of his spirituals for their temporals. The twenty pounds, the price of my Redemption, was raised by some *Boston* Gentlewomen, and M. *Usher*, whose bounty and religious charity I would not forget to make mention of. Then, Mr. *Thomas Shepard* of *Charlstown* received us into his House, where we continued elven weeks; and a Father and Mother they were unto us. And many more tender-hearted Friends we met vvith in that place. We vvere novv in the midst of love, yet not without much and frequent heaviness of heart, for our poor Children, and other Relations, vvho vvere still in affliction.

The week following, after my comming in, the Governour and Council sent forth to the *Indians* again; and that not without success; for they brought in my Sister, and Goodwife *Kettle*: Their not knowing where our Children were, was a sore trial to us still, and yet we were not without secret hopes that we should see them again. That which was dead lay heavier upon my spirit, than those which were alive amongst the *Heathen*: thinking how it suffered with its wounds, and I was no way able to relieve it: and how it was buried by the *Heathen* in the Wilderness, from amongst all *Christians*. We were hurried up and down in our thoughts; sometimes we should hear a report that they were gone this way, and sometimes that; and that they were come in, in this place or that: we kept inquiring and listning to hear concerning them, but no certain news as yet. About this time the Council had ordered a day of publick *Thanks-giving*: though I thought I had still cause of mourning; and being unsettled in our minds, we thought we would ride toward the Eastward, to see if we could hear any thing concerning our Children. And as we were riding along (God is the wise disposer of all things) between *Ipswich* and *Rowly* we met with Mr *William Hubbard*, who told us our Son *Joseph* was come in to Major *Waldrens*, and another with him, which was my Sisters Son. I asked him how he knew it? he said the Major himself told me so. So along we went till we came to *Newbury*; and their Minister being absent; they desired my Husband to Preach the *Thanks-giving* for them; but he was not willing to stay there that night, but would go over to *Salisbury*, to hear farther, and come again in the morning; which he did: and Preached there that day. At night, when he had done, one came and told him that his Daughter vvas come at in *Providence*: Here vvas mercy on both hands. Novv hath God fulfilled that precious Scripture, vvhich was such a comfort to me in my distressed condition. When my heart vvas ready to sink into the Earth (my Children being gone I could not tell whither) and my knees trembled under me, and I was vvalking through the valley of the shadow of death: then the Lord brought, and now has

fulfilled

fulfilled that reviving word unto me: *Thus saith the Lord, Refrain thy voice from weeping, and thy eyes from tears, for thy work shall be rewarded, saith the Lord; and they shall come again from the Land of the Enemy.* Now we were between them, the one on the East, and the other on the West: our Son being nearest, we went to him first, to *Portsmouth*, where we met with him, and with the Major also: who told us he had done what he could, but could not redeem him under seven pounds, which the good People thereabouts were pleased to pay. The Lord reward the Major, and all the rest, though unknown to me, for their labour of love. My Sisters Son was redeemed for four pounds, which the Council gave order for the payment of. Having now received one of our Children, we hastened towards the other going back through *Newbury*, my Husband preached there on the Sabbath day: for which they rewarded him manifold.

On Monday we came to *Charlstown*, where we heard that the Governour of *Road-Island* had sent over for our Daughter, to take care of her, being now within his Jurisdiction: which should not pass without our acknowledgments. But she being nearer *Rehoboth* than *Road-Island*, Mr. *Newman* went over, and took care of her, and brought her to his own house. And the goodness of God was admirable to us in our lovv estate; in that he raised up compassionate Friends on every side to us, when we had nothing to recompence any for their love. The *Indians* were now gone that way, that it was apprehended dangerous to go to her: but the Carts which carried Provision to the *English* Army, being guarded, brought her with them to *Dorchester*, where we received her safe: blessed be the Lord for it, *for great is his power, and he can do whatsoever seemeth him good.* Her coming in was after this manner: she was travelling one day with the *Indians*, with her basket at her back; the company of *Indians* were got before her, and gone out of sight, all except one Squaw: she followed the Squaw till night, and then both of them lay down: having nothing over them but the Heavens; nor under them but the Earth. Thus she travelled three days together, not knowing whither she was going: having nothing to eat or drink but water, and green *Hirtleberries*. At last they came into *Providence*, where she was kindly entertained by several of that Town. The *Indians* often said, that I should never have her under twenty pounds: but now the Lord hath brought her in upon free cost, and given her to me the second time. The Lord make us a blessing indeed, each to others. Now have I seen that Scripture also fulfilled, *Deut.* 30. 4, 7. *If any of thine be driven out to the utmost parts of heaven, from thence will the Lord thy God gather thee, and from thence will he fetch thee. And the Lord thy God will put all these curses upon thine enemies, and on them which hate thee, which persecuted thee.* Thus hath the Lord brought me and mine out of that horrible pit, and hath set us in the midst of tender-hearted and compassionate Christians. 'Tis the desire of my soul that we may walk worthy of the mercies received, and which we are receiving.

Our

Our Family being now gathered together (thoſe of us that were living) the South Church in *Boſton* hired an houſe for us: then we removed from Mr. *Shepards* (thoſe cordial Friends) and went to *Boſton*, where we continued about three quarters of a year: Still the Lord went along with us, and provided graciouſly for us. I thought it ſomewhat ſtrange to ſet up Houſe-keeping with bare walls; but as *Solomon* ſays, *Mony anſwers all things*; and that we had through the benevolence of *Chriſtian* friends, ſome in this Town, and ſome in that, and others; and ſome from *England*; that in a little time we might look, and ſee the houſe furniſhed with love. The Lord hath been exceeding good to us in our low eſtate, in that when we had neither houſe nor home, nor other neceſſaries, the Lord ſo moved the hearts of theſe and thoſe towards us, that we wanted neither food, nor rayment, for our ſelves or ours, Prov. 18. 24. *There is a Friend which ſticketh cloſer than a Brother.* And how many ſuch Friends have we found, and now living amongſt? and truly ſuch a Friend have we found him to be unto us, in vvhoſe houſe vve lived, *viz.* Mr. *James Whitcomb*, a Friend unto us near hand, and afar off.

I can remember the time, vvhen I uſed to ſleep quietly vvithout vvorkings in my thoughts, vvhole nights together: but novv it is othervviſe vvith me. When all are faſt about me, and no eye open, but his vvho ever waketh, my thoughts are upon things paſt, upon the awful diſpenſations of the Lord towards us; upon his wonderful power and might in carrying us through ſo many difficulties, in returning us in ſafety, and ſuffering none to hurt us. I remember in the night ſeaſon, how the other day I was in the midſt of thouſands of enemies, and nothing but death before me: it was then hard work to perſwade my ſelf, that ever I ſhould be ſatisfied with bread again. But now we are fed with the fineſt of the Wheat, and (as I may ſo ſay) with honey out of the rock: Inſtead of the husks, we have the fatted Calf: the thoughts of theſe things in the particulars of them, and of the love and goodneſs of God towards us, make it true of me, what *David* ſaid of himſelf, *Pſal.* 6. 6. *I water my Couch with my tears.* Oh the wonderful power of God that mine eyes have ſeen, affording matter enough for my thoughts to run in, that when others are ſleeping mine eyes are weeping.

I have ſeen the extream vanity of this World: one hour I have been in health, and wealth, wanting nothing: but the next hour in ſickneſs, and wounds, and death, having nothing but ſorrow and affliction.

Before I knew what affliction meant, I was ready ſometimes to wiſh for it. When I lived in proſperity; having the comforts of this World about me, my Relations by me, and my heart chearful: and taking little care for any thing; and yet ſeeing many (whom I preferred before my ſelf) under many trials and afflictions, in ſickneſs, weakneſs, poverty, loſſes, croſſes, and cares of the World, I ſhould be ſometimes jealous leaſt I ſhould have my portion in this life; and that Scripture would come to my mind, *Heb.* 12. 6. *For whom the Lord loveth he chaſteneth, and ſcourgeth every Son whom he receiveth*;

but

but now I see the Lord had his time to scourge and chasten me. The portion of some is to have their Affliction by drops, now one drop and then another; but the dregs of the Cup, the wine of astonishment, like a sweeping rain that leaveth no food, did the Lord prepare to be my portion. Affliction I wanted, and Affliction I had, full measure (I thought) pressed down and running over: yet I see when God calls a person to any thing, and through never so many difficulties, yet he is fully able to carry them through, and make them see and say they have been gainers thereby. And I hope I can say in some measure, as *David* did, *It is good for me that I have been afflicted.* The Lord hath shewed me the vanity of these outward things, that they are the *Vanity of vanities, and vexation of spirit*; that they are but a shadow, a blast, a bubble, and things of no continuance; that we must rely on God himself, and our whole dependance must be upon him. If trouble from smaller matters begin to arise in me, I have something at hand to check my self with, and say when I am troubled, It was but the other day, that if I had had the world, I would have given it for my Freedom, or to have been a Servant to a *Christian.* I have learned to look beyond present and smaller troubles, and to be quieted under them, as *Moses* said, *Exod.* 14. 13. *Stand still, and see the salvation of the Lord.*

FINIS.

A

SERMON

Preached at *Weathersfield*, *Nov.* 21. 1678. By Mr. *Joseph Rowlandson*, it being a day of Fasting and Humiliation.

The Preface.

To the Courteous READER, (especially the Inhabitants of the Town of *Weathersfield*, and *Lancaster*, in *New-England.*

GOds forsaking of such as he hath been near to, is a thing of such weight, and solemnity, and hath such bitter effects, that it is a meet Subject, (especially in a dark and mourning day) for Ministers to speak to, and for People to hear of: that the one may warn of the danger, and the other avoid the judgment. As Gods presence is the greatest glory to a People on this side Heaven, so his absence is the greatest misery on this side hell; this therefore must needs be a concerning point, to such as will concern themselves in their concernments. The ensuing Sermon *will appear a solemn word, if duly considered: the subject matter is very solemn and weighty, (Treating of Gods being with, or forsaking a people) the time when it was delivered was a solemn time, (a day of* FAST *throughout the Collonies) the reverend* Author *that composed, and Preached it; was one solemn and serious above many others, and that which adds one great circumstance to its solemnity, is, in that it was the last word he spake to the World, being but about two dayes before he left it. As it is solemn, so 'tis seasonable, and pertinent. It is a time wherein we have given God just cause to forsake us, a time wherein God is threatning to forsake us. A time wherein God hath in some measure forsaken us already, and what can be more seasonable, than to shew the evils that befall a forsaken People, that we may yet be awakened, and re— that the Lord do not forsake us utterly.*

As for the Reverend Author, *there needs nothing to be said in his commendation, he was known amongst the Churches in the Wilderness, and known to be a workman that needed not to be ashamed. That his Name (which was sometimes precious amongst those that knew him) may not be forgot, and that being dead he may yet speak to a land that have in some measure forsook their God, and are in danger of being forsaken, is the ground-work of the publishing this small part of his labours. It is commended especially to the perusal of the Inhabitants of* Lancaster *and* Weathersfield: *He was a man well known to you, the one had his Life, the other his death, and both his loss; you cannot easily forget his name, and 'tis desired that you may not forget the labour and travel he hath had amongst you; the Word which he Preached to you was acceptable whilst he was living, and it is presumed it will be accepted with the like candor now he is dead. Indeed had it been intended and fitted by himself for the Press, you might have expected and found it more large and pollished; but as it is, it is thought fit not to be lost, and may be of great use, and benefit, to open to us the danger of forsaking God, to humble us for all our coolings, and declinings from God, to quicken us in our return to, and close walking with God. And that it may attain this end, is the hearts desire, and prayer of him, who abundantly wishes thy welfare, and prosperity in Christ Jesus.*

B. W.

Jeremiah

Jeremiah 23. 33.

And when this People, or the Prophet, or a Priest, shall ask thee, saying, What is the burden of the Lord? thou shalt then say unto them, What burden? I will even forsake you, saith the Lord.

IN the Words there lies before us, *(First)* A Question, supposed to be propounded, wherein there is two things: 1. The Questionists, this People, or a Prophet, or a Priest: 2. The Question it self, or the matter of it, *What is the burden of the Lord?* *(Secondly,)* There is an Answer, and a solemn Answer too, which is put into his mouth by the Lord, and which he is to return as the Lords Answer to the Question; *Thou shalt then say unto them, What burden? I will even forsake you, saith the Lord.*

In which Answer there is three things.

1. An expression of Indignation, *What burden?*
2. An Assertion, by way of Answer to the Question, *I will forsake you.*
3. A Seal of ratification, in the last words, *Saith the Lord.*

God having before dealt with the Pastors, that did destroy, and scatter the flock, as in the beginning of the Chapter, *Wo be to the Pastors that destroy and scatter the sheep of my pasture*, & ver 2. *I will visit upon you the evil of your doings, saith the Lord*: and also with the false Prophets, *that prophesie lies in his Name*, as ver. 9. *My heart within me is broken because of all the Prophets*, & ver. 32. *Behold I am against them that prophesie false dreams, saith the Lord, and do tell them, and cause my people to erre by their lies, and by their lightness*: which sort of Prophets went without their Commission, as *ver.* 21. *I have not sent these Prophets, yet they ran.* He proceeds from the head Rulers, to the people that were seduced by them: for by this means their hands were strengthened in sin, so as that they did not return from their wickedness, as *ver.* 14. It was an usual thing for the Prophets of the Lord to begin their Sermons (the matter whereof was minatory, wherein the Lord threatned them with just judgements) with that Phrase, *The burden of the Lord*, as will easily appear if you consult, *Isai.* 13. 1 & 15. 1. & 22. 1. & 30 6 Now they do in the words of the Text, or are supposed in mockery to demand, what *Burden* he had from the Lord, for them?

For the opening of the words; *And* or *moreover*, because he enters upon new matter: *this People*, or the prophane sort of them, whom the False Prophets had seduced; to which he joyns the Prophet, and the Priest, in that they

 were

were alike prophane, as *ver.* 11. *for both Prophet and Priest are prophane, yea in my house,* saith the Lord: and when Prophets are prophane there is wont to be a pack of them, as *Jer.* 5. 31. *The Prophets prophesie falsly, and the Priests bear rule by their means; and my people love to have it so:* shall ask thee saying, *viz.* in a deriding way, not out of a holy end, or desire, *What is the burden of the Lord? or from the Lord?* so were the Prophesies stiled, that contained in them, *Threatnings, Judgments, and Plagues,* 2 King. 9. 25. as if they had said; *what hast thou further mischief in thy head to declare? further Woes and Threatnings to pronounce? hast thou nothing else to prophesie, but Mischief and Calamity? What is the burden now?* Thou shalt then say unto them, the Lord knew what they would say to him, and tells him what he should say, by way of reply, *What burden?* a retorting by way of holy indignation; ask ye indeed, *what burden?* and that in a way of derision; are you of that strain, and spirit? I will even forsake you saith the Lord: a burden heavy enough, and you are like to feel it so ere long, heavy enough to break your Backs, to break your Church, and your Common-wealth, and to sink your haughty Spirits, when this Burden shall come upon you, in its force and weight.

Doct. *That the Lord may even forsake a People that have been near to him, and he hath been near to, though for the Lord thus to do, is as fearful and hideous a judgment as can be inflicted on any People.*

The Doctrine is double, it hath two parts:

First, That the Lord may do thus.

Secondly, When he doth, it is a very sad and heavy burden. It may be prosecuted as two distinct points.

1. God may forsake a People that hath been near to him, and that he hath been near to. This may be spoken to in this order.

1. What is meant by Gods forsaking a People.

2. How may it appear that God may forsake even such a People as the point speaks of?

3. The Reasons.

4. The use.

1. What doth Gods forsaking mean? what is intended thereby?

Sol. It means Gods withdrawing himself, as the Prophet *Hosea* phraises it, *Hos.* 5. 6. *They shall go with their Flocks and their Herds to seek the Lord, but shall not find him, he hath withdrawn himself from them.* They shall seek him, and not find him, and there is a good reason, he hath withdrawn himself, he is gone, in respect of his gracious presence. We must here distinguish betwixt Gods general presence, and his precious presence. In respect of his general presence, he is not far from any one of us, *for in him we live, and move, and have our being, Act.* 17. 27, 28. We have not only our beginning from, but our being in him. As the beam hath its being in the Sun. Of this general presence of

God,

God, we read, *Psal.* 139. 7. There is no flying from it. *Whither shall I go from thy Spirit, Or whither shall I flie from thy presence?* In this sense God is every where, as it is *ver.* 8, & 9. *If I ascend up into Heaven thou art there: if I make my bed in hell behold thou art there.* He fills Heaven and Earth, and there is no hiding from him, *Jer.* 23. 24. *Can any hide himself in secret places, that I shall not see him? saith the Lord: do not I fill Heaven and Earth? saith the Lord.* He hath Heaven for his Throne, and the Earth for his Footstool, as it is, *Isai* 66. 1. This general presence of God, if believingly apprehended, and strongly believed, might be of Great use.

But it is not this general presence that is meant: but his especial presence, his favourable and gracious presence, the removing whereof, is that that is intended, by the forsaking that the Text and Point speaks of. God is said to forsake a People two wayes.

1. As to affection.

2. As to Action.

1. As to Affection, when he discontinues his love to them, when he takes away his love from a people, then he takes his leave of a people, *My mind is not toward this people,* Jer. 15. 1. a very heavy Judgement, and sad removal. Be instructed, O *Jerusalem, lest my Soul depart from thee.*

2. As to Action, when God takes away the signs of his presence.

1. When he takes away merciful and gracious providences, when he carries not towards them as he was wont to do: but vexes them with all manner of adversity, *Deut.* 31. 17. *I will forsake them, and many evils and troubles shall befall them*: when he ceases to protect them from evils, and enemies, as in times past, and provides not for them, as he was wont to do. When he takes away his Ordinances, and bereaves a people of the glorious things of his house; or take away his spirit from accompanying them, whereby the glory ceases, and the ordinances are rendered ineffectual for the saving good of a people.

2. How may it appear that God may forsake such a People?

It may appear by what God hath threatned. What God hath threatned, to such as the point speaks of, may be inflicted on them: but God hath threatned such judgments to such a people. My anger shall be kindled against them, and I will forsake them, as near as they are to me, and as dear as they have been to me, *Deut.* 31. 17. Many such threatnings are found in the Scripture against *Israel*, who are stiled a people near unto him.

In that such as have been near to God, and he near to them, have complained of their being forsaken by God. Thou hast forsaken us, is one of the bitter moans, on record, that the Church of God did often make unto him.

What God hath inflicted on such, may be inflicted on such again; what God hath done to some, he may do to others, in the same state, and relation: for he is unchangeable. Those that were once the only peculiar people of God, near to God, and had God near to them, yet what is their conditi-

Shen.

on at this day? A forsaken condition is the condition of the Offspring of *Abraham* Gods Friend, a seed whom he had chosen, and hath been so for above sixteen hundred years. God hath been Angry with them, and forsaken them, as they were foretold long ago. Hovv is it vvith the Churches of *Asia*, that vvere once famous golden Candlesticks? that had Epistles vvritten to them? Are they not in a forsaken condition? not the face of a Church to be found amongst them.

In that they may do that vvhich may deserve a forsaking, therefore they may do that vvhich may actually procure it. They may do that vvhich may deserve a forsaking, they may through the corruption and unbelief of their hearts forsake God, and God may in just judgement retaliate, and thereupon forsake them. This is spoken to in the forequoted place, *Deut.* 31. 16, 17. *They will forsake me, and break my Covenant which I have made with them: then my anger shall be kindled against them in that day, and I will forsake them, and hide my face from them.* So again, 2 Chron. 15. 2. *But if you forsake him, he will forsake you*; the first is supposed, *if you forsake him*; the latter is imposed, *he will forsake you.*

But vvhy doth the Lord forsake such a People? The Reasons:

1. To shevv that he hath no need of any, he hath forsaken many, and may forsake many more, to shevv that he hath no need of any. God vvould have all the vvorld to take notice, (that though all men have need of him, yet) he hath no need of any man.

2. To testifie his Sanctity, and severity against sin. He vvill not spare them that have been near him, if they vvill not spare their sin for him. He is a holy God, and if they vvill have their sins, and their lusts, and their vvays, and their lovers, he will vindicate his holiness, by inflicting his judgment on them.

3. To be a vvarning to all that enjoy his gracious presence. That they see they make much of it, and that they take heed that they do not sin against him and forsake him, and provoke him to forsake them also.

Caut. The point is to be understood of a people that are visibly and externally near and dear to him, and these may be totally and finally forsaken of God: and yet here it must be noted, that God may exercise a deal of patience, and forbearance toward such as he is about to forsake; he did so with the old world, he did so with the *Israelites* of old; he did so with the seven Churches of *Asia*: he is not wont suddenly, and at once to forsake a people that have been near and dear to him; but he is wont to give them warning, and in patience to bear a while with their frowardness, and wait to see if there be any returning to him, before he doth inflict this heavy and sharp judgement.

Use. It serves to admonish us, not to bear our selves too high, upon the account of priviledges. It is a great priviledge to have the Lord near us, and to be near unto him: and some lean upon this, though they abide in their

him.

in, *Micah* 3. 10, 11. *They build up Sion with blood, and Jerusalem with iniquity, yet will they lean upon the Lord, and say, Is not the Lord amongst us?* But if our deportment be not according to our priviledges, if we do not carry it thereafter, by becoming an humble, fruitful, and holy people; the Lord will bring forth this heavy burden against us, we shall be rejected, and forsaken of the Lord, whatever our external priviledges be.

But the second part of the Doctrine, or the second Doctrine, may be now spoken to, *viz.*

That it is the heaviest burden, or the sorest of Judgments, for the Lord to forsake a people.

There may be two things spoken to in the management of this Truth. 1. Arguments to evidence it. 2. The Uses of it.

1. If God hath threatned it as a very sore judgment, then sure it is so. Now when God hath been angry with a people, he hath manifested the same by menacing them with his forsaking them: when he hath been designed to do them a deep displeasure, upon the account of some high provocation, he is wont to threaten them, not by taking away this or that outward comfort from them; but by taking away himself from them.

And that is a woe indeed, a woe with a witness, *Hos.* 9. 12. *Yea, woe also to them when I depart from them:* This is the wofullest day that such a people are wont to meet with.

2. Gods forsaking a People is a sore judgment, in that it exposes them to all judgements. Sin is a great evil, in that it exposes to all evil; this is a great evil of punishment, in that it exposes to all punishments. If God be gone, our guard is gone, and we are as a City in the midst of Enemies, whose walls are broken down. Our strength to make resistance, that's gone, for God is our strength. As a carcase without life, is a pray to beasts of prey; so are a people forsaken of their God, to all their devouring enemies, and to infernal and cursed spirits: they are exposed to mischief, and the Malice of all their malignant enemies. When the Lord had forsaken *Jerusalem*, the *Romans* quickly made a prey of it; when they were destitute of God, their habitation became desolate. There is no Protection to a People whom the Lord forsakes; but they are perplexed on every side.

3. Because the evils that are on such whom God hath forsaken, they are only evils. The Prophet *Ezekiel* sometime hath the expression, *Ezek.* 7. 5. *Thus saith the Lord God, An evil, an only evil, behold, is come.* This is such an evil, an only evil to a people. An evil, whilst God is present, may have much good in it, the Lord may sancti[illegible] it for abundance of blessing: there is hopes of this whilst the Lord continues amongst them; but if he be gone, it is an only evil, and the evils that come upon them are such, they have nothing but evil in them.

4. Because no creature can then afford any help; for what can creatures do when

when God is departed; he makes the Creatures useful and helpful, but without him they can do us no good, stand us in no stead: they may say to thee, as the King of *Israel* said to the Woman, that cried *Help O King*, He answered, *If the Lord dont help, whence shall I help thee?* all creatures may say if God be departed, *we cannot help*: Nay the very Devil cannot help, if God be gone: when God departed from *Saul*, he sought help from the Devil, 1 *Sam.* 28. 15. *Wherefore* (saith the Devil) *askest thou of me? seeing the Lord is departed from thee.*

5. It appears to be a sore judgement, by the anguish and distress, that such have been in, that have been sensible that God hath forsaken them. Sin hath flown in the face of such, and terrified them: Oh the blessed God is gone, and if he is gone, mercy is gone; and Oh for such and such sins, that ly upon me! what shall I do? what a moan have Saints themselves made in such a case? as *David*, Psal. 22. 1, 2. *My God, my God, why hast thou forsaken me? why art thou so far from helping me? and from the words of my roaring? Oh my God, I cry in the day time, but thou hearest not, and in the night season, and am not silent.* Oh how *Saul* roared out his distress! and that on this account especially, that God was departed from him, not so much that the *Philistines* were upon him, had not God been gone, he could have dealt well enough with them; but here was the misery, and the sting of the misery, *God was departed from him.*

6. It is a sore punishment, in that it is a great part of the punishment of Hell. The essential parts of that punishment, is pain of loss, and sense, and the former some reckon the greater.

Use 1. How foolish are sinners that do even bid God depart from them? as we read, *Job* 21. 14 *Therefore they say unto God, depart from us, for we desire not the knowledge of thy wayes.* But do they know what they say? Oh sinners is this your wish? if it be granted, it will prove your woe for ever. Happily Gods presence is now your trouble; but I tell you his absence would be your torment.

2. See here what an evil it is to forsake God; is it a judgment of judments to be forsaken of God? surely then it is the sin of sins to forsake him: the evil of punishment is in being left by God, and the evil of sin is in leaving God. What, forsake God, who is our only good? God who made us, and possest us from our beginning, God that hath been the guide of our Youth, that hath been good to us, and fed us all our dayes? *Jer.* 2. 19. *Know therefore and see, that it is an evil thing and bitter, that thou hast forsaken the Lord thy God.* And there is an aggravation of it, *ver.* 17. *Thou hast forsaken the Lord thy God, when he led thee by the way.* As a guide to direct thee, as a staff to support thee, as a convoy to guard thee, as a Father to provide for thee, that thou hast wanted nothing: well may it be said, *how evil and bitter a thing is it*; that thou hast forsaken the Lord? He adds in the 31. *verse. Oh Generation!* Generation of what? of what you will; God leaves a space that you may write what you please, generation of Vipers, or Monsters, or any thing rather then Ge-

nera-

neration of Gods people. See the word of the Lord, behold your face in that Glass. So your causless apostasies, have I been a Wilderness unto *Israel*? Have you wanted any thing; Oh ye degenerating, crooked, and wilful generation? God may say to such sinners, as *Pharaoh* to *Hadad*, when he would be gone, 1 *King*. 11. 22. *But what hast thou lacked with me, that thou seekest to be gone?* what hast thou laked sinner, that thou seekest to be gone from the Lord? the sinner must answer with him, Nothing, howbeit let me go in any wise. He came to him in his distress, and when his turn was answered, away he packs. They forsake because they will forsake.

3. Wonder not that Gods Saints have been so solicitous with him, not to forsake them. Thus *David*, *Psal.* 119. 8. *Oh forsake me not utterly.* He might well be solicitous in this matter, for he understood what it was to be forsaken of the Lord. They press hard with the Lord, whatever he doth, he would not leave them, nor forsake them, *Jer.* 14. 9. *Leave us not.* And no wonder, there are such means, when the Lord may have seemed to have forsake them.

4. If Gods forsaking be so sore a judgment, it should make us more cautelous, and wary lest we pull down this judgment on our heads Men should be afraid of this heaviest of judgments, more than the Child of whipping.

5. Let Gods dear ones take heed of concluding against themselves, that they are under this judgment. They are readiest to conclude against themselves, and yet really in the least danger. Thus we read, *Isa.* 49. 14. *But Zion said, The Lord hath forsaken me, and my Lord hath forgotten me.* But why said *Zion so*? it was from diffidence: as Saints do not forsake God as others do, *Psal.* 18. 21. *I have not wickedly departed from my God*: so God will not forsake them as he forsakes others, not utterly forsake them: His forsaking of his is but temporary and partial.

But here a question may be moved, What is the difference betwixt a sinner forsaken, and a Saint forsaken? for the Lord doth not forsake both alike. 1. When God forsakes his own, yet they cry after him, he withdraws himself from them sometimes, yet so as that he draws their hearts after him, as a Mother may hide away from her Child, that it may seek and cry the more earnestly after her. 2. They retain good thoughts of him in his withdrawment, or absence. As the Spouse in the *Canticles*, she calls him her beloved still. As the faithfnl Wife, she retains good thoughts of her Husband, and keeps up her respect, though he be gone from home: but the wicked, when the Lord forsakes them, harbour hard thoughts of him. Is this to serve the Lord, and walk in his ways? what good have I got by all I have done? see how he hath served me.

3. They will seek him till he return again: when the Lord forsakes others, they vvill seek after vanities, to make up the vvant of Gods presence. The Adultress in her Husbands absence, vvill seek after other lovers. The true Saint vvill be satisfied in nothing else but the Lord till he return. Moreover there is a difference in Gods forsaking the sinner, and the Saint; vvhen he

 forsakes

the wicked, they are left in darkness: but when he withdraws from his own, he leaves some light, whereby they see which way he is gone, he leaves some glimmering light, by which they may follow after him, and find him.

And again, when he leaves his own, yet his bowels are towards them, *Jer.* 31. 20. *My bowels are troubled for him, I will surely have mercy upon him, saith the Lord*, He hath an eye towards them for much good, in his forsaking them.

Use 2. Of *Exhortation*: 1. To thankfulness to God, for that he hath not yet forsaken us. Whatever he hath stript us of, he hath not yet stript us of himself, he hath not as yet forsaken us. He might have done it, and have done us no wrong; but he hath not yet done it.

2. To do our utmost that he may not forsake us. And here there may be added Motives and Means.

1. Consider Gods lothness to forsake us. This is a thing that he is not desirous of, he doth not willingly afflict us with this sort of Affliction, or grieve us with this grievous stroak. God hath shewed himself loth to depart from those that have departed from him; but hath warned them of his displeasure, that they might stay him. It goes near Gods heart to forsake a People that have been near to him. Methinks I hear him saying thus, *How shall I give thee up, O New-England*! thence speaking to warn us, of our forsakings of him, and to be instructed, why? lest his Spirit depart from us, *Jer.* 6. 8. *Be thou instructed*, O Jerusalem, *lest my Soul depart from thee, lest I make thee desolate, a Land not inhabited.* You may easily stay him, the matter is not so far gone, but you might yet stay him: were we but as loth he should forsake us, as he is to forsake us, he would never leave us. His gradual motions from a people argue his lothness, and unwillingness to leave them.

2. Consider what the Lord is to us, or what relation he stands in to us, while he is with us. He is our friend, we have found him to be so, and a special friend too: men in the World are not willing to forego a Friend, a good Friend: he is as faithful, skilful, powerful, and tender-hearted a Friend as ever a People had, he stuck by us when also we had been in a woe case, *Psal.* 124. 1. *If it had not been the Lord who was on our side, may Israel now say.* And had not the Lord been or our side, may *New-England* now say. He is a Father, and a tender-hearted Father, *Isai.* 63. 16. *Doubtless thou art our Father.* Can Children be willing their Father should leave them? he is a Husband, *Isai.* 54. 5. *For thy Maker is thy Husband*, a loving, careful, tender Husband too; can the Wife be willing to part with her Husband? If the Lord forsake us, we are bereft of our Friend, left friendless, he is all friends in one, none can be our friend, if he be not. If he leave us, we shall be as Orphans, for he is related as a Father, and how sad is the state of Poor Orphans? and we shall be in a state of Widow-hood, a very solitary, and sorrowful state. He is our Guide, and our Pilot; what will become of the blind if their guide leave them? and what will become of the Ship if the Pilot desert it? Thus the Lord is to his, and well may he say, as *Mic.* 6. 3. *O my People, what have I done? or wherein have I wearied thee, or given thee any cause to be weary of me?* 3. Con-

3. Conſider there are ſhrewd ſigns of Gods intent to leave us, unleſs ſomewhat be done. If you enquire what? I anſwer:

1. The ſins for which God hath forſaken others are rife amongſt us. The ſins for which God forſook the Jews, are our ſins.

1. *Horrid Pride*, Hoſ. 5. 5. *The Pride of* Iſrael *doth teſtifie to his face.* Pride in Parts, and pride of Hearts, pride in Apparel, and Veſtures, and in Geſtures, and in Looks, how lofty are their Eyes! *New-England* is taken notice of abroad, for as proud a People, of a profeſſing People, as the World affords.

When a People are humble the Lord will ſtay with them. If our immunities, which are Gods mercies, puff us up, God will empty us: he will blaſt that to us that we are proud of.

2. *Deep and high Ingratitude.* Do you thus requite the Lord? *Deut.* 32.6. So the Prophet *Hoſea* taxes them, *Hoſ.* 2. 8. *God gave her Corn, and Wine, and Oyl, Silver and Gold, but ſhe conſumed them on* Baal. We have been bleſt, but hath God had the glory of our bleſſings?

3. *Oppreſſion.* *Amos* 8. 4. *Ye that ſwallow up the needy.* Theſe Jews were like the Fiſhes, the greater did devour the leſs. Some are like wild Beaſts, like Wolves that tear off the fleece, and eat the fleſh of the Flocks. There is more juſtice to be found in Hell, than amongſt ſome men on Earth: for there is no innocent perſon oppreſſed there.

4. *Wearineſs of Gods Ordinances.* Amos 8. 5. *When will the Sabbath be done?* They that are weary of the ſervice of God, and the Ordinances of God, they are weary of God. God indeed hath fed us to the full as to Ordinances: and we are glutted, and ſurfeited, and have loſt our eſteem.

When mens Commodities bear but a little price in a place, they will remove the Market: if Goſpel-Ordinances are but a cheap Commodity, have loſt their price, and men are weary of them, God will let out his Vineyard to another People. If our mercies become our burdens, God will eaſe us of them.

5. Couſenage in mens dealings, making the Ephah ſmall, and the Shekel great, ſelling the refuſe of Wheat, *Amos* 8. 5, 6. *They pick out the beſt Grain for themſelves, and the refuſe is to ſell.*

6. Idolatry, which is Spiritual Adultery, and is there nothing of this? chuſing of new Gods.

7. Incorrigibleneſs, or oppoſition of a ſpirit of reformation. When God calls to a People to return, by repentance, but they will go on ſtill in their Sin: God calls them by his judgments, and by his Rod; but they will not hear, as 'tis *Jer.* 5. 3. *Thou haſt ſtricken them, but they have not grieved; thou haſt conſumed them, but they have refuſed to receive Correction; they have made their faces harder than a Rock, they have refuſed to return.* When it is thus with a People, God will pluck up and be gone; ſo *Jer.* 7. 13, 14. *Becauſe they would not hear, and would not anſwer the call of God, I will do to this Houſe, as I did to*

Shiloh. Why what did the Lord do to Shiloh? ver. 12. *Go to* Shiloh, *and see what I did to it, for the wickedness of my People Israel.* Go, and view it, and you will see what he did, he left tokens of his wrath upon them, and forsook them.

2. Another sign of his intent to forsake us, is, in that he is dealing with us as he is wont to deal with them that he is about to forsake. He takes away those that are mostly with him. He will take away his *Moses*'s, those that stand in the Gap, and binds his hands with their Prayers, when he is designed to pour out Wrath upon a People: he will remove the lights, when he is about to darken a Land. When men send away their Plate, and Jewels, and choice things; it intimates their intention of Removal.

3. Another sign is our Luke-warmness, and Indifference in Religion: a usual fore-runnner of its removal. When a People care not for God, and the things of God, he hath left them in some measure, already; and if that Spirit abide, he will not tarry long with them.

Use. 1. Of *Direction*. 1. Examine and humble your selves, for all your departures from God, your forsakings of him; humble your selves for them, confessing with bitterness your evil therein, bemoaning your selves before the Lord upon the account thereof. May the Lord hear his People, from *Dan* to *Beersheba*, bemoaning themselves, *Ephraim*-like; then the Lord will hear, and have mercy, and not leave us, for his Names sake.

2. Judge your selves worthy to be forsaken, because of your forsaking of him. If you judge your selves worthy to be forsaken, God will not judge you worthy to be forsaken, 1 *Cor*. 11. 31.

3. Pray the Lord not to forsake you, the Lord is sometimes staid with Prayers: Prayers have prevailed with His Majesty often, and may do again.

4. Forsake your sins, whereby you have forsaken him. Nothing less than this will prevent this mischief, coming upon us. If there be any, either Son or Daughter, that will not leave their sins for God, God will leave such.

FINIS.

A Narrative of God's Gracious Dealings (Wing A 1025), shelfmark 1415.a.10, is reproduced by permission of The British Library. The text block of the original measures 122 × 70 mm.

A

NARRATIVE

34

OF

God's Gracious Dealings

With that Choice Christian

Mrs. *HANNAH ALLEN*,

(Afterwards Married to Mr. *Hatt*,)

RECITING

The great Advantages the Devil made of her deep Melancholy, and the Triumphant Victories, Rich and Sovereign Graces, God gave her over all his Stratagems and Devices.

O Lord! I am oppressed, undertake for me. Esay xxx. 14.

We are not ignorant of his Devices. 2 Cor. ii. 11.

London, Printed by *John Wallis*. 1683.

TO THE READER.

THE Soul of Man hath a singular affection for its own Body, rejoycing in its Prosperity, and sympathizing with it in all its Maladies, Miseries, and Necessities: Hence if the Body be out of frame and tune, the Soul cannot be well at ease: As the most skilful Musician cannot make any pleasing melody upon an unstringed or broken Instrument.

ment. The blood and humours are the Souls Organs, by which it doth exert its actions. If these be well temper'd and kept in a balance, Ordinarily there is an inward calm serenity upon the Spirit. Ordinarily I say: For in some cases the most chearful Temper may be broken down and overwhelmed either by the immediate impressions of God's wrath upon the Soul, or the letting loose of those Bandogs of Hell to affright and terrifie it. This is no strange News to any one acquainted with the Scriptures, or the Records of the Church in its several Ages, or that hath been conversant with the most humble, serious and mortified Christians. Infinite Wisdom hath seen it fitting to keep his Saints from Hell for

ever.

ever, by casting them as it were into Hell for a time. It being too much for the choicest Saints to have two Heavens, one in Earth, and another in Glory. Flesh is kept from Putrefaction by powdring it in Salt and Brine: and Gold loseth nothing of its Worth by being melted in the Furnace. To wave the broken bones of David, *the terrors and distractions of* Heman, *the groans, chatterings, mournings and pressing oppressions of* Hezekiah; *That Mirrour of Patience,* Job, *will tell us how much he suffered and that immediately too from God and his own God. He had as well as Father* Abraham, *an horrour of great darkneß upon him. He was skared with Visions, terrified with Dreams, the poysoned Arrows of the Almighty were ſhot into his very Soul, the venom whereof drank up his ſpirits, and made him chooſe Strangling rather than Life. Poſſibly he had his Temptations to Self-murder as well as ſome others fearing God under horrour. Hence you need not wonder at their impatiency, and in their agonies at blaſphemous expreſſions. When I have heard from the mouth of an eminent and holy Miniſter of Chriſt, that once counted himſelf a Reprobate, undone and to be damn'd for ever, and was no longer able to ſubſiſt under the weight and burden of Everlaſting and Almighty Wrath, (and who indeed can, if God ſhould let it out upon him?)* That he hated God, yea hated him perfectly, becauſe he was his

Judge and Adversary, tho' a most loving and tender-hearted Father to his Saints; *When I read of miserable* Spira's wishing himself above God; *I do not in the least strange at such intemperate expressions, considering that God, and their Enemy doth blow the Coals, and it may be dictate the very words to them.*

Christian Reader, *Peruse such Instances as these, and* this of a Now-glorified Soul presented to thee, *with fear and trembling. How knowest thou but it may be thine own Case? Let him that standeth take heed lest he fall. The peace, the comforts, the quiet, the joys natural and spiritual, they are all from Grace; you have no longer a Lease of them, no longer term of injoying them than the good will and pleasure of him that dwelt in the burning Bush. If God revoke his own gifts, hide his face, let loose the Tempter, awaken that sleeping Fury in thy bosom, let down but the smallest drop of his Wrath into thy Conscience, thy foundations will be shaken, and the mountain of thy peace will be hurled into a gulf of dismal sorrows.*

Learn then to hate Sin, all Sin bitterly and implacably, to avoid it universally and continually. Be humble and vile in thine own eyes, and walk humbly with thy God. Set upon a through Reformation. Because of Leviathan's *up-raising himself, the Mighty are afraid; by reason of breakings, the very Sinners purify themselves. God cau-*

tions

tions Saints, and alarms Sinners by such flaming Beacons. If these things be done in the green Tree, what will not be done in the dry? Keep no Idol, and beware of making inward comfort an Idol. This provokes God to Jealousy. The Christian's Life is not a life of Sense but of Faith. We walk by Faith, saith the Apostle, and not by sight. Faith closing with the precious Promises, feeding upon the All-sufficient Merits of an unseen Jesus, bringeth in through the holy Ghost, peace, that peace of God, which passeth all understanding, into the Believer's Soul. But then too, this Faith doth purify the Heart, expelleth all inward filth, conniveth, indulgeth not unto any the least sin; but puts the Soul up-

on skirmishing with it, and gets through the power of Christ, victory over it. Otherwise the troubles will return, as the Clouds after the Rain. The least briss in the Eye shall create grief. The least core of bitterness in the Wound shall cause it wrankle afresh. The smallest leak in the Ship, not seen, will sink it; and as multitudes have been killed with Swords and Canons, so others with Stillettoes and Needles, with what the injudicious Worldling calls a Peccadillo, lurking in the Soul.

Walk then, Christian Reader, *in thine integrity. He that walketh uprightly walketh safely. Live still in dependance upon thy Crucified Lord. All thy springs are in him, all thy streams are from him. With joy shall you draw waters of Conso-*

Consolations, reviving Cordials from the wounds of thy dear and dying Saviour. Hide thy self always in the clefts of that blessed Rock of Ages, and thou wilt find there as all the Saints have done in all Ages, a glorious high Throne of Sovereign Mercy for thy sanctuary. The secret of the Lord is with them that fear him, and unto such will he reveal his Covenant. Love the Lord Jesus intirely, supremely and transcendently; and remember that such as love him shall be beloved and saved by him.

As to Scoffers and Mockers at such Relations, that Burlesque and Ridicule these great Instances of Divine Providence, I shall say nothing but that 'tis the Sin of our Age, foretold 1600 Years ago, accomplished

plished in our Days, and an Exercise for the present, and possibly for surviving Saints. Here is the Faith and Patience of Saints, to keep the Testimony of Jesus, and walk Evenly in his ways in the midst of thorns and precipices, and when they are reputed the Worlds Monsters, and the Drunkards Song for so doing. Laugh he that laughs last. The Saints are in heaviness through many Afflictions and Desertions for a little time; but Sinners shall be at last overwhelmed by them for evermore. Their joyful Comedy will have a most Tragick issue. Our blessed Lord hath inform'd his Disciples, that they should weep and lament, but the World should rejoyce; that they should be sorrowful, but their Sorrow

row should be turned into Joy, and their Joy no man should take from them. But the wicked is driven away in his wickedness: Before the Pots can feel the thorns, God shall take them away as with a Whirl-wind, both living and in his wrath.

Thy Soul-friend and

Servant for *Jesus* sake.

London Feb. 3.
1681.

SATAN'S

Methods and *Malice*

BAFFLED, *&c.*

I *Hannah Allen*, the late Wife of *Hannibal Allen* Merchant, was born of Religious Parents; my Father was Mr. *John Archer* of *Snelston* in *Derby-shire*, who took to Wife, the Daughter of Mr. *William Hart* of *Uttoxeter Woodland* in *Stafford-shire*, who brought me up in the fear of God from my Childhood;

Childhood; and about Twelve Years of Age, for my better Education, ſent me up to *London* in the Year 1650, to my Father's Siſter Mrs. *Ann Wilſon*, the Wife of Mr. *Samuel Wilſon*, Merchant, then Living in *Aldermanbury*, and after ſome time ſpent there, and at School, I being not well in Health, had a deſire to go down for a time to my Mother, being a Widow, (my Father dying when I was very young) where I ſtaid almoſt two Years. In which time and a little before my going down, it pleaſed God to work in me earneſt breathings after the ways of God, but the enemy of my Soul ſtriving to cruſh ſuch hopeful beginnings in the bud, caſt in horrible blaſphemous thoughts and injections into my mind, inſomuch that I was ſeldom free day or night, unleſs when dead ſleep was upon me. But I uſed to argue with my ſelf to this purpoſe, Whether if I had a Servant that I knew loved me, and deſired in all things to pleaſe me, and yet was ſo forced againſt his will to do that which was contrary to my mind, whether I would think ever the worſe of him, ſeeing I knew what he did was to his grief. And by ſuch thoughts as theſe, it pleaſed God to give me ſome ſupport wherein his goodneſs did the more appear in caſting ſuch thoughts into my mind; I being young, and alſo bearing

this burthen alone, not ſo much as acquainting my Mother with it, but by degrees theſe Temptations grew to that height, that I was perſwaded I had ſinned the Unpardonable Sin: With theſe dreadful Temptations I privately conflicted for ſome Months, not revealing it (as I ſaid) to any one, thinking with my ſelf that never any was like me, and therefore was loath to make my Condition known: I would often in my thoughts wiſh I might change Conditions with the vileſt Perſons I could think of, concluding there was hopes for them though not for me: that Scripture in the 57. of *Iſa.* the two laſt Verſes, did exceedingly terrify me, *But the wicked*
are

are like the troubled Sea, when it cannot rest, whose waters cast up mire and dirt. There is no peace to the wicked, saith my God. In this ſad and perplexed ſtate, upon a Sabbath day, my Mother having been reading in the Family in one of bleſſed Mr. *Bolton's* Books, and being ready to go with them to Church; I thought with my ſelf, To what purpoſe ſhould I go to hear the Word, ſince, as I thought, all means whatſoever for the good of my Soul were in vain, but the ſame time I careleſly turning over Mr. *Bolton's* Book as it lay on the Table, lighted on a place that directly treated on my Caſe; which it pleaſed God ſo to bleſs, that I was ſo much comforted and ſtrengthned, that I recovered for that time from my Deſpairing condition, and ſo continued for ſeveral years with good hopes of the love of God in Chriſt towards me, yet ſtill continually aſſaulted with Temptations, but with leſs violence than before. After my abode in the Countrey almoſt two years with my Mother, I returned to *London* to my Uncle and Aunt *Wilſon*; by whom about a Year and four Months after, I was diſpoſed of in Marriage to Mr. *Hannibal Allen*, but ſtill lived with my Uncle and Aunt *Wilſon* till after my Uncle dyed; and was about this time admitted to the Sacrament by Mr. *Calamy*, with good approbation: And in the time of

his

his Life, I was frequently exercised with variety of Temptations, wherein the Devil had the more advantage I being much inclined to Melancholy, occasioned by the oft absence of my dear and affectionate Husband, with whom I lived present and absent about eight Years; and soon after he went his last Voyage, I went into the Countrey to live with my Aunt *Wilson*, who was now a Widow, and returned to live at *Snelston* with my aged Mother, she being Married again and living elsewhere; but in few Months after I heard of the death of my Husband (for he dyed beyond Sea) I began to fall into deep Melancholy, and no sooner did this black humour begin to darken my Soul, but the Devil ſet on with his former Temptations, which at firſt were with leſs violence and frequent intermiſſions, but yet with great ſtruglings and fightings within me; as I would expreſs it (to my Aunt) I am juſt as if two were fighting within me, but I truſt, the Devil will never be able to overcome me; then I would repeat ſeveral promiſes ſuitable to my condition, and read over my former experiences that I had writ down, as is hereafter expreſſed, and obligations that I had laid upon my ſelf, in the preſence of God, and would ſay, Aunt, I hope I write not theſe things in Hypocriſie, I never intended any Eye ſhould ſee them; but

but the Devil ſuggeſteth dreadful things to me againſt God, and that I am an Hypocrite. At the firſt I began to complain that I found not that comfort and refreſhment in Prayer as I was wont to do, and that God withdrew his comforting and quickening Preſence from me.

When I had ſeen the Bible, I would ſay, oh that bleſſed Book that I ſo delighted in once! the Devil was ſtrongly aſſaulting my Faith, and I ſeemed ready to be overcome, I anſwered the Tempter within my ſelf in the bitterneſs of my Spirit; *Well, if I periſh, God muſt deny himſelf.*

See the difference betwixt the voice of Faith, and the Language of Despair. At another time I cannot be saved because God cannot deny himself; The truth is, it had been most of all worth the Publishing my Expressions in the time of my Combating with Sathan at the beginning of my Affliction, but those passages are most of all forgotten. One hour my hope was firm, and the next hour ready to be overwhelmed.

This began in *Feb.* 63. but it grew worse and worse upon me notwithstanding such means was used both by Physick and Journeys to several Friends for Diversion. The last Journey I took upon this account, was to a good Friend of mine, a Minister, Mr. *John Shorthose*, who

was

was related to me by Marriage, who lived about Thirty Miles distance, where I still grew much worse, and my continual course there, was to be asking him Questions whether the truth of Grace could consist with such sins, for then I began to fear I was an Hypocrite, and that place I thought upon with much dread, in *Job* viii. 13. *The Hypocrites hope shall perish*; nor had I any ease longer than I was thus discoursing with him, for though he often silenced my Objections, and I seemed for the present to be much satisfied, yet he was no sooner gone from me, but my troubles returned afresh, insomuch that his Wife would often send for him home when he was but gone into the Fields. While I was there the Devil would ſuggeſt ſomething to this purpoſe to me, *That when I was gone from him, he would torment me.* After ſome ſtay there, I returned home again, where quickly I began to grow into deep Deſpair. It was my cuſtom for ſeveral years before to write in a Book I kept for that purpoſe in Short-Hand, the Promiſes, together with my Temptations and other afflictions, and my experiences how God delivered me out of them, mixing therewith Prayer and Praiſes, which practice I continued till I was overwhelmed with deſpair, ſome few paſſages whereof are here inſerted as they were written in my deep diſtreſs.

This

This Book in my Affliction I would oft say, would rise up in Judgment against me. As I was walking with my Cousin, Mrs. *Shorthose*, a Woman cursed and sware sadly; *Ah Cousin*, said I, *I have abhorred such Company all my Life, therefore I hope they shall not be my Companions to Eternity.*

This being the 20th. *Feb.* 63. is a time of great trouble and bitter Melancholy, and one great cause is for want of the light of God's Countenance; and for fear that if I should have any mercy shewed me, I should abuse it; and my wretchedly deceitful heart be drawn aside from God (for I am only fit for the School of Affliction;) and on the other hand, if if God ſhould ſend ſome further trials, I ſhould ſink under them; and my Life be made a burthen to me.

But (Lord) ſure this is the voice of my wretched unbelieving heart; The Lord for Chriſt's ſake, fit me for what ever thou wilt do with me, that I may have power again Sin and Satan, and enjoy the light of thy Countenance, and then do with me what thou wilt: Oh that I might prevail with my Lord, for Chriſt's ſake, for graces ſuitable to every condition, and that I may be able to improve every mercy, and every affliction, to thy glory and the comfort of my poor Soul, and that I may be uſeful in my Generation and not be burthenſom; Lord pity my ſtate for

Chriſt's

Christ's sake, who hath never left me in my trials.

The sixth of *April* 64. The truth is I know not well what to say, for as yet I am under sad Melancholy, and sometimes dreadful Temptations, to have hard thoughts of my dearest Lord (The least assenting to which by his grace I dread more than Hell it self) Temptations to impatience and despair, and to give up all for lost; and to close with the Devil and forsake my God, which the Almighty for Christ's sake forbid: These Temptations were with dreadful violence. Besides, my Melancholy hath bad effects upon my body, greatly impairing my my Health: Truly there is ſometimes ſuch a woful confuſion and combating in my Soul, that I know not what to do; And now my earneſt Prayer to my Lord is this, (which I truſt for Chriſt's ſake he will not deny me, though I cannot beg it with ſuch earneſt affections as I ſhould, yet I hope my heart is ſincere) that for my ſweet Redeemer's ſake he would preſerve me from Sin and give me ſtrength of Faith; and Self-denial and patience to wait upon him, and ſubmit to him; and let him do with me what he pleaſeth:

My God, I know thou haſt (for ever adored be thy Majeſty) appeared for me in many great and ſore

sore straits; for the Lord Jesus sake now appear in mercy for me; that I may have exceeding cause to bless thee for this thy mercy also, and give me an assurance that thou art mine, and that thou wilt never leave me, till thou hast brought me to thy Self in glory.

The 12th. of *May, 64.* Still my time of great distress and sore trials continues, sometimes the Devil tempts me wofully to hard and strange thoughts of my dear Lord; which (through his mercy) I dread and abhor the assenting to more than Hell it self; in a word, every day at present seems a great burthen to me; My earnest Prayer is, 'For the Lords sake, that if

'it

'it be thy holy will, I might not
'perish in this great affliction
'which hath been of so long
'continuance, and is so great
'still notwithstanding means used,
'however for the Lords sake, let
'it be Sanctified to my eternal
'good, and give me grace suitable
'to my condition, and strength
'to bear my burthen, and then
'do with me what thou wilt; I
'know not what to say; the
'Lord pity me in every respect
'and appear for me, in these
'my great straits both of Soul and
'Body; I know not what to do, I
'shall be undone; This I write
to see what God will do with
me, whether ever he will deliver me out of such a distress as
this; that I may have cause to
praise

praiſe and adore his name in the Land of the Living; 'Lord, 'comfort me and ſupport me and 'revive me for Chriſt's ſake.

May 26th. 64. 'I deſire (which 'the Lord help me to do) ex- 'ceedingly to bleſs and praiſe 'thy Majeſty that hath yet in 'ſome meaſure ſupported me un- 'der theſe dreadful trials and 'temptations, which do yet con- 'tinue and have been woful upon 'me, for almoſt four Months toge- 'ther; For Chriſt's ſake pity my 'caſe, or elſe I know not what 'to do; and do not deny me 'ſtrength to bear up under my 'burthen; and for the Lord's 'ſake grant, whatever thou doſt 'with me, that one Sin may not

'be

'be in me; unrepented of or
'unmortified; Do with me what
'thou wilt as to the Creature, so
'thou wilt subdue my sins, and
'chain up Sathan, and smile up-
'on my Soul; Lord, I know
'not what to do, only mine Eyes
'are up to thee, the Devil still
'keeps me under dreadful bon-
'dage, and in sad distress and
'wo, but blessed be my God,
'that he doth not lay npon me
'all afflictions at once; that my
'Child is so well, and that I have
'so many other mercies, which
'the Lord open my Eyes to see;
'especially that Christ is mine,
'for the Lord's sake, and then
'I have enough.

After

After this I writ no more, but this and much more I writ before my last Journey aforesaid, for by that time I came back, I soon after fell into deep Despair, and my language and condition grew sadder than before. Now little to be heard from me, but lamenting my woful state, in very sad and dreadful Expressions; As that I was undone for ever; that I was worse than *Cain* or *Judas*; that now the Devil had overcome me irrecoverably; that this was what he had been aiming at all along; Oh the Devil hath so deceiv'd me as never any one was deceived; he made me believe my condition was good when I was a cursed Hypocrite.

One night, I ſaid there was a great clap of Thunder like the ſhot of a Piece of Ordnance, came down directly over my Bed; and that the ſame night, a while after, I heard like the voice of two Young Men ſinging in the Yard, over againſt my Chamber; which I ſaid were Devils in the likeneſs of Men, ſinging for joy that they had overcome me; and in the morning as I was going to riſe, that Scripture in the 10th. of *Heb.* and the laſt words of the 26th. Verſe, was ſuggeſted to me from Heaven (as I thought) *There remains no more Sacrifice for ſin*; And this deluſion remained with me as an Oracle all along; that by this miracle of the Thunder,

and

and the Voice and the Scripture, God revealed to me that I was Damned: When my Aunt asked me, *Do you think God would work a Miracle to convince you that you are rejected? it is contrary to the manner of God's proceedings; we do not read of ſuch a thing in all the Scripture.*

My Anſwer was, *Therefore my condition is unparalell'd, there was never ſuch an one ſince God made any Creature either Angels or Men, nor never will be to the end of the world.*

One night as I was ſitting by the fire, all of a ſudden I ſaid I ſhould dye preſently; whereupon my Aunt was called; to whom I ſaid, *Aunt, I am juſt dying, I cannot live an hour if there were no more in the world*; in this opinion I continued a great while, every morning ſaying, *I ſhould dye before night*, and every night, *before morning*: when I was thus in my dying condition, I often begged earneſtly of my Aunt to bring up my Child ſtrictly, that if it were poſſible, he might be ſaved, though he had ſuch a Mother.

Many places of Scripture I would repeat with much terrour, applying them to my ſelf; as *Jer.* vi. 29, 30. *The bellows are burnt, the lead is conſumed of the fire; the Founder melteth in vain; Reprobate ſilver ſhall men call them, becauſe the Lord hath rejected them*; Ezek. xxiv. 13. *In thy filthineſs is lewdneſs, becauſe I have*

I have purged thee and thou wast not purged ; thou shalt not be purged from thy filthiness any more, till I have caused my fury to rest upon thee : Luke xiii. 24. *Strive to enter in at the strait gate, for many I say unto you, will seek to enter in and shall not be able :* This last Scripture I would express with much passionate weeping, saying, *This is a dreadful Scripture, I sought, but not in a right way ; for the Devil blinded mine eyes, I sought to enter but was not able.*

When both my inward and outward distempers grew to such a height, my Aunt acquainted my Friends at *London* with my condition, for at *London* I had formerly had four loving Un-

 cles,

cles, my Father's brethren ; two whereof were then living, and a Brother of my own, that was ſet up in his Trade: Theſe adviſed to ſend me up to *London*; there being the beſt means both for Soul and Body; in order to which Mrs. *Wilſon* ſent to intreat my Mother to accompany me to *London* ; (for at that time ſhe could not leave her Family ſo long) who accordingly came, but ſhe found it a hard work to perſwade me to this Journey ; for I ſaid *I ſhould not live to get to the Coach, but I muſt go and dye by the way to pleaſe my friends:* I went up in the *Tamworth* Coach, ſo that it was Twenty two Miles thither ; *Tueſday* was the day we ſet forwards on ; and

on

on that day in particular, the Devil had suggested to me (the *Friday* before) *that I must dye and be with him*; and this the more confirmed me in my fear: My Aunt went with me that days journey, which was first to *Tamworth* on Horse-back, and from thence Nine Miles farther in the Coach to *Nun-Eton*, which was a long journey, for one so weak and ill as I was. My Aunt complaining of weariness; *Ah*, said I, *but what must I do, that must have no rest to all eternity:* The next morning I would fain have returned back with my Aunt, but there we parted, and I went forward with my Mother, and a very sad Journey my Mother had with me, for every

Morning ſhe had no ſmall trouble to perſwade me to riſe to go on my Journey; I would earneſtly argue againſt it, and ſay, *I ſhall ſurely dye by the way, and had I not better dye in bed? Mother, do you think people will like to have a dead Corps in the Coach with them?* but ſtill at laſt my Mother with much patience and importunity prevailed with me: As I paſſed along the way, if I ſaw a Church, as ſoon as I caſt mine eyes upon it, it was preſently ſuggeſted to me, that's a Hell-houſe with a kind of indignation; and this I thought was from my ſelf, and therefore never ſpoke of it till after my recovery, for I thought if it had been known how vile I was, I

muſt

must have been put to some horrible death: When I saw any black Clouds gather, or the Wind rise (as we went along), I presently concluded that some dreadful thing would fall out to shew what an One I was.

When I came to *London*, I went to my Brother's House in *Swithens-lane*, where my Mother staid with me about three Weeks or a Month, in which time I took much Physick of one Mr. *Cocket* a Chymist that lived over the way, but still I was, as I thought, always dying; and I yet wearying my Mother with such fancies and stories; One Evening my Mother said to me, *Well, if you will believe you shall be saved if you dye not*

this

this night, I will believe all that you ſay to be true if you do dye this night ; to this ſhe agreed, and in the night about one a Clock (as we thought) the Maid being newly gone out of the Chamber to Bed, but left a Watch-light burning, we both heard like the hand of a Gyant, knock four times together on the Chamber door, which made a great noiſe (the Door being Wainſcot ;) then ſaid I, *You ſee, Mother, though I dyed not to night, the Devil came to let you know that I am damn'd*; my Mother anſwered, *but you ſee he had no power to come into the Chamber.*

Soon after this my Mother returned home into the Countrey, and left me in my Brother's

houſe,

house, who was a young Man unmarried, and had only a Man and a Maid, and he much abroad himself about his occasions; and now my opinion of Dying suddenly began to leave me, therefore I concluded that God would not suffer me to dye a natural death; but that I should commit some fearful abomination, and so be put to some horrible death: One day my Brother going along with me to Doctor *Pridgeon*, as we came back, I saw a company of Men with Halberds, *Look, Brother*, said I, *you will see such as these (one of these days) carry me to Newgate*: to prevent which I studied several ways to make away my self, and I being so much alone, and in in a large ſolitary Houſe, had the more liberty to endeavour it; firſt I thought of taking *Opium* that I might dye in my Sleep, and none know but that I dyed naturally, (which I deſired that my Child might not be diſgraced by my untimely end,) and therefore ſent the Maid to ſeveral Apothecaries ſhops for it, ſome ſaid they had none, others ſaid it was dangerous and would not ſell it her: Once ſhe had got ſome, and was coming away with it; the Maſter of the Shop coming in, asked what ſhe had, and when he knew, took it from her; (this the Maid told me:) When I had ſent her up and down ſeveral days, and ſaw ſhe could get none; then I got Spiders

ders and took one at a time in a Pipe with Tobacco, but never ſcarce took it out, for my heart would fail me; but once I thought I had been poyſoned; in the night awaking out of my ſleep, I thought I felt death upon me, (for I had taken a Spider when I went to Bed) and called to my Brother and told him ſo, who preſently aroſe and went to his Friend an *Apothecary*, who came and gave me ſomething to expel it; the next day my Uncles and Brother (conſidering the inconveniency of that loneſome Houſe) removed me to Mr. *Peter Walker's* Houſe, a Hoſier at the Three Crowns in *Newgate-Market*; (whoſe Wife was my Kinſwoman) who received me

very

very courteoufly, though I was at that time but an uncomfortable Gueft.

In the time I was at my Brother's, I had ftrange apprehenfions that the Lights that were in Neighbouring houfes were apparitions of Devils, and that thofe Lights were of their making; and if I heard the voice of People talk or read in other houfes, I would not be perfwaded but that it was Devils like Men, talking of me, and mocking at my former reading, becaufe I proved fuch an Hypocrite.

Madam,

As for the time I was at my Coufin Walker's, *I refer your La-*
dyfhip

dyſhip to them, or any Friend elſe that may aſſiſt you; only I have here ſet down ſeveral paſſages, as they came to my mind which paſſed there, which your Ladyſhip may make uſe of as You pleaſe.

One time while I lay at my Couſin *Walker's*, having promiſed a Friend that was very importunate with me to go to a Sermon with her; about two or three days after, the Devil began to terrifie me for making that promiſe, and ſuggeſted to me, *that I had much better break it than keep it, for I had enough Sermons to anſwer for already*; and ſitting in great diſtreſs, contriving how I might put off my going, the Devil found me out a place a place on the top of the Houſe, a hole where ſome boards were laid, and there I crowded in my ſelf, and laid a long black Scarf upon me, and put the boards as well as I could to hide me from being found, and there intended to lye till I ſhould ſtarve to death; and all the Family and others concluded I had ſtoln out at the Door unknown to them to go loſe my ſelf in ſome Wood, which I much talked of; but when I had lain there almoſt three days, I was ſo hungry and cold, it being a very ſharp Seaſon, that I was forced to call as loud as I could, and ſo was heard and releaſed from that place.

While

While ſhe was at Mr. *Walker's* houſe, a Miniſter being deſired to come and diſcourſe with her, did come; and finding her in a more dejected ſtate than any he ever ſaw, did oft viſit her, and perceiving little viſible good effect of his conferences with her, propoſed to Preach a Sermon to her, that might ſuit her condition, hoping God might bleſs that Ordinance to her, that ſhe might hear the voice of Joy and Gladneſs, that ſo the bones that God had broken might rejoyce; ſhe conſented to hear his Sermon, and when upon the day appointed he came to diſpence the word, he found her writing the enſuing Lines to diſſwade him.

Sir,

This is to beseech you as you would detract a few scalding drops of the fury of the Almighty from my poor miserable and ever to be abhorred Soul to all Eternity, that you cease your study upon any subject on my account, and likewise your Prayers, and instead of that pray to God to rid the World immediately of such a Monster, who am not only guilty of all the sins of the Devil, but likewise of such crimes as he is not capable of, which you will say is incredible, but woe and alas 'tis true.

This is all she had written, the Minister coming in unexpectedly prevented what she further intended to write.

After-

Afterwards the Minister invited her to his House, where she was above a Week, but very loath to engage in any Duty: The Minister's Wife did sometimes importune her to pray with her, but could not prevail, she always excusing herself from her unfitness to take the holy and reverend Name of God within her polluted lips; *Dead Dog, Damn'd Wretch, she dare to speak to the great God*; she expressed so great an awe and dread of the glorious and fearful Name of God, as discovered much grace in her most desponding state, to them that conversed with her. Some years after her recovery, she returning to *London*, came to the aforesaid Minister and his

Wife, declaring to them God's great Goodneſs to her in maniſeſting himſelf to her Soul, and returned hearty thanks to them for their tenderneſs to her in her dejected ſtate. From his Obſervation of the ground of her Trouble, he adviſes all Chriſtians to mortifie inordinate Affection to lawful things. *Col.* 3. 5.

I would ſay that *Paſhurs* doom belonged to me, that I was *Magor-Miſſabib*, a Terrour to my ſelf and all my Friends; that I was a Hell upon Earth, and a Devil incarnate; for that which I prayed againſt in hypocriſie, God had brought upon me in reality: for I uſed to have frequently in my Prayers ſuch an expreſſion as this

Jerem. 20. 3.

(an

(apprehending the vileness of my Nature) *if God should leave me to my self, I should be an Hell upon Earth; a Terrour to my self and all my Friends*; and because this was in Hypocrisy, therefore God had brought it on me in reality.

Sometimes when they had told me I had been Prayed for, I would say, *they did not pray for me, for I was not to be prayed for*; for the Scripture said, *That they who had sin'd the sin unto death, were not to be Prayed for*. And when a good Friend of mine Mr. *Blake* came daily and unweariedly to see me; I would Ask him, *Why he yet came, seeing I rejected his Counsel*; And, *Christ bid his Messengers shake the dust of their Feet off against such*. I would ſay *Becauſe I have built my Fabrick upon the Sand ſo high, therefore my fall is ſo dreadful* : When I was told of ſome that were poſſeſt with the Devil and were by Prayer diſpoſſeſt, I would reply, *What tell you me of Poſſeſſion, I cared not if I were poſſeſt with a Thouſand Devils, ſo I were not a Devil to my ſelf* : When ſome had told me that I had been Prayed for, I would Anſwer, *I was the leſs beholding to them, for it would but ſink me the deeper into Hell.* I would often ſay, *I was a thouſand times worſe than the Devil, for the Devil had never committed ſuch Sins as I had ; for I had committed worſe Sins than the Sin againſt the Holy-Ghoſt* ; ſome would anſwer, *The Scripture ſpeaks not of of worse sins, and can you be guilty of greater Sins than the Scripture mentions?* Yes, said I, *My Sins are so great, that if all the Sins of all the Devils and Damned in Hell, and all the Reprobates on Earth were comprehended in one man; mine are greater; There is no word comes so near the comprehension of the dreadfulness of my Condition; as that, I am the Monster of the Creation:* in this word I much delighted.

I would say, *Let him that thinks he stands, take heed lest he fall: I once thought my self to stand, but am miserably fallen.*

When *I* was forc'd to be present at Duty, *I* would often stop my Ears, my Carriage was very rugged and cross, contrary to my natural temper; Here *I* practised many devices to make away my self, sometimes by Spiders (as before) sometimes endeavouring to let my self blood with a pair of sharp sizers, and so bleed to death; once when the Surgeon had let me blood, *I* went up into a Chamber and bolted the Door to me, and took off the Plaister and tyed my Arm, and set the Vein a bleeding again; which Mrs. *Walker* fearing, ran up stairs and got into the Chamber to me, *I* seeing her come in, ran into the Leads, and there my Arm bled upon the Wall; *Now* (said *I*) *you may see there is the blood of a Cursed Reprobate.*

I pleased my self, often, with contriving how to get into a Wood

Wood and dye there; and one morning *I* cunningly got out from my Cousins and went into *Smithfield*, where *I* walked up and down a great while, and knew not what to do; at last *I* tryed to hire a Coach but liked not the men there; then *I* went into *Alderſgate-ſtreet*, and asked a Coach-man what he would take to carry me to *Barnet*, (for then I meant to go into a Wood) but the man upon ſome ſmall occaſion ſadly Curſed and Swore, which ſtruck ſome Terrour into me, what thought *I*, muſt ſuch as this be my Companions for ever? and ſo went away from him; and found one with a good honeſt look, and with him *I* agreed; and was to give him

Eight

Eight Shillings; who carryed me a good way beyond *High-Gate*, and as *I* went along, *I* thought, am *I* now going to Converse with Devils? with such like Thoughts as these *I* was discouraged from going on; and called to the Coach-man, and prayed him to drive back again, and told him it was only a Melancholy Fancy: By these and several other ways *I* thought to put an End to my Life; but the watchful Eye of the Lord always graciously prevented me.

When *I* heard any dreadful thing cryed about the Streets in Books; *I* would say, *Oh what fearful things will be put out of me ere long in Books!* I would say, *I should be called* Allen *that*

Cursed

Cursed Apostate. When I had tryed many ways to make away my self, and still saw God prevented my designs; I would say to my self; *Well, I see it cannot be, it must not be; God will have me come to some fearful End; and its fit it should be so, that God may glorifie himself upon such a wretched Creature.*

As I was going along the Streets, a Godly Minister passing by me; *Oh,* thought I, *with what horrour shall I see that face at the great day!* so would I think by many others of Gods people that I knew, either Relations or otherwise; I said, *I exceedingly wondred that such a Pious man as I heard my Father was, should have such a Child.*

I used

I used to say, *I would change conditions with* Julian, *and that he was a Saint in comparison of me; Nay, That the Devil himself was a Saint compared with me;* I would say, *That the hottest place in Hell must be mine; nay, did you know me, you would say it were too good for me; tho' I poor Creature cannot think so.*

When I complained of those dreadful Sins I said I was guilty of; some would Ask me, *If I would be glad to be rid of 'em, and to be in another Condition?* *Yes,* said I, *so had the Devils; who do you think would not be happy? but I cannot desire it upon any other Account.* I would say, *I now saw that my Faith was only a Fancy, and that according to*

an

an Expreſſion of Mr. Baxters *in a Book of his ; That the Love I formerly had to God, was Carnal and Diabolical.*

I would ſay to my Couſin *Walker, Tho' I am a damned Reprobate, yet from me believe (for ſometimes the Devil ſpeaks Truth) that there is a God, and that his Word is true, and that there is a Devil, and that there is an Hell; which I muſt find by woful Experience.*

I would often Ask my Couſin *Walker, What thoſe that came to viſit me, thought of my Condition?* he would Anſwer, *Very well* ; I much wondred at it ; and would do what I could to diſcourage 'em from coming ; yet if at any time I thought they neglected me, I would

would be ſecretly troubled; as afterward I ſaid.

I was wont earneſtly to Enquire whether it was poſſible that the Child of ſuch a Mother as I could be ſaved; yet I would ſay I was without *Natural Affection*; that I Loved neither God nor Man; and that I was given up to work all manner of wickedneſs with greedineſs; *We ſee no ſuchthing by you*, would ſome ſay; I would Anſwer, I, but it is in my heart; *Why doth it not break out in Act?* ſay they, It will do ere long; ſaid I.

The Devil would bring many places of Scripture to my mind, eſpecially Promiſes; as I ſaid, to Jear me with them, because once I thought I delighted in them;

but

but was miserably mistaken; which did much terrifie me.

I would with Dread think with my self, if the men of *Beth-she-mesh* were so destroyed, 1 *Sam.* vi. 19. but for looking into the Ark, what will be my Condemnation that have so often medled with the Holy Ordinances of God, as the Word and Sacraments; and now proved to be only a *Cursed Hypocrite*, and nothing to do with them; I thought with my self then, I would not partake of the Sacrament of the Lords Supper for a thousand worlds.

When any Friend desired me to go to hear the Word of God; I would earnestly beg of them to let me alone, saying, I had

Ser-

Sermons enough to Anſwer for already, and that it would add to my great Account; if they offer'd to compel me to go, I would deſire them to let me alone, and I would go with them the next time, if I lived till then; but my aim was to make away my ſelf juſt before the time came, for I thought I had better go to Hell ſooner, than hear the Word ſtill, and thereby encreaſe my Torment, and heap up wrath againſt the Day of wrath, as I often expreſt it.

I would ſometimes ſay to my Couſin *Walker*, will you not pity me, that muſt as ſure as that there is a God, for ever burn in Hell; I muſt Confeſs I am not to be pitied, for did you know me me, you would abhor me, and ſay Hell was too good for me; yet however pity me as I am your fellow - Creature; and once thought my ſelf not only a Woman but a Chriſtian, and tho' I was ſuch a dreadful wretch as now it appears; yet I did not know it, I verily thought my ſelf in a good condition; and when you ſee me come to my horrible End, which I am ſure will be ere long; tho' you muſt loath me, yet I ſay, pity me.

Yes he would ſay, *if I thought it was true I would pity you, but I do not believe it.* I uſed to ſay, God could not ſave me, and the reaſon I gave was; that God could not deny himſelf.

I found within my ſelf (as I

prehended) a ſcorning and jeering at Religion, and them that profeſt it, and a deſpiſing of 'em, when I came to the heighth of my diſtemper, the ſtrugling and fighting that was in me continually at firſt (while I combated with Satan) left me: When I complained how vile I was, my Friends would tell me, *It was not I, but the Devils Temptations*, I would Anſwer, No, it is from my ſelf; I am the Devil now, the Devil hath now done his work, he hath done tempting of me; he hath utterly overcome me: *Then why are you ſo troubled?* would ſome ſay; I would Anſwer, Have I not cauſe to be troubled, (think you) that am aſſuredly given up to the Devil and Eternally

nally Damn'd. I would write in ſeveral places on the walls with the point of my Sizers, *Woe, Woe, Woe and alaſs to all Eternity* ; *I am undone, undone for ever, ſo as never any was before me.*

Upon ſome ſudden occaſion I would ſometimes ſmile, but when I did ; I would exceedingly check my ſelf, and be the more troubled afterwards.

Mr. *Walker* endeavoured to get Mr. *Baxter* to come to me, but he ſtill miſſed of him when he came to Town ; No, (ſaid I) God will not let Mr. *Baxter* come to ſuch a Wretch as I am ; but I had then a ſecret deſire to ſee him, rather than any one elſe. And to my beſt remembrance my Couſin *Walker* told me that he asked me if I would believe better of my ſelf, if Mr. *Baxter* told me my condition was ſafe; and that I anſwered, Yes.

When another Chriſtian Friend Mr. *Maſon*, brought me acquainted with any of Gods People, I would ſay, *Alaſs Mr.* Maſon, *you'l dearly repent this; and how muſt I Curſe you in Hell for all that you did in kindneſs to me.*

What is here writ of Mr. Blake *and Mr.* Maſon, *is but to hint what may be ſaid of my Carriage towards them.*

The next Spring which was in *May*, 1665. My Aunt *Wilſon* came up to *London*, being reſtleſs in her mind till ſhe ſaw me;

when

when I heard that my Aunt was come to *High-Gate* to her Brother's Houſe, and did not come to *London* till Monday, I often ſaid I hoped to have ſeen my Aunt before I dyed; but now I ſhall not; this fire within me, will kindle and burn me before Monday; on Monday my Aunt came, I being taken with the firſt ſight of her, went with her to dinner to a Friends houſe in the *Old-Jury*; but was at my old Language ſtill every Day, That the Fire would kindle within me and burn me: the Sickneſs then encreaſing, my Aunt reſolved to take me down again into the Countrey, which I was very glad of; for there I thought

Mr. *Hatt's* Houſe, who afterwards Married her.

I ſhould live more privately, and be leſs diſturbed; (for ſo I accounted of the kind viſits of Friends.) A week before Midſummer we ſet forward toward *Darby-Shire*, and an uncomfortable Journey we had, for by the way I would not eat ſufficient to ſupport Nature; when I was come to *Snelſtone* again, I was where I would be; for there I could do what I pleaſed, with little oppoſition; there I ſhunned all Company tho' they were my near Relations; nor could I endure to be preſent at Prayer, or any other part of Gods Worſhip, nor to hear the ſound of reading, nor the ſight of a Book or Paper; tho' it were but a Letter, or an Almanack.

The

The Lady *Baker* was pleased to write me several Letters which I would not so much as look on, nor hear read by others; one being brought me, and I prest much to receive it, tore it in pieces. Nay I would strike the Horn-book out of my Childs hand; but that would trouble me as soon as I had done it: I would wish I had never seen Book, or learned letter; I would say it had been happy for me if I had been born blind; daily repeating my accustomed Language, that I was a Cursed Reprobate, and the Monster of the Creation.

One Sabbath-day being disturbed about some small trifle, I fell into violent passion; weeping even

even to roaring, and cry'd out, I was made to be damn'd, God made me to that very end, to ſhew the power of his Juſtice more in me than in any other Creature.

My Aunt ſometimes would tell me; that my expreſſions were ſo dreadful ſhe knew not how to bear them; I would anſwer roundly, but what muſt I do then, that muſt feel them; I would often ſay to my Aunt, *Oh, you little know what a diſmal dark condition I am in; Methinks I am as dark as Hell it ſelf*: my Aunt would ſay, *Couſin, would you but believe you were melancholy it might be a great means to bring you out of this Condition*; *Melancholy*, would I ſay, *I have Cauſe to be Melan-*

Melancholy, that am as assuredly Damn'd as that there is a God; and no more hopes of me than of the Devils; I have more Cause to be Melancholy than they have, it's a fearful thing to fall into the hands of the Liviug God. *Heb.* x. *vers.* 31.

My Aunt would persuade me to seek God in the use of means, from that Argument of the resolution of the four Lepers, in the 2 *King.* vii. 4. *I* would Answer with scorn, *I have heard that often enough.*

One fit my humour was such, that when Friends would have argued with me about my condition, I would not speak, but only give them some short scornful Answer and no more; but I would

I would be ſometimes in one temper and ſometimes in another; my Aunt would take the advantage of my beſt humour, to talk with me then, and the main thing ſhe deſigned in moſt of her Arguments with me was, to convince me of the fallacy and deluſion that was in my Opinion; That it was ſo infallibly revealed to me that I was Damn'd; but alaſs all took no place with me; but when ſhe began to ſpeak with me of ſuch things, I would generally fling away in a great fume, and ſay; *Will you not let me alone yet, methinks you might let me have a little quiet while I am out of Hell*; this was almoſt my daily practice while I was with my Aunt: I was uſually

very

very nimble in my Anſwers, and peeviſhly pettinacious to pleaſe my own croſs humour.

My Aunt told me ſhe believed God would not have exerciſed me ſo with Afflictions, from my Child-hood, if he intended to reject me at laſt; I anſwer'd, *Do you not remember what Mr.* Calamy *uſed to ſay, That unſanctified Afflictions par-boyle the Soul for hell*; *Oh*, ſaid I, *that I had gone to hell as ſoon as I had been born, (ſeeing I was born to be damned) and then I had not had ſo many ſins to have anſwer'd for, then I ſhould not have lived to be a Terrour to my ſelf and all that know me; and my Torments in Hell would have been far leſs.*

When

When my Grandmother had told me of the depths of the Mercy of God in Christ: I would answer with indignation; *What do you tell me of a Christ; it had been better for me if there had never been a Saviour, then I should have gone to Hell at a Cheaper Rate.*

Towards Winter I grew to Eat very little, (much less than I did before) so that I was exceeding Lean; and at last nothing but Skin and Bones; (a Neighbouring Gentlewoman, a very discreet Person that had a great desire to see me, came in at the back-door of the House unawares and found me in the Kitchen, who after she had seen me, said to Mrs. *Wilson, She cannot live, she*

ſhe hath death in her face) I would ſay ſtill that every bit I did Eat haſtned my Ruin; and that I had it with a dreadful Curſe; and what I Eat encreaſed the Fire within me, which would at laſt burn me up; and I would now willingly live out of Hell as long as I could.

Thus ſadly I paſſed that Winter, and towards Spring I began to Eat a little better.

This Spring in *April*, 1666. my good Friends Mr. *Shorthoſe* and his Wife, whoſe Company formerly I much delighted in, came over, and when I heard they were come and were at their Brothers houſe, half a mile off, and would come thither the Fryday after; *Ah*, ſays I, *that I dreaded*,

dreaded, I cannot endure to see him, nor hear his voice; I have told him so many dreadful Lyes; (meaning what I had formerly told him of my experiences, and, as I thought, infallible evidences of the Love of God towards me; and now believed my self to be the vilest Creature upon Earth) *I cannot see his face*; and wept tenderly, wherewith my Aunt was much affected, and promised that when he came he should not see me; (I would have seen neither of them, but especially my He-Cousin) On the Fryday, soon after they came in, they asked for me, but my Aunt put them off till after Dinner, and then told them, she had engaged her word they should not see me me, and that if ſhe once broke her promiſe with me, I would not believe her hereafter; with ſuch perſuaſions ſhe kept them from ſeeing me, but not ſatisfied them; for that Night Mr. *Short-hoſe* was much troubled, and told his Wife if he had thought they muſt not have ſeen me, he would ſcarce have gone to *Snelſtone*; the next day they Supped at Mr. *Robert Archer*'s Houſe, Mrs. *Wilſon*'s Brother that then lived in the ſame Town, where my Aunt Supped with them; at the Table ſomething was ſaid of their not ſeeing Mrs. *Allen*, but after Supper Mr. *Shorthoſe* and his Wife ſtole away from the Company to Mrs. *Wilſons*, where they came in at the back-ſide of the Houſe

House suddenly into the Kitchen where I was; but assoon as I saw them, I cryed out in a violent manner several times; *Ah, Aunt* Willson *hast thou serv'd me so!* and ran into the Chimney and took up the Tongs; *No*, said they, *Your Aunt knows not of our coming*; *What do you do here?* said I, *We have something to say to you*, said they, *but I have nothing to say to you*, said I, Mr. *Shorthose* took me by the hand and said, *Come, come, lay down those Tongs and go with us into the Parlour*, which I did, and there they discoursed with me, till they had brought me to so calm and friendly a temper, that when they went, I accompanied them to the door and said; *Methinks*

I am

I am loth to part with them; Mr. *Shorthose* having so good encouragement, came the next day again, being Sabbath day after Dinner, and prevailed with me to walk with him into an Arbour in the Orchard; where he had much discourse with me, and amongst the rest he entreated me to go home with him; which after long persuasions both from him and my Aunt, I consented to, upon this condition, that he promised me, *he would not compell me to any thing of the Worship of God, but what he could do by persuasion*; and that week I went with them, where I spent that Summer; in which time it pleased God by Mr.

Shorthose's means to do me much good both in Soul and Body; he had some skill in Physick himself, and also consulted with Physicians about me; he kept me to a course of Physick most part of the Summer, except when the great heat of the Weather prevented, I began much to leave my dreadful expressions concerning my condition, and was present with them at duty; and at last they prevailed with me to go with them to the publick Ordinance, and to walk with them to visit Friends, and was much alter'd for the better.

A Fortnight after *Michaelmas* my Aunt fetch'd me home again to *Snelston*, where I passed that

that Winter much better than formerly; and was pretty conformable and orderly in the Family; and the next Summer was much after the same manner, but grew still something better; and the next Winter likewise still mending though but slowly, till the Spring began, and then I changed much from my retiredness, and delighted to walk with Friends abroad.

And this Spring it pleased God to provide a very suitable Match for me, one Mr. *Charles Hatt*, a Widdower living in *Warwickshire*; with whom I live very comfortably, both as to my inward and outward man; my husband being one that truly fears God.

As my Melancholy came by degrees, so it wore off by degrees, and as my dark Melancholy bodily distempers abated, so did my spiritual Maladies also, and God convinced me by degrees; that all this was from Satan, his delusions and temptations, working in those dark and black humors, and not from my self, and this God cleared up to me more and more; and accordingly my love to, and delight in Religion, increased; and it is my desire that, lest this great Affliction should be a stumbling-block to any, it may be known, (seeing my Case is publish'd) that I evidently perceive that God did it in much mercy and faithfulness to my Soul; and though for the present it was a bitter Cup, yet that it was but what the only wise God saw I had need of according to that place, 1 *Pet.* i. 6. *Tho' now for a season, if need be, ye are in heaviness through manifold Temptations.* Which Scripture did much comfort me under my former Afflictions in my first Husbands days.

These Promiſes which are here ſet down were great ſupports and refreſhments to me in the time of my various Temptations and Afflictions all along, till I fell into deep deſpair, for from my Child-hood, God Exerciſed me with manifold Trials.

Iſaiah, xliii. 1, 2.

B*UT now thus ſaith the Lord that Created thee, O* Jacob, *and he that formed thee, O* Iſrael, *fear not for I have redeemed thee; I have called thee by thy Name, thou art mine.* Verſ. 2. *When thou paſſeſt through the Waters, I will be with thee, and through the Rivers*

James v. 11.

Behold we count them happy which Endure; ye have heard of the Patience of Job, *and have seen the End of the* Lord; *that the* Lord *is very pitiful and of tender mercy.*

1 John, iv. 4.

Ye are of God, little Children; and have overcome them, because greater is he that is in you, than he that is in the World.

THE END.

An Account of the Travels (Wing A 410), shelf reference Box 11, is reproduced courtesy of the Library Committee of Britain Yearly Meeting, Library of the Religious Society of Friends (London). The text block of the original measures 120 × 65 mm.

11

Anne Fry

An Account OF THE TRAVELS, *Sufferings & Persecutions* OF

Barbara Blaugdone.

Given forth as a Testimony to the Lord's Power, and for the Encouragement of Friends.

Printed, and Sold by *T. S.* at the *Crooked-Billet* in *Holywell-Lane*, *Shoreditch*, 1691.

An Account of the Travels, Sufferings and Persecutions of *B. B.* &c.

IN my Youth and Tender Years, I feared the Lord, and was afraid to offend him; and was zealous and diligent in the Profession I was in, and sought the Lord earnestly, although I knew not where to find him, until I was directed by Friends that came from the North, *John Audland* and *John Camm* by Name, whose Behaviour and Deportments were such, that it preached before ever they opened their Mouths; and it was then revealed to me, That they had the Everlasting Gospel to Preach in this City: And when they did open their Mouths, I was made to bless God that I had lived to hear the everlasting Gospel preached; and they directed my Mind unto the Light of Christ, therein to wait, which I was diligent to do, and found the Vertue of it; and as the Evil was made manifest, I departed from it, and willingly took up the Cross, and yielded Obedience unto it, in plainness of Speech and in my Habit: & the People were so offended with it, when I went into their Publick Places and Steeple-houses to speak, that they took away their Children from me, so that I lost almost all my Imployment; and they kept me in Prison a quarter of a Year at a time: And great was my Sufferings in that Day, but the Lord so filled me with his Power,

Power; that I was preserved through it all: And the Diligent and Faithful did prosper then, and so they do now.

And therefore my Counsel to *Friends*, is, that they keep in God's Power; for there is no other way to be preserved, nor to receive Life and Salvation; its my Testimony for God: For whosoever shuns the Cross, and goes out of the Power, they lose their way, and dishonour God; but whosoever keep in the Faith, and abide in the Power, they are in Safety: I have had living Experience of it, therefore I mention it, and it has been with me a pretty while to publish it, for the benefit of those that are passing through, and are yet to pass through the Sufferings, and therefore do I declare my Experience.

And so, *dear Friends*, the Cross is the Way to the Crown of Life, and to the Crown of Glory; and they that continue Faithful and Obedient, they obtain the Eternal Crown, which they that are disobedient, lose. I speak my Experience of the Dealings of the Lord with me, in my Travels and passings through my Spiritual Journey, for the benefit of those that Travel rightly after. And I can speak it to the glory of God, he never moved me to any thing, but that he gave me Power to perform it, and made it effectual, although I past through much Exercise in the performance of it. And the Power of God wrought in me long before I knew what it was; and when Friends came, that my understanding was opened, I soon took up the Cross and came into the Obedience, and the Lord cleansed me by his

Power,

Power, and made me a fit Vessel for his Use.

And when I had laboured pretty much at home, he called me forth to labour abroad, and I stood so in the dread, awe and fear of the Lord, that his Spirit strove much with me, before I could open my Mouth; and the Word of the Lord came unto me in a Meeting, *That the Lord would have War with* Amalek *from Generation to Generation:* And the Power and Spirit of the Lord was so strong in me, that it set me upon my Feet, and constrained me to speak the words; for I was never hasty nor forward.

And then the Lord caused me to abstain from all Flesh, Wine and Beer whatsoever, and I drank only Water for the space of a whole Year; and in that time the Lord caused me to grow and to prosper in the Truth: And then

I

I was made to go and to call the People forth from among the dumb Idols, and suffered much Imprisonment for it; but yet I was made to go till the Lord gave me dominion, so that I could go into their Places, and say what I had to say, and come forth again quietly. And as *Mary Prince* and I was coming Arm in Arm from a Meeting, that was at *George Bishop*'s House, there was a Rude Man came and abused us, and struck off *Mary Prince* her Hat, and run some sharp Knife or Instrument through all my Clothes, into the side of my Belly, which if it had gone but a little farther, it might have killed me; but my Soul was so in love with the Truth, that I could have given up my Life for it at that day.

And then I was moved to go to *Marlborough*, to the Market-

place

place and Steeple-house, where I had pretty much Service, where they put me in Prison for six Weeks, where I Fasted six Days and six Nights, and neither eat Bread nor drank Water, nor no earthly thing; then I came to a feeding upon the Word, and had experience that man doth not live by Bread alone, but by every Word that proceedeth out of the Mouth of the Lord. And when I was released, I went to *Isaac Burges*, the man that committed me, and discoursed with him; and he was really Convinced of the Truth, but could not take up the Cross; but was afterwards very loving to Friends, and stood by them upon all occasions, and never Persecuted a Friend any more: and when he came unto this City, he came unto my House to see me, and confest, That he could not take

up

up the Croſs, although he knew it was the Truth.

And a while after I was made to go into *Devonſhire*, to *Molton*, and *Baſtable*, and *Bediford*, where I had a Priſon in all thoſe Places: and I went to the *Earl* of *Bathes*, where I had formerly ſpent much time in Vanity, to call unto them to come out of their Vanity; and I asked to ſpeak with the *Conteſs*, and they refuſed to let me in, but one of the Servants that knew me, bid me go to the Back-Door, and their Lady would come forth that way to go into the Garden; and they ſent forth a great Wolf-Dog upon me, which came fiercely at me to devour me, and just as he came unto me, the Power of the Lord ſmote the Dog, ſo that he whined, and ran in crying, and very Lame; ſo that I ſaw clearly the Hand of the Lord in it for my preſervation,

tion, blessed be his Name: and then the Lady came forth, and stood still and heard me all that I had to say unto her; and when I had done she gave me Thanks, but never asked me to go into her House, although I had eat and drank at her Table and lodged there many a time.

And then I was moved to go to *Great-Torrington* in *Devonshire*, unto the Steeple-house there, where was a very bad Priest indeed, though I had little to him, but to the People; and when I had spoken in the Morning, I went to my Lodging, and what I had not room to clear my self of, I went to Writing, and the Constables came and took away my Writing, and commanded me to go along with them to their Worship; and I answered them, That they would not suffer me to speak there, and that I knew

no

no Law would compel me to go twice in a day, and they all knew that I was there in the Morning; and ſo I would not go. So the next day the Mayor ſent for me, and when I came the Prieſt was there, and the Mayor was moderate, and loath to ſend me to Priſon, but the Prieſt was very eager, and ſaid, *I ought to be Whipt for a Vagabond.* And I bid him prove where ever I askt any one for a bit of Bread; but he ſaid, *I had broken the Law by ſpeaking in their Church.* So he was ſo eager with the Mayor, that he made him make a *Mittimus*, and ſend me to *Exeter*-Priſon, which was Twenty Miles diſtant, where I remained for ſome time, and was commanded of the Lord to Faſt fourteen Days and fourteen Nights, without taſting Bread or Water, or any earthly thing, which I performed for a Wit-

neſs

ness against that dark professing People; and there I was until the Assizes, and was not called forth to a Tryal: but after the Assizes was over, a petty Fellow sent for me forth, and read a Law, which was quite wrong, and did not belong to me at all, and put me to lodge one Night among a great company of *Gypsies* that were then in the Prison; and the next day the Sheriff came with a Beadle, and had me into a Room, and Whipt me till the Blood ran down my Back, and I never startled at a blow; but the Lord made me to rejoyce, that I was counted Worthy to Suffer for his Name's sake, and I Sung aloud; and the Beadle said, *Do ye Sing; I shall make ye Cry by and by:* and with that he laid more Stripes, and laid them on very hard. I shall never forget the large Experience of the Love and Power of of God which I had in my Travels, and therefore I can speak to his Praise, and glorifie his Name: for if he had Whipt me to Death in that state which then I was in, I should not have been terrified or dismayed at it; *Ann Speed* was an EyeWitness of it, and she stood and lookt in at the Window, and wept bitterly. And then the Sheriff, when he saw that the envy of the man could not move me, he bid him *forbear, for he had gone beyond his Orders already.* So when he had left me, *Ann Speed* came in and drest my Wounds; and the next day they turned me out with all the *Gypsies*, and the Beadle followed us two Miles out of the City; and as soon as he left us, I returned back again, and went up into the Prison to see my Friends that were Prisoners there at the same time: So I took my

leave

leave of them, and went to *Topsom*, where there was a fine Meeting of Friends, among whom I was sweetly refreshed, and staid there one Night, and then I came home to *Bristoll*; and in my Travels I went several Miles upon long Downs, and knew nothing of the way, but as the Lord was with me, and did direct me; and in all this I have experience of the Love and Power of the Lord to me wards, blessed be his Name for ever: I cannot forget his Loving-kindness to me in my Distress.

And in my Travels near *Bridgewater*, I went to speak to a Priest that I had formerly known, one *Edward Piggot*; and when I came back to the Inn, where I had bespoke my Lodging, they would not let me come in; so I lookt about for shelter to keep me from the fierceness of the Frost, and

I found the Pig-ſtye ſwept very clean, and the Trough turned up, and never a Pig in it, and I ſate me down on the Trough, and that was my Lodging all that Night: and the next Night I could get no lodging, but was fain to lodge in a Barn: and in all this the Lord exerciſed me in the Patience.

Then I went to *Bediford*, and there I was put into the Town-Hall, and they ſearched me to ſee whether I had Knife or Sciſſers about me; and the next day they brought me before the Mayor for ſpeaking in a private Meeting, and he diſcourſed much with me, and had a ſence of what I ſaid unto him, and received it; and at laſt he ſet open two Doors, one right againſt the other, and ſaid, *He would give me my choice which I would go forth at? whether I would go to Priſon again,*

or

or go home? And I told him, that I should choose Liberty rather than Bonds: So I went homeward, and then he took his Horse and came and followed me, for there was some tenderness in him; and he would have had me Rid behind him, but I found that when any Body which he knew did meet us, then he would draw back and lag behind, and as soon as they were gone, he would come up to me again; so therefore I would not ride behind him, but he rode three or four Miles with me, and discoursed me all the way; and when we parted, I was made to kneel down and pray for him, in which time he was very serious; and afterwards he grew very solid and sober, and in a little time he dyed, but I writ to him once before he dyed, a little after I came home.

And then I was moved of the Lord to go to *Bazing-stoke*, to endeavour the Liberty of two Friends, (*viz.*) *Thomas Robison* and *Ambrose Riggs*, which were taken up at the first Meeting that Friends had there; and when I came, they would not let me come in to them; and I having a Letter from *John Camm* unto them, put it in at a Chink of the Door to them; and then I went to the Mayor to desire their Liberty, and he told me, *That if he should see the Letter which I brought them, they should have their Liberty*; and I told him he should, so I went and fetcht it to him, and he read it, and could see no hurt in it: So he told me, *I should have my Brethren out, but he would not let them out presently.* Neverthelefs we had a fine Meeting the next day, being First Day, and coming from the Meeting,

Meeting, I met with the Prieſt, and told him his portion, and in a few days the Friends had their Liberty: and thus the Lord made my Journey proſperous.

And then the Lord moved me to go for *Ireland*, and I went in a Veſſel bound for *Corke*, and the Lord ſo ordered it, that the Ship was carried about to *Dublin*, and we had much foul Weather, ſo that the Sea-men ſaid, That I was the cauſe of it, becauſe I was a *Quaker*; and they conſpired to fling me over-board; but it being made known to me, I went to the Maſter and told him what his Men had deſigned to do, and told him, that if he did ſuffer them to do it, my Blood would be required at his Hands. So he charged them not to meddle with me: And afterwards we were in a Storm upon a Firſt Day, and I was moved to go upon Deck, and ſpeak among them, and Pray for them; and they were all made very quiet, and ſaid, *They were more beholding to me then they were to their Prieſt, because I did Pray for them, and he could not open his Mouth to ſay any thing amongſt them.* We were ſix Days and ſix Nights at Sea, and the Maſter himſelf did not know where he was, nor which way he was going, until we were put into the Harbour at *Dublin*; and although we had abundance of very Stormy Weather, yet we ſuſtained no manner of loſs nor dammage; ſo that the Maſter ſaid, He could never ſay before that he was in ſo much foul Weather, and received no hurt: And we were put into *Dublin* the very ſame day that *Francis Howgill* and *Edward Burrough* were Baniſht from thence. And then I ſaw my Ser-

vice

vice there, and was moved to go to the Deputy, and when I came there, the People said, their was no speaking with him for me; for did I not know that he had Banisht two of our Friends out of the Nation but yesterday. But in the Faith I went, and the Power of the Lord had great weight upon me, and I met with the Secretary, and I desired him to help me to the Speech of the Deputy. And he answered me, *That he did think he could not*. And I told him, if he would be so civil, as to go up and tell the Deputy, that there was a Woman below, that would speak with him; and then if he refused, I was answered. So he went up, and their came a Man to fetch me up into the with-drawing Room; and after I had been there a while, their came a Man out of the Deputy's Chamber, and they all stood bare-headed before him, because they knew I never saw the Deputy ; but I had a sence it was a Priest ; and there was almost a whole Room full of People, and they askt me, *Why did not I do my Message to their Lord.* And I answered, When I do see your Lord, then I shall do my Message to him. So in a little while he came forth, and sate down on a Couch, and I stood up and spake to him that which the Lord did give me to speak, and bid him beware, that he was not found fighting against God, in opposing the Truth, and Persecuting the Innocent, but be like Wise *Gamaliel,* To let it alone, and if it be of God, it will stand ; but if it be of Man, it will fall ; and the Enmity did not lie so much in himself, as he was stirred up to it by Evil Magistrates and bad Priests ; and that God's People are as dear to him now as

ever,

ever, and they that toucht them, toucht the Apple of his Eye. But in his Name, and by his Power their was much hurt done to the People of God all the Nation over, and it would lie heavy upon him at the last; and that the Teachers of the People did cause them to Err, and he knew the Priests portion; and when I toucht upon that, he would say, *There's for you Mr Harrison*, to the Priest that stood there. And the Power and Presence of the Lord was so with me, that it made the Man to be much concerned. And when I had done, he asked the Priest, *What he had to say to that which I spake*: And the Priest said, *It was all very true and very good, and he had nothing to say against it, if we did speak as we meant*. Then I told the Priest, that the Spirit of God was true, and did speak as it meant, and meant as it spoke; but

but men of Corrupt Minds did pervert the Scriptures, by putting their own Imaginations, and Conceivings, and Apprehensions upon it, and so did deceive the People: but holy men of God spake the Scriptures, and gave them forth as they were Inspired by the Holy Ghost, and they are of no private Interpretation; but none understood them, but those that read them by the same Spirit that gave them forth. So I returned to my Lodging, which was at one Captain *Rich* his House, and he came home, and said, *That the Depety was so Sad and Melancholly, after I had beed with him, that he would not come forth to Bowls nor no Pastime at all.*

This my Service for God was great, and he made it to prosper; And then I went to *Corke*, where my Motion was at first, and great were

were my Sufferings there, for I had Prison almost where-ever I came; and I was made to call to my Relations and Acquaintance, by the Word of the Lord, and was made to follow them into several Steeple-houses; and great were my Sufferings amongst them, but where-ever the Lord opened my Mouth, there were some that received me, and would plead my Cause against my Persecutors; and I was in Jeopardy of my Life several times, but the Lord prevented it. And I was made to speak in a Market-place, and there was a Butcher swore he would cleave my Head in twain; and had his Cleaver up ready to do it, but their came a Woman behind him and caught back his Arms, and staid them till the Souldiers came and rescued me. And those that were my former Acquaintance, with whom I had formerly been very con-

conversant, and spent much time and lodged at their Houses several times, even those now were afraid of me, and would not come near me; but the dread of God was upon me, and it made some of them to Tremble; and some said, I was a Witch: and when I would go to their Houses to reprove them, they were so mad that they would run away, and then their Servants would come and hale me out; and when I would go to sit down, they would drag me along upon the Stones, and hale me out and shut the Doors: So I came to witness that a Prophet is not without Honour, save in his own Country. So when I found my self pretty clear there, I returned home to *Bristoll*.

And in a while after I was moved to go for *Ireland* again, and then I was in great Perils by Sea, where I saw the Wonders of the

Lord

Lord in the Deep; and there was one man Friend, and one woman Friend then in the Ship besides me, and the Ship was broken near *Dungarvan*, and it foundred in the Sea, something near the Shore, and we were all like to be cast away; and I was ordered of the Lord to stay in the Ship, until they were all gone out of her, and the Master and the Passengers got into the Boat, (all save one Man and one Woman, which were cast away) and they got to Shore, and stood there to see what would become of me, who was still in the Cabbin, and the Waves beat in upon me in abundance, almost ready to stifle me: And so when I found freedom I went and stood upon a piece of the Deck that was left, and then the Master of the Vessel & the Man Friend called to me, and told me, *If I would venture to leap down, they would venture to come*

into

into the Water to save me: So they came into the Water up so far as their Necks, and I leaped down to them, and they caught hold of me, but I being intangled in the Ropes in leaping down, was drawn from them again; but as the Lord ordered it, a Wave came and beat the Ship out, whereas if it had beat in, it would have killed us all three, but beating out, they recovered me again, and drew me to Shore: So the Lord's Power and Mercy was wonderfully shown at that time for my preservation; I cannot but bless his Name for it.

So then I went to *Dublin*, where I spake in the High-Court of Justic. amongst the Judges; and then they put me in Prison, where I lay upon Straw, on the Ground, and when it Rained, the Wet and Filth of the House-of-Office ran in under my Back: And they Arraign-

Arraigned me at the Bar, and bid me plead Guilty, or Not Guilty: And I answered, that there was no guilt upon any ones Conscience for what they did in Obedience unto the Lord God: And the Judge could not speak to me, but spoke to another Man that stood by him, to speak to me. So I could not say as they bid me, and they returned me to Prison again, where I had very hard Exercise. And there was a Man that could not injoy some Land, except he could prove that his Brother was dead; and he brought a Man into Prison, that said, *he would prove that he was killed at such an Inn, and buried under a Wall.* He accused the Inn-keeper and his Wife, and their Man, and Maid, and a Smith, to be guilty of this Murther. So I went to him, and sate down by him, and spake a few Words to him, and askt him,

how

how he could conceal this Murther so long, when he was as guilty of it as either of them, if it were true. He trembled, and shook exceedingly, and his Knees smote one against another, and he confest, That *he never saw the People with his Eyes, nor never was at the place in his Life, nor knew nothing of it, but only he was drawn in by the Man that was to have the Land, and was persivaded to Witness it.* And the Prisoners heard this his Confession to me; so I sent to the Deputy, to send down his Priest, that he might hear his Confession: So he came, and he confest the same to him as he had done to me: and the five Persons which he accused was then in Prison, but only the Maid in the Prison with me; and the Man confest the same once before the Judge: But the Man that brought him in,

came

came to him every day, and fill-ed his Head with Drink, and caused the Goaler to lock me up, that I might not come at him: So I writ to the Inn-keeper and his Wife, and the Coach-man; and I writ to the Judge also, and told him the Day of his Death did draw nigh, wherein he must give an Account of his Actions; and bid him take heed how he did condemn so many Innocent People, having but one Witness, in whose Mouth their were so many Lyes found; (and they all said they were Innocent.) They called him Judge *Pepes* who Condemned them all. Then a Priest came to speak with the Maid that was Condemned, which was with me in the Prison; but she would not see him, but said, *Nay, he can do me no good; I have done with Man for ever;*

But God, thou knowest that I am Innocent of what they lay to my Charge. So they were all Hanged, and the Man that accused them was hanged up first, for fear he should confess when he saw the rest hanged: And a heavy day it was, and I bore and suffered much that day. Then there were some Friends of mine, namely *Sr. William King*, Colonel *Fare*, and the Lady *Browne*, these hearing I was in Prison, came to see me, and they would needs go to this Judge, to get me released; so when they came, he told them, that *he was afraid of his Life*. And they laughed, and told him, *they*

had

had known me from a Child, and there was no harm in me at all. And they were all very earnest to get my Liberty, and at last they did obtain it. And then I was moved to go to the Steeple-house, where this Judge was, and the Lord was with me, and I Cleared my self of him; and he went to Bed and Died that Night: And one of the Prisoners had writ the Letter which I sent to him, and when they heard he was dead, they all said, *that I was a true Prophetess unto him.*

And thus as an Instrument in the Hand of the Lord, to do his Work, I was faithful and obedient unto his Power,

and

and he caused me to grow and prosper through my great Sufferings; blessed be his Name for ever, that I had great experience of his love and power. *Elizabeth Gardiner*, and *Rebecca Rich*, and *Samuel Clareges* Wife knew all this to be true.

And then I went to *Limrick*, where I had some Service, and they put me in Prison. So in a while I was released, and then I took Shipping for *England* again, and then there was a great Storm took us at Sea, and the Lord moved me to go to Prayer; and I went to Prayer, and in a little time the Storm ceased; and we

were

were preſerved; And coming towards *Mineyard*, we met a Pirate, which had abundance of men on board, and I began to conſider, whether there was any Service for me to do among thoſe Rude People, but I found little to them: ſo they came on Board us, and took away all that I had, and one of my Coats from off my Back; but they were not ſuffered to do me any further harm. So they took away the Maſter with them, until he ſhould pay them a ſum of Money for the Ship and Goods. And ſo we came home to *England*.

But

But in all my Travels, I Travelled still on my own Purse, and was never chargeable to any, but paid for what I had. And much more could I declare of my Sufferings which I passed through, which I forbear to mention, being not willing to be over-tedious.

And I have written these Things that Friends may be encouraged, and go on in the Faith, in the Work of the Lord: For many have been the Tryals, Tribulations and Afflictions the which I have passed through, but the Lord hath delivered me out of them all; Glory be given to him, and blessed be his Name for ever, and evermore.

Barbara Blaugdone.

THE END.

A Small Account (Wing B 3163A), classmark Broughton 471, is reproduced by permission of the Syndics of Cambridge University Library. The text block of the original measures 140 × 80 mm.

A Small

ACCOUNT

GIVEN FORTH

By one that hath been a

Traveller

For these 40 Years in the Good

OLD WAY.

And as an Incouragement to the Weary to go forward; I by Experience have found there is a Rest remains for all they that truly trusts in the Lord.

Psalms 31. 14. *I trusted in thee, O Lord, and said, thou art my God.*
24. *All ye that trust in the Lord, be strong, he shall establish your Hearts.*

S. B.

Printed in the Year 1698.

AS God by his Grace having inclined my Heart to be Merciful, and I have had the Comfort of doing Good, whilst I had an opportunity, in the things as he in this Life is pleased to commit to my Care: I have, as in his sight, walked in the uprightness of my Heart, and as in those things partaining to this Life, I have endeavoured to keep a good Conscience. So in Love to all that may have the Reading of this small Book, I am willing to give them an understanding, as I have found where it is to be attained; as Christ said, *There is but one good, and that is God*; and as we come be guided by his good Spirit, it will lead us into all things that are good; without which we cannot inherit *Eternal Life*. And whatever any may think of me, who look with an evil Eye, yet to my *Friends* that looks with an Impartial Eye, it will be received, as it is intended good will to all; and to those remain a Friend.

S. B.

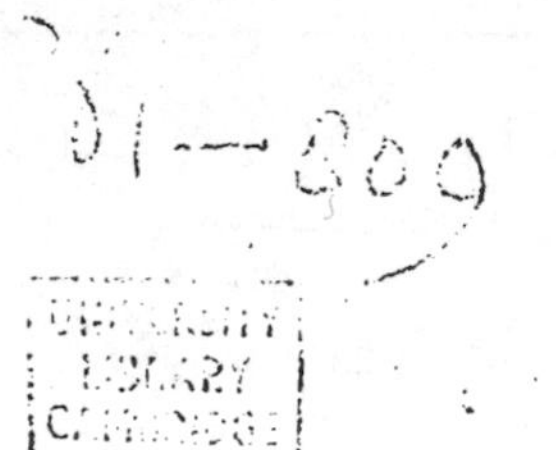

The

The Fear of the Lord is the beginning of Wisdom.
A good understanding have all those that keep his Law.

AND as a *Traveller* to the good Land of *Rest* and *Peace*, and having in measure attain'd thereunto, by that *Heavenly* Guide *Christ Jesus* the true *Light*, that hath been my Instructer and Helper, without which I am nothing, nor can do any thing as I ought to do; I am made free to relate something of my attainment thereunto. I was Born of good Parents, Educated according to the *Church* of *England*; and tho' Young, Zealous therein; yet could not my Immortal Soul be therewith satisfied, but a desire was begotten in me, to know the true God, the which to attain I endeavoured the best way I could, by Prayer and Fasting in secret, not to be seen of any: But God, whose Eye saw me, and my true desire therein; knowing herein I was not safe, tried me, and by one thought which arose in my Heart concerning God, which I could not help, dashed all my Building to pieces,

 and

and I thought my ſelf the worſt Creature living; thus night and day I had great trouble within, but reſolv'd in the midſt of all, and made it my reſolution to follow the thing that is good, and that God that ſaw me, though I ſaw not him; I was by this often comforted, and it became my Song, *Great are the Troubles of the Righteous*, but *the Lord delivers out of them all*; and ſometimes betwixt Hope and Fear, I travelled from Twelve Years of Age to Eighteen; about which time, by Providence I was led into the *North*, at which time, by wonderful changes wrought in them (by which they had the name given them) called *Quakers*, a People ſo contrary to my Education; and the many ſtrange Reports, that were raiſed of them, was rather frightful, than deſireable to me; but that God, that ſaw the great deſire I had to know him, the only true *God*, and *Jeſus Chriſt* his Son, led the blind by a way I knew not, and by one not called a *Quaker*, but one true to the *Church* of *England*, and a ſufferer for King *Charles* the firſt.

I received a true *Account* of the Principles and good Lives of theſe People, which in Simplicity of Heart was related

ted to me, of which I was made seriously to consider; and in a short time, felt a Power arise in my Heart, and I said this is it I have waited for, and with great Power it rent the Vail, chased away my dark thoughts, gave me some understanding of the Scriptures, and I could say, *I have heard of thee, and have read of the Wonders thou didst for the Children of Men;* but that was not mine, but now by thy great Power and Change thou hast wrought in me, I came to know thee O God, and by this, and in no other way can I be satisfied, and that thou the Immortal God, may'st have the Glory of thy own *good Work,* which I never received of Man, neither did I ever see or hear any of them called *Quakers,* till three Years after or more, but returned into my own Country (*North-Hamptonshire*) to my Relations, and not long after came to *London,* and made it my business, and went secretly amongst all persuasions (except *Papists* and *Ranters*) to see if I could find any, that had the sence to know God, and his Son *Jesus Christ* within them.

But, I could find no outward thing could give my Soul satisfaction, neither then, nor now, and in that State I walked alone three Years, but being at a Meeting in great *Allhallows*, one *Edw. Burroughs* came in, and stood up, and spoke; at which I with others was amazed, having never seen nor heard any of them before; but was resolved to hear him again; but by the many strange reports raised of them, I was afraid, but I Prayed to the Lord my God in whom I trusted, that I might not be deceived, for he knew I had nothing in my Eye, but to have a further manifestation of *Him, whom to know is Life Eternal*, of the which he resolved me, and with Signs and Tokens of his *Love*, confirmed me, and I could, and can say it was, and is of God, and is the *Truth*, and proceeds from the same *Rock*, from which all the *Patriarchs, Prophets*, and *Apostles*, had their teaching, *Christ Jesus* the *Rock*, the *Mystery hid from Ages and Generations, is made known unto us*, of which Knowledge I have learn'd, as they did, who said, what is to be known of God, is *manifest in them*, which is the *Key* of *David*, which opens and shuts, and gives the true Understanding of the Mystery of the Kingdom of Heaven, and the true knowledge to all those,

who

who have in true Obedience submitted to his Yoke, and their Wills subjected to his Will; these shall find his saving Virtue of Life, which Life being received, and joyned too with all the Heart, it will endow them with the Heavenly Virtue, in *Christ Jesus* our *High Priest*, and Captain of our Salvation: And with Righteousness, Peace and Joy, in the Holy Spirit of God, and those that willingly give up all they have unto him, shall find in it more than they can believe, or the Carnal Mind can apprehend, for they knew what they said, that the Carnal Mind knows not the things of God, for they are Spiritually discerned, and to be carnally minded is Death, but to be spiritually minded is Life and Peace, which is a certain Truth, and according to the Holy *Scriptures*, from which I desire neither from Them, nor my Neighbour to borrow Words, or a Profession; but to have a right to them, and be made one with them, by the same Spirit of *Jesus Christ*, the Lord of all our Mercies; and as in him they lived, moved, and had their being, who gave them forth, he is so to the faithful this day, and what I have heard and seen, I declare, that he is the true God, *And*

the

the Poor in Spirit receive the Kingdom of Heaven, and see a nothingness and emptiness in themselves, without a dayly supply from him, and they are led and made to understand the Mystery of *Election* and *Reprobation*, as in the two Seeds and Births, the one *elect* and *blessed* of God before the World was; if the mind of Man joyns to *Christ*, who is God's Elect, *Isa.* 42. they are saved by him, and *Works out their Salvation with Fear and Trembling*; and this is the *Elect* and *Corner-Stone*, *Christ Jesus*, whom soever Builds thereon, *The Gates of Hell shall not prevail*, and will over turn overturn till *he come whose righ: is to Reign*; and as unto this *Elect* and *Precious Seed* we Unite, we are therein and thereby blessed of God: this is not of our selves, but the free Gift given of God, by which we make our *Calling and Election sure*, and in this we have learn'd to know the Reprobated, and the *Enemy* of all Mankind, that leads the mind from God, into the *Lust of the Eye*, the *lust of the Flesh*, and the *Pride of Life*, and all other Evils, which if joined unto the Evil conceived in the mind brings Death, and separates Man from God his Maker, and

here

here the strong Man keeps the *House*, and by his Temptations therein, prevails on Man to eat the forbidden *Fruit*, by which he breaks the Law of God, and falls under Condemnation, from which State there is no coming; nor the *Figg-leaf* Garment, nor nothing without will cover, but a turning to the blessed Appearance and Gift of God in the Soul, and there find the Mystery, *Christ within, the Hope of Glory*, who hath many Names, and his Kingdom is compared to a *little Leaven*, the *lost Groat*, a *grain of Mustard Seed*, and many other Parables, and it is vailed from Man, who is in the first nature of the Earth, Earthly, but revealed in the second Man, who is the Lord from *Heaven*, which gives us to know the first Man *Adam* a living Soul, and the last Man *Adam* a quickning Spirit, by which, unless we be Born again of the true incorruptible Seed, which enlightens us, we cannot see the Kingdom of *Heaven*, nor the Glory thereof, which Man in the first Nature have strove to know; but we must receive that knowledge by the ingrafted Word of God, not in our will and time, these things God gives us to know, but being acquainted with

with his Mercies, and the Temptations of the evil *One*, as we may read and learn of *Christ*, who left us an example, as all true Travellers ſhall find in themſelves, him near in their beſt performances; as I have ſeen, and do ſee his approach, and when I have heard, or ſeen any on the high Mountains, in their Imaginations, who pretend they ſee all the World, and their ſelves in conceit above all, for which I have been grieved, as well-knowing the danger of that State, and willing I was to have adviſed them, but knowing they was ſo highly ſet up in themſelves, my voice could not reach them, calling that God which is not God, taking the Name of the Lord God in Vain, for which he will not hold them guiltleſs, ſome of them having blown a loud Trumpet, *Jehu* like, ſaying, *Come and ſee my Zeal for the Lord of Hoſts*, which I have been grieved to ſee in ſome, both Men and Women, and have lived to ſee divers fall, which I well knew as they ſtood could not hold out to the end, and many of *Martha's* Spirit I have ſeen, and now do, which runs, and ſerves, and cumbers themſelves with ſtriving to utter Words, and have got the

the true Notion in their Heads, but the true Seed hath not taken root downwards; and those are they which are stumbling-Blocks, who have been by some encouraged,. as I might have been, but the Lord my God kept me out of that Temptation, and many others not loving Hypocricy, nor a feigned imitation whereby I might deceive others, in what I was not truly to God, who called me to take up the Cross, to that which my Heart loved, whether they were Idols of Silver, or Gold, or other things tho' useful, yet if over-valued they fill the Heart, of which there must be an emptying, to make room for the Heavenly *Jesus*, under whose Reign, *Israel* shall safely possess their Souls in Peace, and have the new Name given them, and the *White Stone* which none knows, nor can believe, but those that have it, and those are they that are come through great Tribulations, and are washed with the Blood of the *Lamb*: and all those of this Faith, I dearly salute, as being Children of one Father, whose *Voice* I know from the Voice of a *Stranger*, and I thank God, who hath raised up the Poor in Spirit, all that are therein gathered, will out-last all other

Notions,

Notions, and the Lord give Wiſdom to them, that have not as yet thereto attained, to know the true Miniſtration and the right Seaſon, when they ſhould, and when they ſhould not, which in ſome hath been lacking; which cauſes the weak to ſtumble, and keeps out more than it brings in.

Thus have I given a ſhort but true Account as I have paſſed through the Wilderneſs of this World, and have ſeen many fall on the Right Hand, and on the Left, where alſo I might but have had for my preſervation, the cloud over me by day to keep me low, that I might not be exalted, neither by Viſions, Sights, nor Revelations; many have been hurt thereby, and caſt that on others, which concerned themſelves: And as the cloud ſtood over me, it kept me low from ſelf-exaltation, to know my ſelf nothing, but what I received from the God of all my Mercies: and as I ſee the *Cloud by day*, I alſo ſee the *Pillar of Fire by Night*, which cauſed me to ſtand ſtill, and ſee the Salvation of God, and the bright appearance of his Glory. I am ſorry for ſome that are backſliden, and may ſay to them, what have you or your Fathers found in the

the God of *Jacob*, that you ſhould depart from him? But let all the ſtrong will'd, know little *David*, who truſts not in Bow nor Sword, but in the living God; he by his Sling and ſmooth *Stone*, ſhall hit the Head of thoſe that defies the Armies of *Iſrael's* God.

And to all you workers of Iniquity, who have charged us that we deny *Chriſt Jeſus* come in the *Fleſh*, the Holy *Scriptures* and the *Reſurrection*, and ſay we are *Heathens*, and *Hereticks*, all which we know to be falſe, and can appeal to God in the integrity of our Hearts therein, and with him we can with Joy leave our Cauſe, as well-knowing he is able in his time to plead it, tho' there may be evil doers amongſt us. If *Chriſt* had one in twelve, that was not enough for the Jews and ſome that followed him, to ſay he was not in the Truth, becauſe *Judas* betrayed him, and *Peter* deny'd him, and he in that Agony bearing our griefs, *Iſa.* 53. to cry out, *My God my God why haſt thou forſaken me*, all this muſt needs ſtumble the Eye that looked out, but they remembred his promiſe, and waited at *Jeruſalem* for the fulfilling of it, who ſaid, he would come, and he did come, which confirmed

confirmed them, and so it hath done us.

And now something to you my dear Children, whom I never deck'd in the extreams of formality, to make my self, or you seem what you were not; but this was, and is my desire for you, seek first the Kingdom of Heaven, and the Righteousness thereof, and all other things shall be added unto you, be sure to *Remember your Creator in the days of your Youth*, and you shall find the Comfort of it in your Old Age, or at your Death, when all the Glory of this World will stand you in no stead: And though some of you have met with some Disappointments, yet you shall find (as I have done) all things work together for good, and bring you nearer to God, which I have ever desired for you, more than for Silver or Gold, tho' therein some of you have had a blessing beyond my desire, and my comfort is, you all set your Faces *Sion-ward*, and to your Parents have been Dutiful, Loving and Obedient, for which God will bless you, as you continue in his Grace.

This is written by one that hath been called a *Dissenting Quaker*, which I desire not to be from faithful Friends, for

I

I never knowingly diſſented from the Truth, but loved it, and though in ſome things was not ſatisfied, yet kept as near as I could in Word and Deed to hurt no *one*, but endeavoured to anſwer a good Conſcience towards God and all Men, in which I have found him near to help me, and the bleſſing to my Soul and Body, and have a true Love to all the ſincere in Heart, by what name ſoever called.

And as through Diſpenſations and Adminiſtrations and Gifts, (which are all by the ſame Spirit) God is pleaſed to give a further manifeſtation of Himſelf, who is a Spirit, in that way ſhews Himſelf to Man as he can receive him, which was, and is his great Love, knowing how happy he is made by it, and unhappy without it, and God's great Condeſcenſion therein, who ſeeks Man, before Man ſeeks Him, becauſe he is good, and would have Us be like unto Him, and take delight in Us, and we in Him: and in this way he led all his faithful People, before the *Law* and after, which *Law* was given by *Moſes* by Divine Inſpiration, many Years after ſome of thoſe things were done, which all had their ſignification, and pointed at *Chriſt Jeſus* coming in the Fleſh,

Flesh, who, when come, said, *before* Abraham *was I am,* and they in the Wilderness drank of the same Spiritual *Rock*, which *Rock* is *Christ*, the Messenger of God and of the New Covenant, the Law written in the Heart, unto Him must all come, that will truly know the Interpretation of what's contained in both Old and New Testament, which was declared from the Spirit and Power of God in the true *Seed*, and that were left to be profitable, especially to the Man of God, through *Faith* in Christ Jesus, by which we may see (as our Minds are turned to God) the Examples of those that followed the Lord their God, and there make a true spiritual Application, and see how far we are come into the good work of God, in the proving of our Hearts; as *Abraham* Offered up *Isaac*, so must every one offer up what God requires, to manifest our love to God; and for all such who by Faith walk, God will provide himself a Sacrifice; and so *Jacob* the wrestler with God, sent from his Father's House to go into a strange Land, and have no dependency on any outward or visible thing in this his Journey, yet Travels on, and the Sun sets, night comes on, on this Stone

lays

lays his head, and thus rests on the faithfulness of God to him in all conditions, and then is the ladder of true experience seen, where the *Angels* of God ascend, and descend, at the foot abode, and you will say God was here and I knew it not; and here *Jacob* received his blessing, to whom Children was given, and there was a striving, as by the best Mind and Spirit, you shall find the eldest by Nature will seek to rule, and strive against the beloved of the Father: And *Joseph* the true born Son sold into *Egypt*, to provide Corn for *Jacob* and his Sons, but they must go down to fetch it; and this is to be known in its time and season, and the Scripture fulfilled, and the spiritual meaning therein known: As *Saul* the first King over *Israel*, for stature and appearance Beautiful, annointed of the Prophet to be King; but God saw beyond outward appearances into the Heart, and they that go out from God their strength, their defence is gone, and they shall become weak as *Saul* did, and their Enemies prevail; then contemptible *David*, who by his Brethren dispised, him God saw, and by the Arm of God's strength had killed the *Lyon* and the *Bear*, and in that Power by which he o-

 vercame

vercame the Latter, by believing in the same Power he overcame the greatest of his Enemies, and this made him King in *Saul*'s stead, though with him he had long Wars to Fight the Lord's Battle: but *Solomon* by the true Wisdom of God must Build the House, in whose Reign there is Peace and Safety, and he shall Judge and give true Judgment betwixt the Mother and the Child; and *Christ*'s Kingdom (Typified in *Solomon*'s) consists of Righteousness, Peace and Joy, which is very delightful and desirous, because, the satisfaction the Soul receives thereby, and hath a true sight of the Love of God in all he doth, is but to make his Creature Man happy, which Love is so great it cannot be expressed, for the which, all those that have received it praise God, and all that have not come out of themselves, and seek the Kingdom of Christ, not in words, but in Truth, that they may partake with thy Saints in Glory, and thereby see the Emptiness and Vanity of this World, whether it be Profession, Pleasure, Riches, Honour; the Excellency of this Excels them all.

And to all you sincere hearted, as *Cornelius* was, to whom *Peter* was sent, who said,

ſaid, *I ſee of a Truth, God is no reſpecter of Perſons*; but amongſt all that truly ſears God, and works Righteouſneſs, are therein accepted, yet God was pleaſed by *Peter*, to Preach and Teſtifie unto Jeſus Chriſt as his anointed, who was crucified, and to his Reſurection from the Dead, *Acts* 10. that in and through him they might believe, and receive the Gift of the *Holy Ghoſt* and of Power, and thereby the inward cleanſing from Sin and Pollution, and by the Power and Work of *Chriſt*, to become the Sons of God, which no outward thing can do; but whoſe therein believes, ſhall find Power in that Gift which God hath given, which is a true diſcerner of the thoughts and intents of the Heart, to which, I would perſuade all that are weary and heavy laden to come unto, and they ſhall aſſuredly find Reſt to their Souls, by Chriſt Jeſus the Subſtance, unto which all Men muſt bow in the inwardneſs of their Hearts, for the day of his bright Appearance is at hand; and *Behold he comes with Clouds*, *Rev.* 1. 7. yet they that are gazing abroad, cannot ſee him, being veil'd from that Eye and Mind, as he was unknown to the *Jews* formerly, who had a great expectation of the coming of the *Messiah*, who came in the will of God at the appointed time; yet he not coming in that Glory, and great Appearances they expected him, they could not believe nor think that it was he, and now there is great expectation in some of his second appearance, some saying, *Lo here*, and some *Lo there*, and yet still are disappointed, and strangers to his appearance in Spirit: but to them who truly look for him, he shall appear the second time without Sin, unto *Salvation*, and there the true inward Christians shall see him in his Glory, and enter into his Kingdom, which exceeds all the glory of this World, neither can the wise imaginary part in Man give a true description thereof, but as God's Wisdom rises up into the Throne, and hath the Government of the Mind, they shall know the depth of these things from him that gives it; and give him the Praise, who hath brought them into so happy estate, who desires well for every Creature, both Man and Beast, who groans for deliverance: And as a Man comes to be gathered into the light, and changed into the Nature of Jesus Christ, the whole Creation will reap

great

great benefit thereby, and as many as have seen the beginning of the good Work of God in what he did, *He divided the Light from the Darkness*, and *saw the Light*, and *it was Good*; and so he went on in every day's Work, till the whole Creation was finished; and as we read in the Old, we must find it in the New, for he saith, *I will make a new Heaven, and a new Earth, wherein shall dwell Righteousness.* And as in the first, he went on in order in his Work, so you shall find him now; and though by him called into the Vine-yard to work, it shall find in many a high and strong will, which would obstruct the good Work of God, and that *Hammon*-like gets upon the Kings *Horse*, but he's not *Mordica*, that sits low in sackcloth at the gate, and where this is, in what pretence so ever, in whom Pride rises and prevails, it will (if suffered) destroy the Seed of the *Jews*; but he that sees in secret will reveal the matter, and that Spirit shall be brought down, let its cloathing be never so glorious: God hath decreed to exalt *Mordicai*, who is of the true Seed, he is found worthy, and the Lord lives; he shall Reign whose Right it is, though the *Heathen* rage, and the People imagine a vain thing, yet will he set his Son upon the holy hill of *Sion*.

I could not well omit one thing more, to give satisfaction to some, who may think, I am one that goes under the name that ministers to the People, but I am not; but this I give as my experience, to all that are traveling to find rest with God in his *Kingdom* of *Peace*; but to appear in a *Publick Assembly*, there to speak, I never did; and I am of the *Apostle*'s mind, *Let such Women* (*as want Instruction, or would usurpe Authority over the Man*) *keep Silence in the Church, and give place to Man, to whom God hath given Preheminency, and made fit for that great Work*; in which Work, had not I satisfaction in my self, and been strengthened by those worthy good *Ministers*, through the weakness of some others who thereto pretend, and, as I well know, run when they are not sent, I might have stumbled; but I saw, how ever Justified by others, divers of them were not, nor are not upon the right Ground, and some of them have been blown away like Chaff with the Wind, not but that I know there is many Good and Vertuous *Women*, who are appointed for good Examples in their

Families,

Families, who in *Modesty*, *Sobriety*, *Charity*, and *good Works*, a *good Life*, and *Conversation*; with these I joyn, and in that Life I desire to Preach to my Children, Friends, Neighbours and Servants; and they that in this rightness of Heart Live, shall deceive none, but gain to themselves a lasting Establishment, which shall be of good Savour, never to be repented of; and as in this I desire to do unto all as I would be done unto, and that in Truth and Sincerity I have here writ, may be for the good of all; to help the Feeble, and strengthen the Weak, and that from the ground of Integrity, and in Good Will to all Men; and it being received in the good Mind, will cover any Weakness herein contained, and make that use of it as it is intended, *Good Will to all, and Glory to God.* Yet as there was formerly, so there is now, *he that is born after the Flesh, Persecutes him that is born after the Spirit*, whose Censures I expect not to escape, it being so natural to the Litteral *Jews*, when they could find nothing to accuse Christ of, whilst upon the Earth, sought what they could to intrap him in his Words; but God gave him that Wisdom to see in them, and cautioned his

Disciples, *not to give the Childrens Bread to Dogs, nor Pearls to Swine, least they trample them under Foot, and turn again and Rent you*; under Christ's Protection I leave my self.

This writ by one that hath waited at *Wisdom's Gate* for Instruction, who hath given me an entrance to know as I have here declared, and all that would go higher to see the Bride, the Lambs Wife, must be guided thereto by the Meek and Humble Spirit of *Jesus*, without which there is no Safety, though they may understand all Mysteries, and give much to the Poor, and have all those Gifts the Apostle mentions (in the 13 of the 1. Epistle to the *Corinthians*) and yet if the most excelent gift of Charity be wanting that thinks no Evil, which boasteth not, *&c.* but Suffereth, Believeth, Hopeth, and Endureth all Things, and rejoyceth in God alone, he that is here will out-last all other let their pretences be what it will, and they that come not here let them change their Habits, their Customs, and as some call it the *Worlds Fashions*, yet if they come not to see the *World's Covetousness* (unto which the Heart of Man is naturally inclined) rooted out, the Earth will open

and

and swallow up that Mind, and the Heart will be dead to God, and they will loose their part in the blessed Inheritance.

Some on the other hand notwithstanding they may have seen the good way, set forward therein, but soon forgot what the Lord did for them, who brought them out of the *Land of Darkness*, from under their hard *Taskmasters*, who put them to make *Brick* without *Straw*; their Hearts not being throughly Converted, they lusted for the *Garlick* and *Onions* again, their old Diet; and though they had past the *Sea*, many dyed in the *Wilderness*, and all them that delighted in the Sins of *Sodom*, and make a mock at the good *Angel*, that God hath sent to pull just *Lot* out of *Sodom*, they shall be struck Blind, and the Fire of God's Wrath shall destroy all such that come not in at the right Door of him who said, *I am the Way, the Truth, the Life, and the Light*; who ever striveth by any other way will be found Theives and Robbers, and deprive the Soul of its Inheritance with God.

This by one who for many Years hath been counted a *Dissenter*, being never forward to intrude into those things I had not seen nor adhered to, what I had not a

clear

clear sight as my duty to God, and there I stand still waiting on God to reveal to me; yet that God that sees the inside, the Heart, hath rewarded me according to the sincerity thereof; and I have found his Love so great and unexpressible, which hath made up all again more than I have lost by any Man, and hath safely preserved where Man could not see me, whose Eye is abroad and looks at the outside appearance; but as God's Eye, who beholds both Evil and Good, so have I seen in both Parties things acted and done, which my Soul had no Pleasure nor Unity with, but was willing the Lord should bring me off from those from whom he was departed, and that the sincere hearted of both sides might be Reconciled, for the accomplishing of which I have used my best Endeavours, desiring there may not be a looking at what is past, but an endeavouring for the good of all, as I have really done, as may be seen in this following *Letter*, which I writ in answer to a Friend, who was and is dissatisfied with some for appearing therein; but let thembe what they please, I am well satisfied in this good Work.

But

But I have seen the new Wine put into the old Bottle, it not being well seasoned there becomes a Sowerness, and the good Relish thereby seems to be lost, that is in it self good; in which state there is many that keeps to the old Leaven of the *Pharisees*; Christ gives this Mark by which they should be known, *They love the uppermost Places, and to be Master, make long Prayers, and to preach in their own Wills, different in their Robes, makes a fair show in the Flesh, that they may appear well unto Men*; this hath been and is a great grief to the Just, but I am comforted in this, I see many right-hearted and good Christians, who speaks from the Truth the anointed of God, those God will bless, and he will appear in them who reigns in Righteousness, and all such shall reign with him for ever and ever; and as I have seen this Good, I have also seen this Evil, which Man is prone to, and apt to set a great value upon themselves, and they not see it, and let the Truth be never so plainly discovered, and from the Spirit of the Living God dictated; yet if it comes not in their way, and after their manner, as they have set it up in themselves, there is no room for any thing to enter

enter, though never so good; of this I have made to my self a good Caution, and said, *O Lord if this Iniquity remains in me, search it out; for I see it looks ill in others, and so it will in me if I am found therein.*

S. B.

How mean soever I may appear to Man,
A Witness in my Soul there lives that can,
Bear Record to the Father *this, that I*
Seek *not Mortals praise, but Immortality;*
That Crown of Rest and Peace I may receive,
Which Mortals have not in their Power to give;
Which he must do who sets me free from Sin,
And being clean in Peace there Rules that King,
Who will not joyn unto Iniquity,
But love's Uprightness and Integrity.
Thinks Human Wisdom, *I can easily see,*
The Scripture *can this thing declare to me;*
But 'tis not known by Pleasure, Ease *or* Sleep,
Who find this Pearl, *must dig low and deep;*
And who finds before it be his own,
They must sell all to purchase that alone,
And cast up all his Stock and look within,
Before to Build this House he doth begin,

And

And learn by true experience rightly for to know,
The thing that's realy good from what's but good in
Remember Babel, *do not build too High,* *(show*
Nor make a Tower to reach unto the Skie,
Nor look thou out, but turn thy Eye within,
See *Christ there laid, then build thy House on him.*
Who build not on that Rock *shall surely fall,*
For he is that Corner Stone *uniteth all.*
Cease then a while you Humane Learned Men,
That know your Wisdom cannot find out him.
Thou Willing and Obedient, know it's thee,
Whose Vale is rent to see this Mistery,
It's not the prudent learned Wit that shall
Him comprehend who is the Light of all,
The Lamb of God, who comes in love to gain
And bring lost Man (stray'd from God) back again;
And make Man happy, the greatest good that can
Befall to Mortals, or the Sons of Men;
Which if not rightly known, what e're we do
Wants the good Oil, and God's acceptance too.
He sees the Heart and what rules there full well,
Whether it be Pride or Passion, Husk, Fame or Shell;
Of all that cumber we must come to see,
Man strip'd of all and Christ alone to be
The true conducter, from the ways wherein

He'll

He'll not appear, because they lead from him;
And all that goes in this true blessed way,
Shall by his Light be sav'd both Night and Day.
And as I have walk'd unseen and all alone,
In secret to my God I made my moan.
Its restless eye that makes complaint to none,
But unto thee from whom relief must come;
Out of my Troubles, Doubts and Fears,
And send the Harvest which was sown in Tears;
Tho' sorrow may indure for a Night,
Thy morning Presence brings my Soul delight;
Thou art a God of Truth, in all things Just,
And those that know thy Name will in thee Trust.

An Answer to a Letter from a Friend.

THine I received, and have considered thereof, and could have been more large in my own, and my Friends Vindication therein concern'd; but am gathered into that, not to strive, but to commit my Cause to God in well-doing; having in my self, and many others, seen *Pride* to beget *Passion*, and *Passion Prejudice*, by which the *Eye* of the right understanding

derstanding is made Blind: As for rehearsal of all those former failings therein contained, if they were true, yet rightly considered, and impartially weighed; may say, since those Divisions, a great manifestation there hath been of such Spirits, to whom those names may deservedly be attributed; tho' for many Years I have been counted a *Dissenter*. Yet I, nor many more, never took pleasure to lay the Nakedness of any open, but rather to cover for his Names sake, who hath kept us in his Truth, by which we have been preserved.

I have seen, I have seen, an *Enemy* enter the House, and hath not been discover'd till they come into the Cool, out of the Hurry and Noise, and hear the call of the *still Voice*; and herein my Soul, with many other of my Christian Friends, have been Blessed; and by this we are led to Unite, and to be truly reconciled in that *Spirit*, by that Heavenly *Jesus*, that true *Reconciler* of Man to his *Maker*.

And of this, from thy true Friend, be assured, it was not from the Spirit of *Hypocrisie*, *Policy*, or any *carnal* or *selfish End*, no, no, our House is not Built on that *Sandy Foundation*, but on *Christ Jesus*,

that

that *Rock of Ages*, which leads his in the way of Everlasting *Peace*, which *Peace* cannot be declared, but as it is felt, of which *Peace* hath my Soul tasted largely, and can say truly, since into this happy state the Lord hath brought me, I have experienced more of that *Heavenly Joy*, and *Everlasting Peace*, than ever I knew before, but I thank the Lord who gave me a share thereof, under every dispensation he hath led me through, and can say, they were all good in their time, but this excelleth them all, well knowing the Administration of *John* to be Glorious in its Time, yet, *He that is least in the Kingdom of Heaven is greater than he*; into which *Kingdom*, that thou may'st have an entrance after all thy Travels, and come into this *Sabbath* and *Rest* with God, will be a true Joy to thy Friend, of which I can say, with many more of my dear Friends whom I know not, but as I feel them in this Spirit, *It is the Way and there is not another*: And for all those that are otherwise-minded, the Lord send a *Famine* to come on the outward *Knowledge*, that they may know to be led to the Spiritual *Joseph*; whoever comes unto him, he upbraideth no one with what is past,

but

but receives them with his Love, and embraceth them, and they partake with him of the Fatneſs of the good *Land*. Of this I am a witneſs, and remain

Thy True Friend,

S. B.

AS to a *Faſt*, I deſire this may be ſolemnly proclaimed; a *Faſt* from *Strife*, *Malice* and every evil *Work*, as new Born Babes deſire the ſincere Milk of the Word of Life, and grow thereby, in which we ſhall be accepted of God, and truly reconciled to one another.

S. B.

Poſtſcript.

I Did not intend to have Printed this *Letter* I ſent to a *Friend*, but finding he hath Printed the *Letter* he ſent to me, as an Anſwer to *W. R*'s Book I ſent him, which Book I had g od Unity with, and with all that are of a reconciling Spirit, which to my Comfort, I find many ſincere hearted therein, and as the vail of Prejudice comes to be taken of the Heart, we ſhall ſee one another as God ſeeth us, to whom I approve my Heart, let Men Judge of me as they pleaſe; it is not from any Evil or Inſinuating ſelf-end, I can truly ſay for my ſelf, and many more true *Chriſtian F iends*, whoſe Hearts in this matter of Reconciliation is not to gain Praiſe of Men, God is our witneſs; but we are led to Unite by that bleſſed Spirit, who hath ſhewed us of what and in what the *Kingdom of Heaven* conſiſts, of which is true Righteouſneſs, Joy and Peace in the holy Spirit, which I with many more have taſted, and could be glad all that oppoſe would come and taſte and ſee how good the Lord is, and with what the *Immortal Soul* is Refreſhed.

I could never find ſatisfaction in any viſible thing, till I received the *Word* of *God*, in which *Word* I find the *Key* of *David*, *Which opens and none can ſhut, and ſhuts and none can open*; and that is that, that opens the *Myſtery of the Kingdom of God*, in which the *Father*, *Son* and *Spirit* is to be koown; which *Word* of *Faith*, gave the true underſtanding to the *Prophets* and *Apoſtles*, and to all the *Faithful* of *God* to this day: *And in that way which*

which some call Heresie, Worship I the God of my Fathers, believing all the Law and the Prophets, and in Jesus Christ, *who is the Author and Finisher of our Faith.*

S. B.

O Lord! Out of the deep I cried unto thee, and thou pluckedst my feet out of the Mire and Clay, and hast set them in the right way: And being converted, strengthen my Brethren. Unto which I have this further to add, when I first heard the confused noise, made by *G. K.* and *T. B.* which appearance was, and is to me like the *Golden Calf*; and beholding many I knew, which I thought had been more grafted in the *Word* of *Life*, than to go after it, for which I was greatly troubled, but the heavenly *still Voice* gave me this Satisfaction, fret not thy self, be still, it is a Cloud I suffer, the Wind thereof shall blow away the *Chaff*, but I will gather my *Wheat* thereby nearer together; and this I know to be a certain Truth, by which my Heart hath been often refreshed, for which my Soul, *Praise thou the Lord.*

S. B.

And unto all thoſe who have raked up the miſcarriages and evils, and printed it, and given it abroad to defame the People called *Quakers*, whoſe Principles ſhall out-laſt their Malice; and was ſome of us of their Spirit, to render evil for evil, revileing for revileing, might ſay that of ſome of them that would cauſe ſhame, who covered their fooliſh actions with the name of the Lord, but it was, and is ſuch a Lord, of which there is many, but not the true God as ſome can witneſs, but cover'd it from Men, hopeing time might work them to ſee their weakneſs, and know the true Lord over-ruling all their falſe Imaginations, who may be truly compared to *Saul*, when gone from the true *God*, he goes to the *Witch* of *Endor*, and ſhe raiſed up what he would ſee, but not what he ſhould ſee; ſo he was never the better for it, but his Enemies prevailed, and he fell by his own Sword; ſo ſhall envy ſlay the wicked Man; and they in darkneſs ſhall grope for the door, but ſhall not find it: All this is true, and I own before all Men the Principle of the *Quakers*. And have this to ſay for my ſelf, and many more I well know, however our Enemies may render

us;

us; vve knovv this by our ſelves, and our Conſciences bears us vvitneſs, vve have in good Converſation vvalked before God and Men, vvhich vvill ſpeak for us in the gates of our Enemies; and vve find the anſvver of a good Conſcience a continual Feaſt, who have not received the Truth by obſervation, but by the true adminiſtration, by which we have learn'd vvhat lets into the Kingdom of our God, and vvhat keeps out, let Mens pretences be vvhat they vvill; they that makes lies there refuge, and takes avvay Mens good names, ſhall be found vvorkers of Iniquity.

I having in this ſmall account hinted of many States, and ſeveral ways of the Lord's working in Man, that he may come to know him, and on him rely in all eſtates. I have one thing further to add; I have lately ſeen an excerciſe at hand, but when or in what I know not, but leave it to God and his appointed time, let it be in Mercy or in Judgment, I believe all is for good, as I have ever found all his dealings to me, it was unpleaſant to the fleſhly part, but I turn'd in, and ſaw God's preſervation near to all that truly on him relies; and in nothing elſe was there ſafety, and therefore I deſire all

to

to draw their minds from Vanity and consider their latter end, that it may go well with them, what change so ever comes; for the glory of this World passes away, therefore *Work while the Day lasts, for the Night cometh wherein no Man can Work:* I have also by my experience learned that in Sights and Visions, without watchfulness, there is a Temptation near, there being a readiness in Man to cast that on others, which God intends for our selves, if vve could patiently wait till the Vision speaks; for vvant of that many have run fiercely into things without, and have fail'd, and have brought Reproach on themselves, and God not glorified thereby: this I have also seen, and is often before me, and as there is no outward thing I more truly rejoyced in than to hear the Faithful Ministers of Jesus Christ, in the which I am Comforted, that *God* hath given such a manifestation of his Heavenly good Spirit to instruct his People in the Right and Everlasting Way, which *God* will Establish in the Earth; though I could be glad for the sake of many who take offence and are kept back, because it is very discernable, *Martha*'s Spirit speaks when they had better be Silent,

goes

goes hastily forward, but would find a greater gain in themselves, if they learn'd to obey, and stand still and see the *Salvation of God*; such may be angry that others rise not up and serve after their manner, but *Jesus* that rightly knows the Spirits of all, saw *Mary* sit at his Feet, low in her self, she chose the better Part, which shall never be taken away, and the Seed sown in that good Ground shall bring forth Fruit to the *Lord of the Harvest*; but there is several sorts of Ground in vvhich the good Seed is sown, and there are many Obstructions in the Ground which hinder the Prosperity of *Gods* holy and good Seed; but the *Harvest* will come, and the good *Husband-man* will discern the *Tares* from the *Wheat*, vvhich none else can do, there being such a likeness; the Administration of *John* vvas Glorious, in its time, but he said, *Behold the Lamb of God, that takes away the Sins of the World*, shall be preferr'd before and above all appearances, be they vvhat they vvill, here *many that are Last shall be First, and the First Last:* these are *Christ*'s ovvn Words, and are certainly true, and beleived by one vvho vvishes vvell to all.

S. B.

I

I, being incouraged by the *Immortal God* to Print this, and the matter contained therein, and gave it to ſeveral *Friends*; and it coming into the hand of *T. C.* he came to me, and asked me, Whether I meant *George Keith?* To whom I replied, *I did*; who made this Application, becauſe he Preached up the Man *Chriſt Jeſus*; therefore he ſaid, I made him the *Golden Calf*; and ſo he reported it: And to all that ſhall hear this Report, I have this to ſay, and take Almighty God to be my Witneſs, I do believe *Jeſus* of *Nazareth*, Born at *Bethlehem*, according to God's Divine Appointment, to be the *Eternal Son* of *God*, and all thoſe things to be true, as the Scriptures declare of him, and have received ſo great a benefit by him, as my Tongue cannot expreſs; and for this falſe Aſperſion and wrong Interpretation of *T. C.* I leave God to plead my Cauſe, whom I know is able, and in his time will do it; but muſt ſay, as I have once before, *He that is born after the Fleſh Perſecutes Him that is born after the Spirit.*

FINIS.